# MY VIEW FROM THE HOUSE BY THE SEA

# MY VIEW FROM THE
# HOUSE BY THE SEA

A Life Transformed by Samoa and the Peace Corps

A memoir

# DONNA MARIE BARR

Print ISBN: 978-0-9941203-1-1
eBook ISBN: 979-8-2013611-1-2
Library of Congress Control Number: 2022903755
www.donnamariebarr.com

Cover design and photos (except as noted) by Donna Marie Barr.
Assistance with interior book design by Eswari Kamireddy.
Author photo by Julie Goettsch.

*Dedicated to*

*Harold Robert Bailey,*
*raconteur extraordinaire,*
*Peace Corps trainer, beloved uncle*

*and to*

*Tuifeamalo Annandale and*
*Si'a Lesaisaea Evaimalo Niualuga Tavita,*
*whose friendship mattered*

"Every book is, in an intimate sense, a circular letter to the friends of him who writes it. They alone take his meaning; they find private messages, assurances of love, and expressions of gratitude dropped for them in every corner. The public is but a generous patron who defrays the postage."

Robert Louis Stevenson in *Travels with a Donkey*

*The coconut tree doesn't bend by itself;*
*it bends because of the wind.*
Things don't just happen.
*Samoan proverb*

# Table of Contents

# Foreword

When the village of Poutasi requested a Peace Corps volunteer in 2007 we had no idea who might be assigned, and I never would have suspected that one day I would be writing the foreword for her book. It is not until someone writes a memoir that you get to fully understand why they did things in a certain way and their true motivation. Donna's Peace Corps projects were successful endeavors, but it is her love for Poutasi and the children of our village that stand out most of all.

Poutasi still remembers her special moments with us, especially the young ones (not so young now) who gained so much during their most impressionable years under her loving counsel and guidance. We are so happy that she has this opportunity to share her 'special story' of which we were an important part, with the rest of the world. May God's Blessings be hers for the 'volunteering spirit' that brought her to Poutasi. Fa'amanuia le Atua i'a te ia ona o lona soifua foa'i mo Poutasi. Malo lava Donna!

—Tuatagaloa Joe Annandale
Ali'i Sa'o, Head Chief of the Tuatagaloa Clan, Poutasi, Samoa

# Preface

After I'd raised three sons and enjoyed an intense and gratifying professional life, I finally realized my lifelong dream to join the Peace Corps. I found myself exploring my own internal pathways while navigating an ancient and unfamiliar way of life in Samoa. Dropped off at the door of strangers, barely able to speak the language, I embarked on a cultural immersion filled with ups and downs, through which I ultimately gained deep insights into myself and the country I come from.

Despite those many challenges—some heart-warming and some hair-raising—along the way I fell in love with Samoa.

As an avid journaler, I always knew that I would write about my Peace Corps service. But I couldn't have envisioned how significant that experience would be, or that writing about it would be equally as enlightening.

What follows is a true story. Some events, however, may not have happened exactly as I recount them, because I didn't always translate the Samoan language correctly and I may not have remembered every detail accurately. More importantly, I saw things from my own perspective, and some of my early opinions changed over time. In places I've written about sensitive cultural matters, and I apologize if any offense is taken—especially by those who so kindly welcomed me to their country, their villages, and their homes.

I've included additional acknowledgments and thanks elsewhere, but at the outset I want to mention my mom, Hope Helen Wild. At eighty years old, she kept up regularly by email, and sent me frequent "care packages" of candy, nuts, dried fruit, and many unexpected treats. Other family and friends were also wonderfully supportive, but Mom was my most faithful correspondent. In the spring of 2006 when I told her I was applying to Peace Corps, she embraced me and said "Go for it! This is the time in your life to do it." Thanks Mom!

And with grateful aloha, I want to thank my Uncle Bob for inspiring me to become a writer, as well as for sharing your joy for life, and your love of Hawai'i. I am who I am because of you.

Both have passed away, although I feel their presence in my life every day.

—Donna Marie Barr, December 2021

# Chapter 1

# Setting Out on the Adventure

*'Ua fa'ala'au tu i vanu*
*"Like a tree standing near a precipice"*
*The future is unknown.*

From the house by the sea, I watched sunset after sunset, never able to capture in words the true beauty of the waning sunlight playing on the clouds and the ocean, marveling at each evening's transformation. As the colors glowed, morphed, and faded into dusk, I'd write in my journal until the lights in my Samoan village came on one by one:

> *I'm watching another breathtaking sunset. The view keeps changing. For the first time here in Poutasi, I feel like I'm home.*

My fiercely red, wire-bound journal was my constant companion throughout my Peace Corps adventure that began in 2007. I chronicled the beauty and kindness of the Samoan people, the challenges of daily life in a foreign country, and my struggles to learn the language and carry out village projects. But beyond the facts, I wrote of the life-changing explorations and discoveries, the tribulations that seemed so overwhelming, and the successes large and small, and hopefully lasting— how it *felt* to be there. I now see my Peace Corps self from a new point of view, as I struggled, learned, and loved while daily life in my small village surrounded me and the house by the sea.

The *fale 'i tai* (fah'-lay ē tī)—the house by the sea—was my place of refuge, solitude, relaxation, meditation, entertainment. My office, meeting place, writing space, and village observation post. I can't imagine my life in the village of Poutasi without the fale 'i tai at the heart of it.

Forty years earlier, like many young Americans in the 1960s, I'd thought about joining the Peace Corps one day. And like most young Americans in the 1960s, I didn't. Luckily, I had a second chance.

In 1961, when President John F. Kennedy said to America, ". . . ask not what your country can do for you, but what you can do for your country," I was a tall, geeky, ponytailed seventh grader. My childhood in the rolling green hills of eastern Nebraska was a classic farm life. We had a red collie dog, barn cats, geese, chickens, milk cows, and sheep. I loved my horse Cocoa, so named because his reddish-brown coat was exactly the color of Hershey's cocoa powder. I rode for hours, daydreaming on his strong back in fragrant alfalfa and knee-high corn fields.

Through eighth grade, I walked with my younger brother to a white clapboard, two-room schoolhouse with one teacher for lower grades and one for upper. After school, I'd often curl up to read on the porch swing, shaded by giant elms. My favorites were stories of adventure in faraway places—*White Fang, The Swiss Family Robinson, Island of the Blue Dolphins*. I was an introspective and energetic girl who got straight As and played piano for choir at the small country church where my grandfather was pastor. In the summers, I planted and weeded in the family garden, worked on 4-H projects for the county fair, and went to Riverview Bible Camp, where I got my first kiss in the glow of the bonfire by the wide Platte River.

In high school I was in the Future Homemakers of America club, played flute in the marching band, and planned to become an English teacher. Attending the small Lutheran university in a neighboring town, I drove my baby-blue 1962 Renault Dauphine to my waitressing job after classes, wrote articles and a column as feature editor for the college paper, and thought I'd marry the handsome sports editor who I'd been dating for two years. Life was proceeding expectedly.

But I was also restless and curious. Maybe I was born that way or wanted to see for myself what was in those books that I loved, or perhaps I needed to satisfy my inquisitive itch to experience the world beyond my provincial upbringing. For all those reasons (and more), in 1970 I joined the United States Air Force instead of the Peace Corps, and had a vastly different, though equally challenging and formative, experience.

The Air Force sent me to Carswell Air Force Base in Fort Worth, Texas, to work in NORS— "Not Operationally Ready, Supply." Our responsibility was to track down replacement parts for F-111 fighter jets in Vietnam. We called bases all over the world to find the required component and ship it to the deployed location (and if necessary, we could cannibalize aircraft not in the theater of operations). I had to drive an assortment of small trucks and a forklift, so I needed a U.S. Government Driver's License. At the base driving school, I met my future husband, the tall, thin, dark-haired non-commissioned officer in charge. It was love at first sonnet. James was also an English major, resuming studies after his return from Vietnam. We began taking literature classes together at Texas Christian University and we married six months later. He was funny, had an inquiring mind and a nearly photographic memory, and was a Texan through and through, born in El Campo, fifty miles from the Gulf of Mexico. The Instamatic camera photos of me romping in the waves on nearby Galveston Beach, my first glimpse of the vastness of an ocean, revealed sheer delight on my beaming face.

After we were discharged from the Air Force, we lived in Baytown on the Houston Ship Channel, leading to one of the busiest seaports in the world. Together we sang along with the new generation of Austin-influenced country music, ate our fill of fried oysters, clams, and shrimp at San Jacinto Inn, and sailed our small boat in Trinity Bay. We both completed our degrees at the University of Houston, where we worked on the McGovern campaign and met his running mate, Sargent Shriver, who was also the first director of the Peace Corps. I received my Bachelor of Arts in English and a Master of Arts in Public Administration.

By 1977, when our son Geoffrey was six, James was a construction manager and I worked as a paralegal at a large downtown Houston law firm, sorting through the massive, yet fascinating, paper records of the contested estate of reclusive billionaire Howard Hughes. Because Hughes didn't leave a will, the disposition of his business empire fell to the courts. Though numerous purported wills appeared, naming heirs that ranged from Western movie actor Hopalong Cassidy to a Utah service-station operator who had supposedly given Hughes a ride in the desert, none was ultimately deemed valid. Long after I left the firm, the case went to the Supreme Court three times and was finally settled in 1984.

### Why Don't You Move to Hawai'i Instead?

James and I had been talking for months about leaving the big city to move to Colorado. My grandparents lived near Denver and my parents and brothers had relocated there. Then my Uncle Bob called, and it changed everything. I vividly remember our conversation as I paced in the kitchen twirling and untwirling the curly cord on the pink Princess wall phone as he asked me, "Why don't you move to Hawai'i instead?"

Uncle Bob was my mom's younger brother—the "black sheep" of the family. When I was a kid, he was the wild and crazy uncle who sky-dived, spent a summer on a sailboat crew in the Bahamas, and drove his red Kharmann Ghia convertible to Colorado when the family gathered at Christmas. I could talk to him about anything, and he always honored secrets. He was brilliant—an exceptional writer, a gifted actor, talented teacher, and a clever amateur landscape architect, engineer, and carpenter. He made me laugh and taught me to examine life beneath the surface.

While an English professor at Laney College in Oakland, California,

Uncle Bob became friends with one of his students—a Portuguese football player from Hawai'i Island, known as the Big Island. After one visit to his friend's house in 1976, within a year he sold his home (a 38-foot ketch in Embarcadero Cove Marina), cashed in his pension funds, and moved to Hawai'i. He built a house on the east side of the Big Island, south of Hilo, and began teaching for the United States Navy Program for Afloat College Education, which gives sailors at sea an opportunity to take college courses tuition-free. After several years on a dozen naval vessels, including three around-the-world voyages, he concluded his teaching career at the University of Hawai'i at Hilo.

After I hung up the phone, James and I talked for about ten minutes, looked at each other, and both said, "Why not?" A year and a half later, in 1978, we moved to the Big Island. I fell deeply in love with Hawai'i and immediately felt like I was home. I was captivated by the abundant rain, sunny beaches, trade winds, the ocean, snow-capped mountains, active volcanoes, tropical flowers, hula, the music . . . and on and on.

I worked as a real estate paralegal at a Hilo law firm and James had a custom furniture and cabinetry business. I immersed myself in Hawaiian culture. I took a language class, went to Hilo's Merrie Monarch Festivals (the competitive "world series" of hula), was captivated by the songs of old and new Hawai'i, and began to study the history and culture of the unique place where we lived, in Volcano Village, one mile from Hawai'i Volcanoes National Park. We often camped and hiked the black lava trails, and I volunteered at the Volcano Art Center in a historic building in the park.

We loved it there, but the cost of living was high, and wages were low. Five years later when our second son Jay was two, we decided to relocate to Colorado as we'd discussed years before that momentous call from Uncle Bob. We knew it would be better economically for our young family. But I never lost the desire and intent to move back to Hawai'i someday, and I visited Uncle Bob frequently. Meanwhile, our third and youngest son, Thomas, was born the year after we moved to Colorado.

Life was busy, and sometimes complicated, and after seventeen years of marriage, James and I divorced in 1987. When we fell in love and married, we really didn't know one another, and although we had a lot in common and were compatible in many ways, we ultimately weren't in numerous others.

Meanwhile, I had a rewarding, successful career as a real estate paralegal and law office manager for the Denver offices of two of the nation's largest law firms, traveling all over the country for my job, while teaching night classes in the paralegal program at the Community College of Aurora. The legal work was challenging and interesting, but the hours were long and the atmosphere stressful. I asked myself, "Where can I use legal, managerial, and real estate experience outside a law firm?" The answer led me to real estate portfolio management, and I loved it! I facilitated large and complex purchases, sales, and leases of real estate in Denver and Colorado, including one major transaction that required that I rush back from a Hawai'i vacation at Uncle Bob's to meet with the governor.

Then in 2004, after our boys were grown, I "retired" at fifty-five from my position as Real Estate Asset Manager for the State of Colorado and decided to "take the (pension) money and run"—back to Hawai'i!

### *If You Wait for the Right Time it Will Never Come*

I make it sound like an easy decision, but it wasn't.

A year earlier while visiting Uncle Bob, I sat on the steps of his guest cottage on a peaceful Sunday afternoon, contemplating my future options while drinking ice water with a squeeze from a freshly picked lemon. The air temperature was perfect, the rainforest around me was verdant, and I itched to play in the tropical gardens and begin to create my own Big Island haven. I'd already purchased three acres on which to build a home someday—a quarter mile down the narrow country road from Uncle Bob. I knew that "someday" had arrived, and I needed to come up with a plan and the courage to do it.

For months I pondered and strategized. I'd be far away from my aging parents, my sons, my only grandson, other family, and friends. I realized that I'd lose my career momentum and leave a well-paying job when I could instead just stay put and be better prepared financially for my long-term future. What would I do with my house? Uncle Bob had graciously offered me the cottage for the immediate future, but what would I do when I got there? I'd nurtured this dream of returning to Hawai'i for twenty years, but would it be what I wanted it to be? What *did* I want it to be? What if I didn't like it? What if it didn't work out? What if, what if, what if . . .?

Synchronous events that guided me in making this momentous decision happened again and again, such as the day in March when my secretary casually tossed the *Denver Business Journal* on my desk with the headline—SOMETIMES YOU HAVE TO MOVE ALL THE WAY TO PARADISE. The story was about a married couple (attorneys in Colorado) who decided to find a way to explore their passions while earning a living in Costa Rica. They said, "It was time to change the whole channel." They left behind family and friends, ate indigenous food, learned to speak Spanish, embraced a completely different culture, and befriended a wide variety of plants, animals, reptiles, and bugs when they slept in a tent for the first six months. They were now running Iguana Lodge, but in the beginning they did whatever it took to get by. The biggest takeaway from the story was: "Realize there is never a right time. If you wait for the right time, it will never come." I too now had the chance to do something else. I could change the channel of my life, and yet . . . what if?

Few would dispute the longing to live in such a beautiful setting, although there are many in the world. For lovely scenery and pleasant temperatures, one could move to Costa Rica, or Florida, or any place warm. But it wasn't just the climate or the beauty, it was *that* place where I needed to be. Every vacation for twenty years, I'd spent with Uncle Bob at his lushly landscaped retreat in the rainforest of the Big Island. I was there when the house was built, and together our family planted the trees and nurtured the land. This was the place that always drew me like a magnet.

That same spring, I happened to see a magazine article written by a local life coach about trusting yourself: "Are you ready to re-ignite your passion for life?" I took it as another synchronous omen and enlisted the author to help me make this momentous decision to leave behind everything that was secure, known, and successful to take off for a too-long-delayed return to Hawai'i. My coach was a support, confidante, listener, and challenger. During one exercise she suggested, I sat on the floor and moved around in a circle to sheets of paper on which I'd written various aspects of my life—job, money, kids, house, relation-ships, friends . . . and in the center, Hawai'i. As I scooted around on the plush carpet, pausing to contemplate each topic, I could feel my body talking to me; my shoulders would tighten, or I'd smile, as I sat eyes closed and thought about how it felt to be in that place. Then at the end, I "moved" to Hawai'i, and I felt the weight lift; I took a deep breath and relaxed.

Everything began to fall into place. I rented my house in Colorado to my youngest son and his roommate. The new strategic plan that I'd authored for the State real estate department was ready to be imple-mented. I had no further strings to hold me back except for my kids and family, and they already lived spread out from coast to coast.

I wrote in my journal:

*If I let my fears influence me more than my desire to be happy, I'll postpone joy and always wonder if I did the right thing. One sim-ple answer remains—just do it!*

I could hardly wait to shed the professional business suits, heels, and panty hose to wear flipflops, blue jeans, and tank tops! I had enough of a plan to calm the nerves of someone who'd always planned everything in detail, even though part of me was terrified with the prospect of being unemployed and not knowing what would come next. I shipped my Jeep Cherokee to Hawai'i, brought along Yamaha, my Golden retriever, had the guest cottage to stay in, and enough money to live the simple Hawaiian life that I'd wished for all these years.

On the flight to Hawai'i I wrote:

*It feels as if I'm jumping ship as soon as the shoreline comes into view and I can safely swim to the island. Along the way I'll be fearful and must be cautious—there'll be sharks, waves, undertow, and my own limitations. But the ship and its baggage will be left behind, and I know I have the strength, the ability, and the will-power to make the swim.*

Three days after I returned to the Big Island in 2005, and exactly one year after reading that *Denver Business Journal* headline, I offered to volunteer again at the Volcano Art Center in Hawai'i Volcanoes National Park. I helped in the office for three months, and then was hired as an education coordinator to organize native plant workshops, escort educational groups around the island, and share the beauty and mystery of the place I loved. I learned volumes about Hawai'i's geology, flora, fauna, and culture, and met many fascinating people.

Another delightful year went by and I was where I wanted to be, living in the rainforest, working at a job that I enjoyed, finally beginning to live the life I'd dreamed of. I loved meeting up with friends at the Volcano Farmer's Market early Sunday mornings, followed by a long walk in the forest with Yamaha excitedly sniffing every new aroma that crossed our path. I cherished my time with Uncle Bob, happily welcomed my son and grandson for a visit, and I brought Hawai'i to the mainland with handmade leis and bouquets for my middle son's wedding. I was savoring my life. And yet . . .

*It's been a year this week since my return to paradise. I've just read my last year of journal writing. It's always good to reflect on the passages in one's life. As happy as I am, I still feel that there's something out there more "meaningful" or "fulfilling." The lure of the Peace Corps still lingers in my mind. A couple of years ago I researched it thoroughly and met with a recruiter in Denver before I retired. But I knew that I had to come back to Hawai'i first and foremost.*

*In* Writing Down the Bones, *Natalie Goldberg said, "Sometimes you have to change something else in your life in order to move further." The idea of doing something totally out of my comfort zone sounds okay right now and may be just what I need. I wouldn't be able to build a house on my property as soon as I'd planned but perhaps that's not as important. I am where I'm supposed to be, just not yet doing what I'm supposed to do.*

After serious soul-searching, I listened to my inner voice. In April 2006, I talked it over with family and friends, and with excited anticipation I submitted my Peace Corps application.

### So You're Going to Somalia?

One couldn't ask for a specific country placement when I applied like can be done now, but I could indicate a preferred region (chances were about 50/50 of getting that choice). With my affinity for the tropics, I asked for the South Pacific. Several months and two interviews later, my recruiter reported that she would nominate me for service pending the background checks, medical exams, and placement opportunities. Feeling hopeful that I would be accepted, that winter I left my job at the art center to spend three months in Colorado, including Christmas gathered with family. Then I returned to Uncle Bob's guest cottage, and nearly one year after submitting my application, still anxiously waiting for an invitation from Peace Corps, I wrote:

*I'm in the doldrums. Such a wonderful nautical word. Waiting for the wind to fill my sails. Keeping warm under the covers until the sun came up this morning, I thought, "What will I do if I don't go to Peace Corps?" And the truth is, I don't know! I have no back-up plan! That's a disconcerting thought, and rare for me.*

One week later, I got an invitation in the mail to go to Samoa! I happily accepted, wondering what my future held.

"So, you're going to Somalia?" people would ask. Or, more commonly, "Are you going to American Samoa?" I always answered, "No, Western Samoa." Although I knew it wasn't called "Western" Samoa anymore, but many people still think of it this way. To tell them where Samoa was, I said, "It's an island nation, south of the equator, near Fiji and Tahiti." After living in the South Pacific, I now know this is like saying that Kansas City is near San Francisco and Miami. Of course, to be fair, most Americans' exposure to the Samoan Islands is via the NFL, the undeniably delicious "Samoas" Girl Scout cookies, or The Rock (Dwayne Johnson, or Seiuli, his Samoan name).

For three thousand years the Samoans lived in relative isolation on their archipelago of small islands, with occasional journeys to and from other island nations in ocean-going outrigger canoes. They were master wayfinders—ancestors of the Polynesian voyagers who later settled in the Hawaiian Islands.

The first known European to sight the Samoan islands was a Dutchman in 1722. Some years later, French explorer de Bougainville, impressed with the Samoans' numerous canoes and skill in handling them, called them the Navigator Islands. While the name didn't stick, since they already had one (ah, the arrogance), it was apt. Samoans were indisputably some of the world's best open-ocean sailors, centuries before Europeans dared to venture out of sight of the shoreline.

In the 1800s, there was a thriving trade by German settlers in cacao and copra (dried coconut meat from which oil is extracted). There are still remnants of the huge coconut plantations, and it's common for Samoan families to have German lineage. However, Great Britain and America were also interested in the islands. In 1899, the three countries agreed to divide the archipelago into German Samoa and American Samoa, and the British were content to colonize elsewhere in the Pacific.

At the outbreak of World War I, at Great Britain's behest, the New Zealand Expeditionary Force invaded the German colony unopposed. After the war, the League of Nations gave New Zealand a mandate to administer the islands and close ties remain between the two countries. Nearly every Samoan has family in New Zealand, English is spoken with a Kiwi accent, and the government and school system are based on New Zealand's.

In 1962, "Western Samoa" became the first small-island nation in the South Pacific to gain independence, and in 1997 the nation officially changed its name to "Samoa."

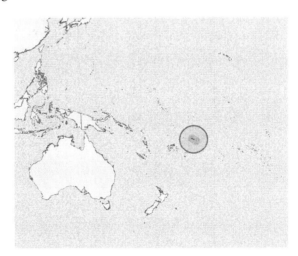

Samoa is located south of the equator in the middle of the Pacific, about even latitudinally with the northern tip of Australia. There are two main islands, Savai'i and 'Upolu; two smaller islands in the straits separating the main islands, Apolima and Manono; and a handful of uninhabited islets. Savai'i is about forty miles by thirty miles. The other major island, 'Upolu (where I lived), is roughly fifty miles long and fifteen miles wide.

The country's capital, Āpia, is on 'Upolu, and was the only town of any notable size. It had a population of thirty-four thousand when I lived there and is only slightly larger today. The remainder of the nation's one hundred eighty thousand people lived in small villages, mostly along the coastlines.

## ISLANDS OF SAMOA

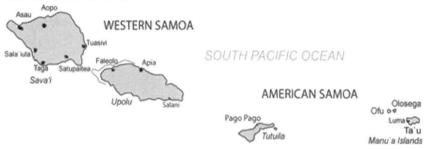

(This photo and the previous photo by Unknown Author are licensed under CC BY-SA.)

American Samoa is sixty-eight nautical miles east of Samoa. Their five tiny volcanic islands and two coral atolls encompass an area of just under eighty square miles, slightly larger than Washington D.C. Tutuila Island, with its deep-water harbor of Pago Pago, became the largest jungle training center in the South Pacific during World War II.

I read every book about Samoa that I could get my hands on and practiced Samoan words (which I hoped I pronounced correctly). On our last Sunday afternoon together, with everything I'd read drifting through my anxious and excited mind, Uncle Bob and I sat in the trade wind breeze at his favorite perch on the balcony facing the ocean. We shared bursts of intense conversation followed by long silences. The next morning, we hugged tightly, and I left with two huge, black suitcases stuffed with lightweight clothing including skirts and dresses for church, snorkel gear, a battery-operated lantern, my laptop and camera, a couple of my favorite books, small gifts for children, crafting supplies, and whatever else I could stick in at the last minute. On the plane I wrote:

> *Here it is. The day. The day I leave my beloved Hawai'i for ports unknown. Yes, there's a physical destination, but I don't know where I'll end up. I know I'll be challenged, moved to tears, exhilarated, rewarded, changed. I'll still be who I am, but I'll return with a new layer added to the composite of me that will make the overall blend new and different.*

## I'm Really Here!

In Samoan it's *le vasa*—the ocean. Although you've been flying for ten and a half hours with nothing below but the vast expanse of the Pacific, the sea captures your attention as you approach Faleolo Airport on the Island of 'Upolu. Waves crash offshore, but inside the fringing reef the water is calm, a nearly phosphorescent, most exquisite, azure. As outrigger dugout canoes float tranquilly, dark shadows below reveal coral colonies. Beneath the surface a whole other world exists.

At daybreak on June 6, 2007, we arrived on Air New Zealand from Los Angeles where our group of sixteen had gathered for two days of orientation. "We" were eight men and eight women in Group 78—the seventy-eighth group to serve in Samoa since 1967—mostly young people, but also two couples my age. Despite the early hour, a dozen cheerful Peace Corps staff and volunteers met us in the airport lobby holding a six-foot long WELCOME! banner. We were delayed when one of the young men in our group was held in customs for half an hour because he brought a plastic bag stuffed with other plastic bags in his suitcase. They thought that was odd and searched his bags thoroughly. Knowing now what we didn't know then, it *was* odd. We didn't know that in Samoa biodegradable bags made of starch were plentiful.

The air was hot and muggy, and we were weary from lack of sleep as we wrestled our luggage to a waiting blue and yellow bus. For forty-five minutes we looked from left to right and back again, trying to take it all in as we bounced along through small coastal villages on the government road that circumnavigates the island. We rode to Āpia Central Hotel where we ate a breakfast of white bread toast, hard boiled eggs, and fresh papaya at a small buffet set up in the hotel courtyard. I unpacked a few things and collapsed in my room for a short nap.

Āpia Central Hotel was a modest, two-story, square building with all rooms opening to the center. Most guests were local, not tourists. It had served for many years as the Peace Corps' site for trainees to stay and learn. My tiny room with a single bed had no refrigerator, phone, or TV. At night I listened to Samoan radio to help learn the language.

The eleven young people shared four rooms, the couples each had a room, and I was given my own—because I was "an older woman." I'd learned that elders were respected in Samoan culture, but I hadn't thought how it might apply to me at fifty-seven. (I later missed the deferential treatment when I returned to America!)

The center courtyard of the Āpia Central Hotel.

That first night I wrote:

*There's so much more to come! I can't even begin to evaluate any-thing. It feels good though. My only real concern is if I'll be able to accomplish a worthwhile project in my village. I'm not sure why I'm anxious about that. I have many skills and I'll get training and support. Maybe it's because, although this will be a great adventure for me, that's not why I'm here. I want to contribute something. We were told that the development projects are just one of the three goals of Peace Corps. The other two are to help promote a better un-derstanding of American people within the country served, and to help promote a better understanding by Americans of other people and cultures. I can do that! Two out of three ain't bad!*

But my first thoughts didn't tell the whole story. Why *did* I join the Peace Corps? Yes, I wanted to travel, have an "adventure," do some-thing out of the ordinary, challenging, and fun, and I wanted to make a difference, somehow, somewhere. However, although I didn't realize the depth of it at the time that I applied, there was an even more com-pelling need behind the decision. Even after moving over three thou-sand miles from Colorado to Hawai'i, I hadn't figured out who I was *now*, and what I wanted to do next. I'd just gotten busy again, working full-time, volunteering . . .

This would be the first time since college that I hadn't worked at a daily job, despite my supposed retirement. Peace Corps is also a job, but in a whole different way. Perhaps I had "run away from home" in a sense. I'd gone from my parents' house to a college dorm, to Air Force barracks, to our married home, and then raised kids for thirty years. When I moved back to Hawai'i, I spent a lot of time with Uncle Bob next door and helped him with chores and errands. I was looking for-ward to finally living alone in Samoa. Maybe "living alone" meant not being responsible for anyone else. As I was to discover, I was given the daunting opportunity to be accountable for my own well-being in a whole new way—and sometimes when you're living with someone else you can feel very alone.

### *Learning the Samoan Way*

The first three months would be rigorous training until we were accepted for service and sworn in as official volunteers. We began classes at the hotel for ten days, and then later we would be bussed to our "training village" of Manunu. There we'd live with local families to be immersed in the language and culture. After we were no longer trainees, each of us (couples together, of course) would be sent to villages on both major islands for our service assignment.

Peace Corps (PC) staff also stayed at the hotel and in the village, teaching us daily classes. Our trainers were local men and women who taught us Samoan language and culture, classes on safety and security, health and medical classes, lessons on funding sources and techniques to use in our later-to-be-assigned villages, and myriad other topics. One of my favorite memories is the day that one of the female trainers taught the women how to discreetly bathe from a five-gallon bucket without removing her *lāvalava* (sarong)—using a little ingenious shifting around and about—in case we needed to bathe that way in our villages.

I hadn't given much thought to pre-service training and was ready to take on whatever came my way, but it was more intense than I'd expected. We started language lessons in the hotel courtyard the morning we arrived. Each day we chased the shade in a constantly moving circle of folding chairs. I was used to warm weather living in Hawai'i, but not like Samoa! In the heat of the day, it was impossible not to sweat while doing nothing more than sitting in the shade. Early on, I bought a fan woven from *laufala* (leaves of the pandanus tree). Every Samoan adult carried a fan on the bus, at the market, at church—and I quickly learned why.

We knew that some of us might not make it through training if we failed language tests or other written and oral exams. Worldwide, about one-third of Peace Corps Volunteers (PCVs) leave early for numerous reasons—from illness to misconduct. Four volunteers were sent home shortly before we arrived for watching porn videos at night in the PC office. In Group 79, which arrived four months after us, one volunteer decided to go home after five days! I never learned why.

Constantly learning, we attended classes at the hotel all day, Monday through Friday and a half-day on Saturday. Each evening, we briefly freshened up then walked together to dinner at a nearby restaurant. Georgie's, one of our favorites, had surprisingly good pizza. We'd skirt around and hop over the drainage ditches along the sides of the streets, watching out for cars, buses, and stray dogs, laughing, commiserating, and practicing our Samoan.

Āpia was actually a conglomeration of villages, like subdivisions of a much larger city, each with its own mayor and village council. The main metropolitan district—government buildings, restaurants, shops, open air markets, a couple dozen or so banks and other office buildings—was about ten blocks wide and twenty blocks long, hugging the waterfront with the primary port facilities at the far end. From Beach Road, the residential areas fanned out in every direction with their own small businesses. On the mountain above town was the last home and resting place of the great storyteller, Robert Louis Stevenson.

There were few sidewalks and only a couple of stoplights. That changed quite quickly though. Three months after we arrived, Samoa hosted the South Pacific Games, now known as The Pacific Games. Held every four years since 1963, it's a multi-sport event much like the Olympics (albeit on a much smaller scale), with participation exclusively from countries in the Pacific region. So, Samoa had to prepare for a relatively huge influx of people and build sporting venues. For this endeavor, the Chinese government stepped in to assist, including installing sidewalks and stoplights.

Large packs of dogs roamed the streets, especially at night, and I'd lay in my hotel room bed listening to them snarl as they fought. In preparation for the games, there was a concerted effort to clear them out, and it got better, but to this day whenever I visit, I'm wary of dogs wandering about at night in Āpia.

Those first days whizzed by with all the intense sensory, phonetic, and cultural input streaming into my brain. Each day was the same: lessons, walk to dinner, back to the hotel to do homework, sleep, and then do it all over again. So we were delighted when we heard that we'd have an outing with PC staff to Matareva Beach on the other side of the island.

*Matareva is a picture-perfect white sand beach lined with palms. I played in the ocean, snorkeled, and saw a stunning blue star fish. Perhaps it was just the beach we were at, but it seemed to me that the fish weren't as large as I'm used to in Hawai'i and there weren't as many. The countryside and villages along the way were bustling with Sunday activity and families walked to church in their white clothes—very picturesque. Tomorrow, it's back to class in Āpia.*

*In four days we go to Manunu. It still feels like a trip, and not a two-year job.*

### Thank You for Welcoming us Pisikoa

Manunu, our training village, was near the Falefa River, inland from the north coast, encircled by lushly green, cloud-shrouded mountain tops. After our bus wound several miles up a muddy, one-lane road, we came to a couple dozen traditional open houses and a few more made of concrete blocks with metal roofs. The homes surrounded a large grassy area in the center called the *malae*, used for rugby, cricket, or large gatherings. Two hundred people lived in the village, with additional *fale* down the road, or back a short way in the bush. Most often "fale" refers to a Samoan house, but it literally means a structure of any kind. A "traditional" fale, or what I sometimes refer to as an "open" fale, is open on the sides and built on a concrete foundation or an elevated wooden platform, on which large posts support a thatched roof, or more commonly one of painted corrugated metal.

When we arrived, it looked as if all the villagers were in the malae waiting to greet us. Kids ran alongside our bus, whooping and cheering. As we disembarked, it suddenly felt real.

We were quickly ushered into a large open fale for an 'ava ceremony, one of Samoa's most significant cultural customs. In training at the hotel we'd been taught how to participate in this important ritual, but now, as I sat there across from the somber high chief with the bottom of his necklace of dried pandanus fruit—painted bright red—resting on his expansive belly, it took on a new significance. The village orator, a "talking chief," theatrically recited tributes to ancestors and welcomed us with formal traditional phrases in his booming voice as I strained to understand a word or a phrase here and there.

An 'ava ceremony to welcome important visitors in a Samoan village.

'Ava, called "kava" in other Pacific countries, is part of the black pepper family. The ground-up roots are mixed with water, then the strained water is drunk. It tasted like dirty licorice to me. I never drank enough to feel it, but I was told that if you drink a lot your tongue and lips get numb, and it's a general relaxant, but not intoxicating. It was consumed in ritual fashion at the beginning of every important occasion, formal gathering, reception for guests, beginning of a meeting of the village chiefs, and even the launch of a rugby tournament. The whole ceremony was carried out with great care and attention to detail, every move deliberate.

Only the village chiefs (*matai*) and honored guests participated, with designated seating arrangements—the high chiefs on one side, the high orators on another side, and the rest seated according to rank. With glancing looks at one another, curiously peering beyond the fale, we solemnly sat as we'd been taught, cross-legged on woven laufala mats spread on the concrete floor. A few feet in front of the long row of chiefs with their backs to the posts sat young men in their twenties or thirties—shirtless, glistening with coconut oil, and wearing only colorfully printed lāvalava. In front of them was the 'ava liquid in a foot-wide circular wooden bowl called a *tānoa,* with small carved legs around the circumference. The 'ava mixer sat behind the tānoa, scooped up the muddy-looking juice in half of a polished coconut shell and handed it to a server. One of the chiefs called out a ceremonial ritual, directing the presentation of the 'ava according to rank.

I nervously waited, reviewing the proper protocol in my mind until it was my turn. The server lifted the coconut shell above his head and strode to the center of the fale. The chief shouted again and the young man walked toward me, holding out the 'ava cup, keeping his left hand with the palm outwards pressed tightly behind the small of his back. With a graceful sweeping motion from right to left, he presented me the cup. I grasped it, said, *"Lau 'ava lea le Atua, manuia!"* (This is your 'ava God, blessings!), then sipped the peppery liquid. The rest of the group responded, *"Soifua!"* (Good health!). I tossed the remainder over my shoulder and handed the cup back to the server who returned to the tānoa to refill it. (The act of throwing the remaining contents over the shoulder is said to be an unspoken wish that all misfortune should likewise disappear; unconsumed 'ava is never returned to the tānoa.)

As the matai continued one by one to welcome us with long speeches and prayers, I was acutely aware that within a matter of minutes I'd meet my host family. Finally, we assembled back on the malae and listened intently. Sa'u, a big jolly fellow who was one of our PC language trainers, announced the name of the family I'd live with for the next two months, and Reverend Roma Enosa and his wife Wilma came forward with greetings of kisses and hugs. They were both short and stout with smiles that lit up a room.

As we split off from the group, I walked nervously with them to their nearby fale of ivory-painted concrete blocks, bright red window and door trim, and a red metal roof. The house was compact—a main living area about twenty-by-twenty feet with a kitchen at one end, and a bathroom and two small bedrooms in an adjoining wing. Pastors, especially Congregational, were high-ranking and influential in the villages and as a result lived in some of the nicer houses, drove better vehicles, and had more food and other amenities. Before arriving in Manunu, I'd been told that I'd live in the Congregational pastor's house and have my own room—as a perquisite, again, because I was an "older" woman.

Roma and Wilma's home had indoor plumbing, a refrigerator, a kitchen range with an oven, and even a microwave. Nonetheless, much of the cooking was done in the *umukuka* (cook house) that each Samoan family had behind the main house. Inside, the house walls were painted bright white and the curtains on the louvered windows were vibrant tropical prints. I perched tensely on the edge of a sofa covered in another delightfully colorful fabric (sealed in plastic, which was common to keep it clean in a climate where mildew grew rampantly) and we began to tentatively get to know each other.

*"Tālofa. O a'u 'o Donna. 'Ou te sau mai Hawai'i."* ("Hello. My name is Donna. I come from Hawai'i.")

*"Tālofa! O a'u 'o Roma."* ("Hello! My name is Roma.")

*"O a'u 'o Wilma."* ("My name is Wilma.")

I was delighted to learn that Roma spoke English quite well and had lived in California for fifteen years (Long Beach has the largest Samoan population on the mainland United States). Wilma's English was limited, but with my ever-improving Samoan and her patience, we said what we needed to say. It was late Saturday afternoon by this time, so after dinner accompanied by small talk, I fell into bed, spent from the nervous energy of the day.

The next morning the village was abuzz with preparations for Sunday religious services. All but four of our group lived with families who were members of Roma's congregation, the only church in Manunu, next door to their house. The others walked about a mile with their families to a Mormon church in the next village. The Congregational Church, whose missionaries came to Samoa in the 1830s, was the largest religion. *Everyone* attended church on Sunday (more than once), and it was a day of rest. Families ate a big meal after the morning service and stayed at home to *mālōlō* (rest or relax). In Āpia, stores and restaurants were closed, and life in the villages was even more circumspect. There was definitely no swimming, rugby, or volleyball on Sunday, three favorite local pastimes.

Roma asked me to say a few words at the service about his sermon topic—Trust in Jesus. I hurriedly wrote what I could manage in Samoan and asked him for help with the gaps in my meager language skills.

*Tālofa. E la'itiiti la'u fa'aSāmoa. 'Onosa'i fa'amolemole.*
*Fa'afetai le fa'aaloalo.*
*'Ou te sau mai Hawai'i. Fiafia tele a'u i Manunu.*
*O le mataupu mo le aso: O ai tatou te talitonu i ai?*

*O nisi taimi tatou te fefefe ma pala'a'ai. Pe fo'i o tatou pisikoa sa tatou le mautinoa.*

*Pei tai 'ua fetalai Iesu, "Talitonu mai ia te a'u."*

*E leai se mea tatou te popole ai. Tatou fa'atuatua ia Iesu. E alofa Iesu ia tatou.*

*Fa'afetai mo 'outou agalelei. Mo le talia lelei o matou pisikoa 'i lo 'outou nu'u.*

*Ia fa'amanuia mai le Atua. Soifua.*

I said:

Hello. I only speak a little Samoan. Patience, please.

Thank you for your hospitality.

I come from Hawai'i. I'm happy to be in Manunu.

The theme for today: Whom do we trust?

We're all afraid sometimes. We *pisikoa* (Peace Corps Volunteers) are nervous too.

Jesus said, "Trust me."

We don't have to be worried. We have faith in Jesus. Jesus loves us.

Thank you for your kindness. Thank you for welcoming us pisikoa to your village.

God bless you.

*It seemed to go well. They didn't laugh too much!*

The malae in Manunu from the steps of the Congregational church.

The author between Roma and Wilma after Sunday morning church in Manunu.

One of our first village assignments from the Peace Corps trainers was to recite the names, ages, and relationships of the members of our Samoan host families, in Samoan of course. In the beginning I didn't understand who was actually part of the family I lived with. Roma and Wilma had three sons, Roma Junior, seventeen, eight-year-old Herman, Enosa, three, and a baby daughter, Urima, who was four months old. Occasionally Kanana, their teenage daughter, stayed with us, although she lived with her aunt and uncle in a village near Āpia.

Fa'apa'ia, thirteen, had lived with them since she was a baby, but her biological mother was someone else in Manunu. There was also Roma's niece, twelve-year-old Foa'i, and Lamanda, twenty, daughter of another family in Manunu. Since Wilma was still nursing tiny Urima, the girls did the laundry, housework, cooked, and babysat before and after school.

Leleiga, twenty-three, son of another family in Manunu, also lived with us full time and was attending the National University of Samoa along with Lamanda (Roma paid their tuition). Lisi, forty-two, was Wilma's cousin, and he, Leileiga, and Roma, Jr., fed the chickens and pigs, took care of the outdoor chores and gardens, and slept in a small fale behind the main house. The older girls slept in another small fale, and the small children slept with Roma and Wilma on the floor under a hanging mosquito net in the living room.[1]

I felt fortunate to have my own room with a comfortable, mosquito-net-draped, four-poster bed (normally reserved for guests) and a mirrored dresser (most of the PC women didn't have mirrors and were a bit envious). Also in the room was a large wooden wardrobe for Wilma's finer clothes and Sunday hats. I had keys to the house and my room. Our group's housing was varied, with some volunteers sharing a traditional open-sided fale with a large family and only a couple of sheets hung to create a "room."

We continued our rigorous training and language sessions, always

---

1  Names of the key people mentioned throughout are listed at the end of the book.

with homework at night and scarcely a moment to ourselves. Every day we sat in our "classroom" in a large open fale on the other side of the church, barefooted and cross-legged on woven mats in the Samoan way. I could only sit like that for a limited time, while for the Samoans it was effortless having done so from childhood. For a break, I tucked my feet under me sideways or stuck them straight out and covered them with a mat, as it was impolite to point your feet at someone. We were taught other cultural customs such as when you moved in front of people, seated or standing, you must say *tulou* (excuse me) and bow slightly. If you wanted to speak to someone seated, especially if that person was older or high ranking, you brought yourself physically down to their level by sitting or crouching so you were at eye level or lower. And it was considered impolite to eat or drink while walking

The most important lesson every Peace Corps volunteer learns is understanding of and respect for the local culture. Our trainers emphasized the need to dress appropriately, the importance of attending church in our villages to assimilate, how to properly address people of different social levels, bus protocol, and many other topics. I learned *Fa'aSāmoa*—"the Samoan way." The word "fa'aSāmoa" covers everything from denoting the Samoan language, to food, clothing, governance, the complex and often baffling levels of social hierarchy, and so much more. Simply put, it's "the way we do things in Samoa."

*Here's an interesting tidbit we learned today about relationships in Samoa, a very religiously conservative country. If you even slightly encourage someone, you're "dating." Friendliness may be misinterpreted, and Western women are particularly desirable. If you're alone with someone of the opposite sex, you are presumed to be intimate. Public displays of affection are discouraged. I don't plan to need that, but good to know!*

We learned that like most of the world's cultures, Samoa is a communal or collectivist society—quite different from our American individualistic culture. Pacific Island cultures fall at the extreme collectivistic end of the continuum, and American culture is at the farthest individualistic end. These differences presented some of the biggest challenges for Peace Corps volunteers.

In America we're all about "the self." We value self-sufficiency, self-determination, self-direction, and self-responsibility. On the other hand, collectivists view people as interdependent. In Samoan culture, everyone should contribute to the whole, work with others to achieve mutual goals, adhere to traditional group values, understand their place within the social hierarchy, and perform their expected roles. Americans view themselves in control of their lives and therefore may blame themselves and feel shame or guilt if they don't meet expectations. Samoans identify strongly with family, church, or village, and they feel shame or guilt if their behavior brings disgrace on the group.

Culture also influences how decisions are made within a family. In American individualism, the ideal is for everyone to be able to freely make their own decisions. Opinions of family elders may be respected, but as youth become adults, they expect and are expected to make decisions about their own lives. In Samoa, elders are revered and often have authority to ensure that family members do what's best for the family, rather than what's best for themselves as individuals. Instead of living independently or going away to college, young adults may be expected to remain home to fulfill roles within the family. Such decisions by authority figures are obeyed with less questioning than is typical in individualistic cultures. In Samoa one's family is an integral extension of one's life.

Americans believe that we should continually improve and advance in our education, careers, and other endeavors. These combined individual efforts are expected to generate progress at the national level, creating a higher standard of living. Long-established collectivistic cultures may not place a strong value on this kind of progress. Time is less like an arrow into the future and more like a circular process, as seasons change and people repeat traditional activities, such as fishing, planting, and harvesting crops. Families and communities faithfully carry on the activities that have sustained their lives over generations, rather than trying to improve the system into which they were born.

A comparison of idioms illustrates it well. Americans will say, "May the best man win!" and the Samoan will answer, "My turn today, yours tomorrow."

*We've been here in Manunu for ten days. When we first arrived, with the awkwardness of meeting my family and settling in, it was the first time I wanted to be back in Hawai'i rather than here. I had a similar moment during the week, but those thoughts pass, and tonight I'm feeling relaxed and happy. Because of the novel environment and the rigorous training schedule, I realized today that I've put out of my mind much of what might have occupied me otherwise, worries or even just routine planning. I simply have to take each day as it comes.*

At daybreak each morning while the air was still, quiet, and cool, I would slip out the side door and walk along the country road leading out of the village. Cattle grazed in pastures on either side until I reached a tangle of giant banyan trees where I usually turned around. When I came back, one of the girls would serve breakfast to Roma and me, he at the head of the table and me on his left, while Wilma tended to Urima, and the other girls did household chores. Since he'd lived in the States, we talked easily about American politics, sports, and of course about family, Peace Corps, or village events. My usual morning fare included two hard-fried eggs, toast and jam, papaya with a squeeze of lime, fresh coconut, and black tea. Then I walked in the dew-laden grass two "doors" down to our classroom fale to listen and learn as much as I could, as fast as I could.

### *Learning the Language is a Constant Process*

Early on, the training staff gave us Samoan names imitating our English names in Samoan. Mine was *Tona* (tō′ nah), but the only people who called me that were the PC trainers and later, grandfather Tamamasui in the village where I'd eventually work and live. Most volunteers went by their Samoan names, and some I still refer to in that way although we've been back in the States for a decade or more.

We were supposed to speak mostly Samoan since that was one of the "jobs" of our host family—to teach us the language and the culture. Even though it seemed like a ceaseless struggle to learn *gagana Sāmoa* (Samoan language) fast enough to become semi-fluent, I genuinely enjoyed that part. I've been fascinated with languages since I was a four-year-old sitting on Grandma's lap memorizing my first German poem—about the cows who give us milk—from a book she'd read as a little girl. It was her first language; she learned English at seventeen and had a charming accent all her life. I studied German in high school, continuing in college, along with Middle English and Old English, and considered becoming a German language teacher. If I were able to do life over, I think I would get a PhD in linguistics and teach at a university. I find it compelling—the etymology, foreign adoptions and adaptations, history, compounds, all of it.

When I moved to Hawai'i at twenty-nine, I took a conversational Hawaiian class and taught myself the basic structure, pronunciation, and rhythm of the language. I couldn't speak it but over the years I learned and listened. I knew that knowing a smattering of Hawaiian would help me learn Samoan. There are notable differences, but the pronunciation is the same, and the alphabet and cadence are similar since they're both Polynesian tongues.[2] (Throughout this memoir I've used the word "Samoa" as it's commonly written in English. However,

---

2  A guide to pronunciation, a glossary of Samoan words, and names of the key plac-es mentioned are included at the end of the book.

in the Samoan language it is "Sāmoa" with emphasis on the first syllable.)

In our classroom fale after we learned about varying subjects in the morning, I'd unbend my elderly knees, stand and stretch, and walk home for lunch with Roma. If I was lucky I had a few minutes to mālōlō before language class in the afternoon. The trainers split us into three groups based on our proficiency. I was always in the middle group, my vocabulary sometimes making up for lack of grammatical finesse.

*Saʻu keeps telling me how well I'm doing "especially for an older person." That irritates me, since I think I'm as intelligent and capable academically as I was when I was younger. I also have more to build on with a lifetime of learning. Some of it's aptitude of course. Maybe historically it's been more difficult for older people to learn the language, but it still annoys me!*

*I got a grade of 95 on my first oral competency exam (interview). I think I actually got points when I said in Samoan, "I forgot" and "Let me think for a moment." Saʻu laughed in surprise for what that was worth. Bits and pieces are falling into place. I get to learning plateaus—I have a breakthrough when it clicks—and then I can go to the next level.*

Some days we sat on our mats with pencils and written tests to puzzle out the peculiarities of the grammar and vocabulary that we were expected to converse with after only three months. Before graduation and village placement, there would be a final language proficiency test that intimidated all of us. I nearly always carried a small, blue glossary and phrase book that I'd created, and constantly added to, with sections such as "Food" or "Animals" or "Ocean Words." Of course, when you're in a foreign country where everyone else is speaking a different language, you become a constant student—in church, shopping, project meetings, on the bus, waiting for the bus.

Modern Samoan has two styles of pronunciation, often termed the T-language (formal) and the K-language (colloquial). The T is the original Samoan spoken when the first Europeans arrived. The K developed as the missionaries attempted to write the language. The change of Samoan from an oral to a written language had an interesting effect on the spoken language. Samoans began to pronounce t as k and n as ng, as in song. This change spread throughout the islands to the point where today's most often spoken Samoan is the K-language. For example: *'Ou te matamata le TV* (I watch the TV) versus *'Ou ke makamaka le TV.*

Nonetheless, Samoans view the T-language as the most correct form and use it when singing, writing, preaching, praying, broadcasting on radio or television, teaching, and speaking to foreigners. It is the language of meetings and parliament. Children learn to speak using the K and began to learn the formal T upon entering school. Native speakers effortlessly switch from one to the other depending upon the situation. Because the K-language wasn't normally written, Peace Corps taught us the T-language. In addition, many Samoans felt that the T was the appropriate form a non-Samoan should speak. I regret that I didn't learn to converse easily in the K-language; I primarily used the T, even for everyday conversations. But at least they could understand me, and as a *pālagi* (also *papālagi*, a foreigner) it was expected.[3]

*In Samoa (and the rest of the Pacific, I presume) Hawai'i isn't considered part of the United States. Of course, they know it is geopolitically, but in ordinary conversation they're mutually exclusive. The trainers taught everyone else to say, "I'm from America," but told me I should say "I'm from Hawai'i." It makes sense when I think about it. Hawai'i was part of their Polynesian culture and civilization long before it was part of our country.*

---

3 *Pā* means to burst and *lagi* is sky. Therefore, the first foreigners "burst" through the sky when their towering sailing ships appeared on the ocean horizon. It isn't a pejorative.

I never felt truly fluent but eventually I could communicate well enough to do anything I needed to do in Āpia. Even though many taxi drivers and shopkeepers spoke English, I always spoke Samoan and wrote down new vocabulary words every day.

"Where do you come from?" they'd ask.

"*Ou te sau mai Hawai'i. 'Ua e o 'o i Hawai'i?*" (I come from Hawai'i. Have you traveled to Hawai'i?)

We all like hearing our own language. Words open doors and make us feel at home. I always asked about Hawai'i because there was an automatic bond created when they knew I was from a Pacific island as well. The response would almost always be something such as: "No, but my brother lives there" or "Once I went to visit my aunty in Waianae."

English is a mishmash, as are Americans. By comparison, Samoan is a language steeped in over two thousand years of tradition, considered to be the oldest form of Polynesian, including ornate and voluminous genealogies, chants, legends, and songs that demonstrate a profound reverence for the past. With varying amounts of mythological elaboration, these tell historic tales of the migrations of a sea-faring people, their adventures on the way, and the anthropomorphic gods who created them.

It was important in Samoan hierarchical society to learn the very formal and respectful *gagana fa'aalo'alo* (respect language) used to address chiefs and other notable persons. Children were taught from a young age how to communicate appropriately and accurately. For example, although the common word for "eat" is *'ai,* when addressing an ordinary chief you would say *tausami*, and when speaking to a high chief, one uses the word *taute.*

Samoans were sometimes ingrained to be so respectful that they talked to please and therefore often told me what I wanted to hear rather than the truth. I suspect that there were many times when I was told, "the carpenter will be here tomorrow" or "we'll be meeting next week" even though it was likely that there was no plan at all. We learned nonverbal communication as well, including gestures, eyebrow raises, glances that carried meaning, and the "tsk tsk tsk" made with a soft clicking sound on the side of one's mouth that signified disapproval.

In a society with a rich and ancient oral tradition, proverbs were an important part of the culture. These unique sayings provided connections to truths beyond one person or any single moment in time, and often incorporated historical events or people. Many of these expressions were studied, memorized, and used only by the village orators (talking chiefs). They were highly valued, guarded, and handed down like family heirlooms, stashed away until necessary to illustrate, celebrate, or provide a moral for the appropriate event. However, every Samoan could quote sayings handed down through the centuries, often reflecting life on the sea or in nature.

At the start of each training day, we'd sit on our fala mats waiting for Sa'u to write "the proverb of the day" on the whiteboard in big black letters, such as: *E lē sua se lolo i se popo se tasi* = You can't make oil from one coconut = All opinions are important.

In addition to gagana Samoa, we learned some basic British English brought with the New Zealand influence. A biscuit was a cookie, chips were French fries, a car park was a parking lot, petrol was gas, a lift was an elevator . . . along with some adaptations such as "plantations" which had come to mean the small family farms of taro, sweet potatoes, and other produce grown in the villages. I found myself spelling words in the British fashion, like "grey," "centre," or "colour."

Up until now Group 78 had been relatively sheltered, staying together at Āpia Central and then with our training families in Manunu. Soon we'd be briefly on our own, partnering up with other PC volunteers throughout the country for some one-on-one training as we continued to prepare for our eventual transition to our assigned villages.

# Chapter 2

## Choppy Seas at the Outset

*E mana'o 'i le ufi 'ae fefe 'i le papa*
*"You want the yam but are afraid of the rock"*
*Whatever you want comes with difficulty.*

*After our first two weeks in Manunu, we're staying temporarily back at Āpia Central for a short training. We heard some negative tales from other PCVs about their experiences in their training villages, but our group's seem to be uniquely positive. I think perhaps Manunu is a very special place. I've come to know and like my family and I know I'll want to keep in touch.*

Before we would return to Manunu and our host families, each of us spent two days and nights with an experienced volunteer. I was assigned to stay with Jordan from Group 76 in her village on the south side of the island. She was a twenty-something petite hippie from Seattle with a pixyish grin and short light brown hair.

Her host family had built a small fale for her on short stilts with a wooden platform and a thatched roof. She'd tacked yards of colorful cloth to the walls and ceiling to keep termite droppings off her bed and makeshift desk. The extended family lived in similar structures nearby; the main house had a rusted corrugated roof instead of thatch. There was a cookhouse, outhouse, and a six-foot-tall white PVC pipe sticking out of the ground with a faucet for shower and all-around household use. I thought I'd probably be living like this if I made it through training, passed all the tests, and was sworn in officially on August 22nd. As it turned out, I was very wrong about that!

Jordan was an Intercoastal Management volunteer with a degree in zoology specializing in fisheries. From her village, she rode the bus daily to a nonprofit in Āpia where she was designing an environmental education curriculum. In the late afternoon sunset we walked barefoot along the beach as she shared firsthand what it was like to be a pisikoa (Peace Corps volunteer), along with helpful phrases such as, *"Aua le kaukala i kiki!"* (Don't talk so cheeky!)

Jordan's fale in Tafitoala on my two-day visit.

The family was welcoming and even though they spoke mostly Samoan, we had a laughter-filled dinner together seated on fala mats in their fale. Later, Jordan and I excused ourselves to her hut and talked into the night about the realities of PC life.

## *Celebrating Independence*

It was the eve of the Fourth of July and the next morning we bussed to Āpia to snorkel at Palolo Deep National Marine Reserve. Established in 1974, it was the first marine conservation area in the South Pacific islands. We floated in the crystal-clear water across the shallow reef admiring the white-tipped staghorn coral, periwinkle sea stars with their arms and legs conforming in shape to the surfaces they clung to, and spiny jet-black sea urchins. Then the sea floor abruptly dropped away to reveal the "deep," a steep-sided lagoon in the middle of the reef flat creating a natural aquarium, a "blue hole" the diameter of a city block. Toothy moray eels poked their heads in and out of the coral-laden walls while tiny anemone fish flitted in and out of the safety of the abundant growth. Green sea turtles and reef sharks swam yards away and there were multicolored schools of fish in every direction I swam. In training we'd learned that many of Samoa's coral reefs, and thus the fish who lived within them, were destroyed in 1990 and 1991 by cyclones (called hurricanes in the northern oceans) as well as by human interference, such as dynamiting or poisoning to catch fish. I'd been disappointed with previous snorkeling but Palolo Deep was still pristine.

That night all the Peace Corps volunteers, along with other guests, were invited by the United States Chargé d'affair to the American Embassy in Āpia for an Independence Day celebration. We stood on the lawn in the soft tropical air and sang as the Royal Samoa Police Band played The Star-Spangled Banner. And there were fireworks!

I was lazily seated on the garden wall sipping a glass of white wine, taking it all in, when Mapu introduced himself. He was tall and naturally muscular in the way of Samoan men, ruggedly handsome with a strong chin. His dark-brown eyes, framed by long black lashes, ambushed me into an engaging conversation that lasted the rest of the evening. A retired U.S. Army colonel from American Samoa, he told me laugh-out-loud funny stories about his travels. He'd lived in Honolulu where he owned property, along with a restaurant in Samoa and a resort in Pago Pago. He wrote his phone number on a napkin and invited me to stop by the restaurant since he'd be in town till the end of the week. I flaunted the napkin to my PC friends and discarded it a few days later. I was wary for a multitude of good reasons, although I was tempted. Ultimately I didn't call because it was too early—I'd only been in Samoa for a month. But I'd also left things unresolved with my ex in Colorado.

Jackson (not his real name) was the longest of my four post-divorce relationships with men who were unavailable in one way or another, by distance or intention. Was that the luck of the draw? Seems unlikely. I kept pursuing a "relationship" and sometimes blamed the lack of one on being a single mom and busy career woman. But with the wisdom of hindsight, I no doubt chose that or unconsciously communicated my own unavailability.

For ten years Jackson and I had been on-again-off-again. He was tall, sexy, and funny, with a shock of blondish hair. From Wisconsin, after twenty years in Colorado he still spoke with the slight Scandinavian inflection of the northern American Midwest. He had a great sense of adventure, evidenced at the time we'd met by his love of flying gliders. We had many similar interests and had a lot of fun; we just couldn't seem to stay together.

We'd said goodbye a few months before I moved back to Hawai'i. Then after two years, he called just before I flew to Colorado to visit my mainland family for three months in anticipation of leaving for Peace Corps. Once there, we fell back into being a couple again, and he came to Hawai'i to see me a month before I left.

*I know it's unrealistic to expect a commitment of some sort, but I feel like I need something to take to Samoa with me. Maybe I should leave it be and if it's real it'll survive two years. But if I dream of coming back to him and he's not there for me . . . What would I ask of him? I don't even know.*

Shortly after the Fourth of July party, I wrote:

*Got an email from Jackson. Same old BS—not ready for a relationship, concerned about my references to future, blah, blah, blah. It's always the same with us and the sad part is that I anticipated it. I sounded pissed off in my reply, but this is a lousy way and time to tell me! Oh well, I'm a big girl and there's a whole world out there!*

I knew this long-standing entanglement kept going nowhere and yet the strings of it came all the way to Samoa with me . . . and, for better or worse, prevented me from exploring anything with Mapu at the party.

### Preparing for Life in my Future Village

That night Jordan and I slept at the home of volunteers who lived in Āpia. The next morning, Meghan, a vivacious brunette from California with dark brown eyes (Group 77), rode the bus with us to her village of Si'umu at the end of the cross-island road. She taught computer classes at the secondary school there and invited me to visit, so I hopped off the bus with her and met up with Jordan later in the day. It was immediately obvious how much she cared for her students. There were fifteen of them and two computers without internet, so they alternated three at a time. Teaching Excel and Access, Meghan walked back and forth helping with computer projects, then to the others seated at a long table in front of a blackboard. The sixteen-to-seventeen-year-old kids sang and danced for me and I sang and gracelessly danced the Hukilau Hula for them, with much good-natured laughter on both sides.

I stayed one more night with Jordan, then headed back to Āpia to meet up with Group 78 fortified with increased confidence, and also with trepidation at the thought that I'd soon be genuinely on my own. Back in Manunu the weeks flew by. In our classes, we learned the basic tools to assess a village's needs and find funding, with occasional field trips such as one to the Ministry of Agriculture where we learned how to compost and saw the experimental sheep farm and vegetable green-houses. We often had guest speakers from relevant government ministries or non-profit agencies. One of the most memorable was Roger. Tall, muscular, and tattooed, the ministry representative wore a red dress, elegant sandals, and dangly earrings with long jet-black tresses. Sometimes a male Samoan chooses to dress and/or behave as a female and is known as a *fa'afāfine*, which means "like a woman." In Samoa, fa'afāfine are respected and accepted members of the community and are privileged to belong to the worlds of both men and women.

In the morning we always had a half-hour tea break. This included actual tea but also coffee and food—always food. Due to Samoa's long-time relationship with New Zealand and thus the British Commonwealth, the custom of "tea" was well-established in offices, business meetings, and pretty much every affair that coincided with morning or afternoon teatime. We were at class by 8:00 AM, followed by mid-morning tea break, lunch with our families, back to class in the fale, afternoon tea break, evening meal with our families, and maybe a little social time before studying for the next test or learning new vocabulary words.

One afternoon instead of our usual classes, one by one we talked with the Associate Peace Corps Director who supervised the Village-Based Development (VBD) volunteers. Within the next few days, she and the PC staff would decide which villages we'd each be sent to. As VBD volunteers none of us knew the specific projects we'd be working on until we got to our villages, so we ranked various types of assignments. We discussed location preferences (I said I'd rather be on 'Upolu Island to be closer to Āpia) and living conditions (I told her I'd rather live alone than with a family).

*Soon we'll be sworn in as official Peace Corps volunteers and go to our villages. The next steps will be vastly different and challenging.*

*Not only will we be faced with getting to know new villages but we'll also be separated as a group for the first time. We've come to know each other well, and although we're unique in many ways, we've bonded. That'll be tough.*

Each evening after the young women served the meal to Roma and me, we frequently watched the local TV news and talked it over. Time with the family was short since I had homework to do and I was tired from a day of intense learning, but I always held Baby Urima at some point during the day. She was born April 19th, only a few weeks earlier than my newest grandson, Jayden, born the day we'd arrived in Samoa.

*I often think of Jayden when I hold Urima. She's so cute and I know he is too. I can see her growing and changing in the short time I've been here. It's a wonderful blessing I might not have had living with another family—I can experience vicariously the stages he's going through. This week she laughed out loud for the first time. It was adorable and we all laughed with her!*

### *"It'll be Okay," I Convinced Myself*

In mid-July I walked eagerly to the large map of the islands posted in our classroom fale where I found the pinned slip of paper that told me my village assignment.

> *I'm going to Poutasi on the south side of 'Upolu! I'll know more about it when I go to the village for a short visit next week. I do know that I'll live in a house of my own right on the beach. Sweet!*

A few days later, Group 78 gathered early in the morning in the courtyard of Āpia Central where we'd spent the night. The hotel often served as a place to re-gather or for additional training purposes. One-by-one village representatives came to pick up each volunteer for our first visits to our assigned villages, while I sat there, still waiting. The Poutasi village mayor arrived two hours late to pick me up. "No worries—fa'aSāmoa," I thought to myself.

He didn't have a car, so he came by taxi. Since most rural families didn't have vehicles, in addition to the buses, taxis were the way to get around. In the rural areas they were available, although limited and expensive by Samoan standards. For a little over an hour we rode awkwardly in the dilapidated white cab, the mayor in the front talking to the driver in rapid Samoan and me in the back. At the end of the cross-island road, we turned left at Meghan's village of Si'umu and drove along the southern coast for several heavily forested miles, passing through three villages. Then as the taxi slowed, I saw a small wooden sign painted red with yellow letters spelling POUTASI.

As we turned toward the ocean, the mayor pointed out the small medical clinic that served the entire district (one of several funded by the government in villages far from Āpia) and the Congregational and Catholic churches, the largest village structures. At the end of the narrow coastal road we made a U-turn, and as we drove by he pointed to an open fale with a red roof and said that would be my house. Then within a few minutes of our arrival, without getting out of the taxi, we were back on the government road and were dropped off in the neighboring village of Sāleilua where he lived, a couple of miles away.

There was a long history and close relationship between the two villages and his family's chiefly title was associated with Poutasi, which explained why someone who didn't reside in the village was mayor. He was a short, wiry old man with no teeth and a face full of wrinkles. I'd been told that I would stay in his house for the two-day visit, along with his son, daughter-in-law, and grandson. The adjacent fale were occupied by various family members, and as usual, people came and went regularly. I was surprised to learn that he spoke English well since he'd totally ignored me in the cab. I gratefully reverted to my native language by afternoon. He was a plant lover like me, so we walked in his garden and he told me the Samoan names for hibiscus, gardenia, croton, and more. We talked about family, local history, and possible projects in the village, including a homework center.

In the evening, he and I sat down to a meal of boiled green bananas, taro, and boiled chicken with ramen noodles. After we finished, his daughter-in-law served us delicious cups of *koko Sāmoa* (fresh roasted, grated cacao beans with hot water and sugar). That night I wrote:

*It's 3:00 AM. I can't sleep. Despite my efforts to remain positive and optimistic there are these moments when it's not easy.*

*As I lay here under the mosquito net, I see on the wall beside me the largest spider I've ever seen in the wild. He's about five inches across from one foot to the other. Do spiders have feet? Not as fat as a tarantula, but a sturdy specimen. I'm not afraid of spiders but I'm grateful that the mosquito net is tucked in tightly under the mattress. I'm glad that I was given a bed in a private room, nevertheless the ceiling of the unpainted concrete block house is sagging overhead. The indoor bathroom is a luxury but we don't flush the paper (which is used bingo sheets) and the shower is a cold-water drizzle straight from the pipe sticking out of the tile wall. I wonder what difference hot running water would make in the lives of the people here? Or is it a sheer extravagance to have hot water? Have we become so accustomed to it that we think it's a necessity? Are dishes washed in cold water just as clean? I didn't think so before, but I have been, and will be, eating off them—so I hope so.*

*The grease-splattered wall behind the propane two-burner cooktop in the grimy kitchen, the dirt in corners everywhere, the mildewed front of the refrigerator where dirty hands touch it every day— these are realities of life here I've become accustomed to already, but are things I couldn't tolerate at home.*

*Of course, if I look at each piece in isolation it may seem negative— the dirt, or the mildew, or the bugs, or the cold water—but at this moment I choose not to see the pieces, but the whole. The natural beauty all around, the warmth and kindness of the people, and the opportunity to be here. To live and learn and share and become more than I am.*

After our brief drive through Poutasi the day before, the mayor had told me that we'd go back there "tomorrow." Mid-morning on the second day of my visit, a taxi took us instead to 'Ili'ili, a beautiful rocky point with stunning, crashing waves. He pointed toward Poutasi nestled in the crescent of the bay between 'Ili'ili and the point at Vaovai, the next village on the other side of the river. The sky and the sea were vivid blue and it was dazzling as the white, foamy spray exploded onto the black lava rock of the low cliff in front of us. Then I walked beside him back to his fale and we barely talked. I thought perhaps I should call someone at PC but decided to go with the flow.

That afternoon I was sleeping (it's what you do in Samoa after lunch) when Teuila, our PC Medical Officer, and Fono, our PC Security Officer, stopped by. They'd been going from village to village checking in with volunteers and had come from Poutasi where they'd been looking for me. I explained that I hadn't actually been to the village other than the drive-through. They talked to the mayor and he arranged for someone to take me.

Within the hour, I was dropped off unceremoniously in Poutasi at the fale of Mataomanu and Meleisea Seti and left to fend for myself. Mataomanu was about my age with wire-rimmed glasses, white hair in a bun, and a merry look about her. She would've looked look like Mrs. Santa Claus if she wore red velvet trimmed with white fur instead of tropical prints. Her husband was Meleisea Seti, one of the high chiefs of the village. For the longest time I couldn't figure out why he remind-ed me of my dad—except for being bald, he didn't look anything like him—but I think perhaps it was because Meleisea Seti, like my dad, always had a smile for everyone. Luckily they had a daughter visiting from Australia who spoke English well, so I enlisted her assistance to walk with me around the village.

I didn't have a plan, and apparently neither did the mayor, so not knowing what else to do, I decided to explore the neighborhood and introduce myself. At the last house at the end of the beach road, I called out tentatively and introduced myself to an elderly woman named Moana, seated cross-legged on the floor as she wove a fala mat. In my halting Samoan I sat beside her and explained that I was the new pisikoa as I answered the questions they taught us to expect in training—where are you from, how old are you, are you married, do you have children? Then I moved on to the next fale and the next, with occasional assistance with my faltering language skills. After a couple of hours had passed, I'd stopped at only a few homes, since each had insisted on serving me biscuits and tea. Then the same taxi drove up and I was whisked back to the mayor's house in Sāleilua where I again spent the night and was picked up by PC in the morning. So much for my village visit.

*It's frustrating, but it'll be okay. I did have a moment—which quickly passed—when I thought, "I'd rather go home than deal with all of this." I walked past the house where the mayor says I'll be living. Two small rooms, with an attached open fale facing the ocean. A fabulous view!*

## The Weeks of Training Come to an End

After our village visits, Group 78 returned to Manunu and suddenly we were only two weeks from the end of our training. I was already thinking about how I'd miss Roma, Wilma, and especially Urima, and I was nervous about moving to my new village.

I'd gotten used to Roma's family. The little boys ran about the village, the adolescent girls were bashful and busy when not in school, and the two young men did chores and went to school. Tiny Urima was the center of attention and everyone wanted to play with her and make her smile.

I enjoyed Wilma's company when she wasn't caring for the baby, but my Samoan was still at the low end of my learning curve, so it was usually Roma and I who sat at the table or in the front room talking. At fifty-five, Roma was almost my age, well educated, and well-traveled. Wilma was younger, his second wife. After they married, he decided to go into the ministry and they'd lived in London for a year and in Jamaica for a year during and after his seminary training. Roma had been pastor in the village for fifteen years when I arrived.

Our final week in Manunu was stressful. I was studying like crazy for our Language Proficiency Interview—the oral exam that would determine whether we could survive in our villages alone. Then one morning we were bussed to Āpia to the Division of Internal Affairs (the Samoan agency in charge of Peace Corps) to meet with the mayors and PC Committees from each of our villages. However, while other PCVs began eagerly talking with their committees and mayors, the mayor was the only one to show up from Poutasi. Again, he mentioned a homework center and again, I eagerly replied that I could do that, even though I didn't know exactly what it would entail.

Then that same day, I got the disconcerting news from the PC office that I wouldn't be living in the beach house in Poutasi as I'd eagerly anticipated. The Associate Director said that I'd live with a village family nearby instead, although I could use "the house by the sea" whenever I wanted. I was told that too many repairs would be necessary for me to live there and in retrospect that made sense. Also, our medical officer Teuila expressed concerns about the building location being right by the ocean for hurricane and tsunami threats. That *didn't* make sense since I ended up living literally across the road. Regardless of the reasons, including the possibility that the mayor got it wrong in the first place, or that the village thought that I deserved better accommodations, I was sorely disappointed. I'd been looking forward to my privacy, fixing up a place of my own, cooking my own meals, and coming and going as I pleased. It turned out that living in someone else's home would be one of the biggest challenges, and one of the biggest rewards, of my PC experience.

> *I still have a lot to learn—it may help to live with a family. I've got to come up with something positive about it. Who knows, it may work out fine. I may like it there, or things may change down the road. It's stressful to think of meeting and living with all these new people. Nobody said it'd be easy, but I did it in Manunu. It's funny how I'd wrapped my mind around the idea of living in the fale by the sea.*

When a village requested a volunteer, they agreed to provide housing that could be locked, with security wire on the windows and mosquito-proof screens. Living conditions amongst volunteers varied widely. Teachers were often provided housing at their school and PCVs working in Āpia shared houses rented by the Division of Internal Affairs.

Some villages built small two-room wooden houses for the PCVs or, like Jordan's, much more modest structures. Others lived with a family who was expected to feed the volunteer, who in turn was obliged to give $200 tala to the family from their monthly stipend of $1,026 tala ($410 USD). I'd already decided that I didn't need anybody's help and would take care of myself.

Finally it was time for the last hurdle before swearing in—the dreaded Language Proficiency Interview, a half hour conversation with a Peace Corps language facilitator. I was relieved to see Teuila instead of a stranger across the long bare table with her open notebook in front of her. She smiled reassuringly and launched right in with the typical Samoan greetings to start the conversation. We were supposed to demonstrate our range of language abilities through a variety of tenses, vocabulary, and the ability to ask and answer questions. I scored an "advanced intermediate level" ranking, which sounds impressive and was among the top of our group, but in reality it was in the range called "limited working proficiency." I had now successfully completed my training and would be officially sworn in as a Peace Corps volunteer in just a few more days.

In Samoan fashion, the Manunu villagers planned elaborate festivities to say goodbye to us. On a sunny Saturday morning, swaying and singing, the women of Manunu walked across the malae wearing matching red and blue dresses. Some tucked flowers in their hair and others wore garlands of sweet-smelling *moso'oi* flowers. Their beautiful voices blended in harmony, wafting to us on the cool breeze. Our small group of pisikoa and staff sat with nearly everyone in the village arrayed before us as the village chiefs took their places in front on fala mats seated according to rank.

The chief orator began to speak in his soaring voice, with a ceremonial braided coconut switch over his shoulder and his carved talking staff held firmly in his hand. The women bowed low and gifted expertly woven "fine mats," laid on the grass before us. Then six young men carried a bamboo platform on their shoulders, covered with banana leaves and a huge, whole roasted pig. He'd been cooked that morning in an above-ground oven with hot rocks and was gently placed in front of us. Other young men brought woven palm leaf baskets with smaller roasted pigs, chickens, and other food. Then as the final honor, they laid banana leaves on the grass and presented to us the head, front, and hindquarters of a cow butchered less than an hour before.

The most significant part of Samoan culture at weddings, funerals, blessings of houses/churches, bestowing of a chiefly title, or any other special event, was the formal presentation of gifts to show respect to the honored parties. The amount and quality of the gifts varied by the event's significance but a typical presentation included coconuts with money stuck in the hole in the top, cases of canned corned beef or herring, and of course pigs, chickens, and sometimes a cow. "Fine mats"—up to one hundred feet long for the most elaborate occasions—were woven from the long, thin leaves of the fala tree and displayed by the women as they carried them aloft.

Following the gifts (our trainers took this booty with them) was a great feast and every family in the village went home with leftovers. Food played a central role in Samoan culture, representing prosperity, generosity, societal rank, familial ties, and community support. A great show of hospitality was always extended to visitors, who were offered food no matter what time of day. Even if not hungry, you were expected eat a small amount of food to convey appreciation.

The festivities continued that night with a *fiafia* on the malae with songs, dances, and skits. The word *fiafia* means happy and to like something, or a celebration with singing, dancing, and food. Everyone in the village attended in their finest attire, both men and women with flowers in their hair, and children so excited it was hard to behave themselves. Our trainers asked me to dance the opening siva, although traditionally a younger woman, such as the daughter of a high chief, would've been the "opening act."

Wilma streaked large red crescents on my cheeks and around my forehead she tied a *pale fuiono*—a headband of shiny beads and red-dyed chicken feathers (in the old days, nautilus shells or mother of pearl and bird feathers were used). Red feather plumes fluttered on a loose belt around my waist.

Photo courtesy of Nick Shuraleff.

Teenaged Kanana tried her best to teach me the intricate hand and foot movements. I have no idea what my dance looked like but it was so much fun! The eight men in Group 78 learned a warrior-like *haka* dance, we women danced a graceful *siva*, and together we did a seated dance clapping and motioning our hands while chanting (called *sāsā*). Groups of villagers reciprocated with their own haka and dances. And there was food—lots of food.

### *An Honor Bestowed: Donna La'itiiti*

The next morning, composed and serious, Roma looked at me across the breakfast table and said, "We've decided to give Urima the name

"Donna." It's a blessing that you came to live with us and you're now part of our family."

I was stunned. At first, I didn't know what to say. I wanted to blurt out, "Really! Wow!" But to match the tenor of the pronouncement, I replied, "I'm so honored. *Fa'afetai* (thank you)!"

On cue, Urima whimpered from the pile of blankets on the floor draped with mosquito netting hung from the ceiling. I reached in and picked her up, holding her tightly, her head on my shoulder and her tiny face close to mine, and deeply breathed in her smell of coconut oil, talcum powder, and babyness. My namesake! Donna La'itiiti—Little Donna.

As on our first Sunday morning two months before, our group stood side by side on the raised stage while Roma eloquently thanked us for the happiness we'd brought to the families in Manunu and prayed for us on the next leg of our journey. This time we knew everyone who gave us a hug or sweet-smelling lei, and soon we were buried in flowers up to our ears and higher. I read an elaborate, touching, three-page prayer of thanks in Samoan that Sa'u wrote on behalf of the group. Compared to the few words that I was able to stumble through at that first service, even I was impressed with my abilities.

*Today the church youth will dedicate the afternoon service to us pisikoa. I've heard them practicing all week but I know I'll still be blown away by the beauty and rhythm of the songs and dances. Some of the volunteers asked how I can sleep and study with the nightly music and singing outside my window. I'm alternately able to tune it out or enjoy it. I don't need to play any music of my own. I suspect I'll miss it greatly.*

Later that week, in the church in Manunu at our swearing-in ceremony, or our "graduation" as the villagers called it, we took our oath in Samoan and English administered by the Chargé d'affair from the U. S. Embassy. Afterward there were speeches by the Peace Corps trainers and village chiefs, followed by presentations of more fine mats and gifts of food to and from the village, Peace Corps, and distinguished guests—and another feast.

Manunu was beautiful in many ways, nestled in the mountains, with the homes in a circle around the grassy malae and a remarkable social network of families, Samoan style. They literally and figuratively surrounded us with their love and kindness.

> *To say that none of us, the people of Manunu or the pisikoa, will ever forget the experiences of the past few weeks is an understatement. The village has told us how much we'll be missed and that we've made a difference by being here. This week, one of the matai said that for some of the people this has been one of the happiest times of their lives. The villagers will tell stories about the pālagi with whom they laughed and played and took into their hearts. And each of us will have stories to tell our grandchildren about how we once lived in a Samoan village and sang in the church choir, danced the siva, killed a chicken for dinner, climbed a coconut tree, had a beau with whom we sat and talked under the stars, made coconut cream from fresh coconut, swam in the pool by the waterfall, taught them how to play softball, lived in a little thatched-roof hut, had a chicken lay an egg at the foot of the bed, or had the honor of a holding a precious baby girl in your arms who was named for you.*

It was time to move on to our "real Peace Corps experience." That last day as I held Donna La'itiiti and looked into her liquid, dark brown eyes, she smiled. I tearfully put her down and hugged Roma, Wilma, and the family. As Group 78 left for Āpia Central for our last night there before our transferring to our new villages, waving out the bus window I shouted, "*O le a 'ou toe sau!*" (I will come back!)

## Chapter 3

## Getting to Know my Village

*Seu le manu 'ae taga'i le galu*
*"Catch the fish but watch for the wave"*
*Be careful in an undertaking and look out for the obstacles.*

For many weeks of training, we'd been busily cramming new words and knowledge into our overloaded minds. But as overwhelmed as I'd felt up to now, I was about to be confronted with a whole new set of experiences—sometimes bewildering, sometimes enchanting, always informative. Every Peace Corps volunteer's story differs depending upon the country, ministry, non-profit governmental organization, school, village, or family that was part of their experience. And every volunteer cannot imagine what it would've been like otherwise.

The next morning, Papu, our forty-something, happy-go-lucky Peace Corps driver, picked me up at the hotel in the fire-engine-red Peace Corps pickup to deliver me to my new village. We drove from Āpia toward the western tip of the island, past the turn to Manunu, into new territory, following the bus route with which I would soon become intimately familiar. Interspersed with waterfall after waterfall, we passed through cloud forests dripping with tree ferns down to the valley below, soon occasional glimpses of ocean through the jungle along the southern coast, and then we arrived in Poutasi.

This arrival felt very different from the drive-through with the mayor. The first thing that struck me was the village's beauty. Glorious colors were everywhere—flowers, leaves, clotheslines, painted roofs, dense rainforest, and vivid, sky-blue ocean. Approximately three hundred twenty-five people lived in a compact rectangle—half beside the government road about one-quarter mile from the ocean, and half along the seashore. A natural spring created a brackish lagoon in the center of the village alongside the malae and district secondary school.

We turned off the government road at F&K General Store, passed the Women's Committee House and small medical clinic on the left, with a handful of homes on the right. At the ocean where we turned left, a fork in the sandy one-lane road led right to the neighboring village of Sāleilua. We drove along the shoreline past the Congregational pastor's house and church hall on the left. Next was the family compound of Meleisea Seti and Mataomanu and then my new home, next door to the Congregational church.

An eye-catching turquoise roof topped a concrete block house painted bright white. All around was beautiful and meticulously-kept landscaping—numerous varieties of palms, plumeria, golden trumpet flowers, hibiscus, breadfruit, and papaya. About fifty feet away, on the other side of the road, was the house by the sea.

My family's house in Poutasi.

Papu introduced me briefly to Niualuga (Niu) Evaimalo and Saina Niualuga—the husband and wife of my new family. Then Papu was gone and again I was literally dropped off at the door of strangers in an unfamiliar village, barely able to speak the language with a totally unknown future. I've never felt so alone and vulnerable.

"Tālofa!" I said with a wide smile belying the anxiety I felt inside.

Saina embraced me repeating "Tālofa!" and welcomed me into the fale. We sat awkwardly in the front room as I told them about myself and they told me about their family. The time was soon cut short when I learned that they both worked outside the village and needed to get back to their jobs. Saina's family owned Mari's Cafe and Bakehouse in Āpia next to their small grocery store, and she worked nights there. During the week she and their two daughters stayed in Āpia at her mother's house and they came home on weekends. Niu worked for the Ministry of Natural Resources and Environment (MNRE) at his office a few miles down the road from Poutasi where he was supervisor at Pupu-Pu'e National Park. To my relief, both were excellent English speakers.

Saina showed me my room and introduced me to 'Ofisa, who smiled shyly. She was the family's house girl who cooked, cleaned, and did other chores. Many families had house girls, even those of only moderate means. Saina told me that 'Ofisa would prepare the evening meal when Niu returned from work and to let 'Ofisa know if I needed anything in the meantime.

I had myself a good cry when I was finally alone in my room. It felt so strange and stark—not like "my" room in Manunu. In one corner was a comfortable mattress and pillows on a simple wooden platform. Along the wall beside the bed was a coffee table. In another corner sat an old ornately carved vanity with a mirror and four tiny drawers, two of which didn't open, and one straight-backed wooden chair. I situated a few things and ate the lunch 'Ofisa gave me—what Samoans called "flying saucers"—a smushed, grilled sandwich with SpaghettiOs in the middle. Not what I would've chosen, but I ate half, drank a cup of tea, and started reading a new story in Doris Lessing's aptly titled *Winter in July*.

After about an hour, I knew that despite my trepidations I needed to go outside, get moving and walk around the village. I went back to my room twice to quell the tears that threatened again, but then I stood up straight and told myself, "One day at a time. Fake it till I make it," and stepped out the front door.

I walked along on the beach road and was instantly captivated by the closeness and expanse of the ocean inside the protected bay and beyond the reef. On the government road I bought a couple of icy-cold, bottled Cokes at F&K store and began to walk back to the house. As I looked toward the Women's Committee House I saw Mataomanu and Tumema whom I remembered from my first brief village visit, so I asked if I could join them. I handed each a Coke and we sat cross-legged and talked about this and that . . . mostly me answering questions. My Samoan was okay, and it felt comforting to be there.

When I got back to my family's home, I walked across the road to the house by the sea—the *fale 'i tai*. It was open-sided, forty feet long by twenty feet wide on a black lava rock foundation with a concrete floor. A faded, rusty-red metal roof was held up by massive stripped and smoothed hardwood logs, with a wide overhang all around. It sat at the edge of the beach in the center of the village, facing the small, protected bay with the homes of Poutasi in both directions along the shore.

The view of Nuʻusafeʻe Island from the fale ʻi tai.

I poked my head into the two small, empty rooms at one end where I'd thought I would live. The scraps of paper, layers of dust, and cobwebs told me it hadn't been used recently. The rest of the fale was open to the air and the sea. In the middle were four wooden Adirondack-style chairs, so I sat facing the ocean. On the far-left horizon the panorama of the small bay spread from Vaovai, where the mangrove-lined river spilled into the sea, to Nuʻusafeʻe, a tiny palm-covered islet a mile in front of me, to ʻIliʻili Point on my far right, and the spectacular South Pacific as far as the eye could see. Next stop—Tonga.

*I read at the fale ʻi tai all afternoon. The ocean calms and soothes me. Maybe if I hang out there enough it'll be okay.*

That evening Niu drove up in his navy-blue Toyota Tacoma double-cab pickup—the family's only transportation (Saina didn't drive). The girls, ten-year-old Hemara and six-year-old Tia, and son, seven-year-old Fetū, tumbled out of the pickup that was loaded inside and in the bed with groceries and supplies. I later learned that they also had a teenage daughter, Aileen, who lived with her aunt and uncle in Āpia.

Niu and Saina were in their forties. Niu was tall and strong with short, curly, reddish-brown hair. He had a certain set to his jaw that said, "Don't mess with me." In an earlier century he would've been a fierce warrior. He had a Bachelor's in Environmental Science from Pacific University in Fiji. Saina was medium height with medium length light-brown hair. She was funny, chatty, and charming, yet I could see that she took her responsibilities to her family, church, and village very seriously.

I immediately hit it off with little Hemara. She had brunette hair that didn't want to be tamed and an adorable smile. She spoke English well and had a certain gravitas that I'm sure she got from her dad. Younger Tia reminded me of her mother, coy and cute with blondish hair; even in first grade I could visualize her becoming Miss Samoa one day. Both girls attended St. Mary's Primary School in Āpia. The boy Fetū looked like his father with curly blondish hair and a shy smile. He attended the primary school nearby. There was also grizzled old Tamamasui. He had been Saina's father's best friend and was like a grandfather to the children.

Three days after arriving, I sat at the fale ʻi tai on Sunday afternoon trying to write while the kids buzzed around me asking questions, playing with my flip flops, my sunglasses, and the lāvalava I'd thrown over the back of the chair—trying to get my attention. I alternately wanted them to leave me alone, and yet welcomed their company and laughter. Finally, I shooed them away and contemplated the scene before me.

*How fortunate I am to be in such a beautiful place! I could be someplace cold and dreary, or dusty and drab. I'm listening to the birds twitter in the nonu bushes and the constant chatter of coconut palm fronds rising and falling in the breeze. I hear the ceaseless roar of the surf as it crashes over and over offshore on the fringing reef. I've quickly become accustomed to the "white noise." But it's always there, loud enough to be clearly heard when you stop and listen.*

*I'm looking at tiny Nuʻusafeʻe Island between the palms in front of the fale, part of the reef formation. It's a postcard version of a Pacific islet, rimmed with coconut palms on a wide, startlingly white coral beach. The sun is slowly setting, leaving a honey-gold path on the sea. As it sinks behind the ballooning cumulus clouds on the horizon, the forest at ʻIliʻili Point is silhouetted, the tallest palms in stark relief above the tree canopy. Soon the brightness will fade to pinks and oranges. Behind me the tops of the green mountain ridges are covered with clouds whose edges look like cotton puffs. It's probably raining at the summit.*

*There's a warm breeze blowing my troubles away, scattering them over the Pacific. I'll replace them with loving, calm, serene, and confident thoughts that are being sent my way from family and friends back home.*

## Two Weeks Down—101 to Go

*The family is genuinely warm and welcoming, and for that I'm thankful, but it's still frustrating to share someone's home. Because it's not my house, I spend most of my time in my room, which gets claustrophobic. I could hang out more with them but it doesn't feel comfortable. Maybe it will in time. Two weeks down, one hundred and one to go. I'm feeling kind of blue tonight. It's lonely and hard. Two years seems like an awfully long time. I sent a text to all of Group 78 today and heard back from most—seems that we're all having a similar experience.*

By Samoan standards Niu and Saina's home was above average, among the best in the village. It was a combination of old and new construction. The newest addition on the ocean side included a front room used only for greeting and entertaining formal guests with a door looking toward the village road and the fale 'i tai. The kids often played there on rainy days but it wasn't an inviting place to hang out in the sense of what Americans call a "living room." It was open in the middle with wooden chairs and plastic covered sofas lining the outer walls. A hallway led to two bedrooms including mine and also opened to the outside.

A center room with two bedrooms on one side connected the front addition to the kitchen. However, no one slept in any of the "bedrooms" other than me. They were used as dressing rooms and for storage of everything non-kitchen related, from racks and suitcases of clothes to the three-foot high stack of fala mats for special events (nowhere in the house were what Americans call "closets"). The TV was in the center room where the family lounged during the day and slept at night on a bed and on the floor on thin mattresses and fala mats. There were two small bathrooms, one of which I shared with the kids.

The kitchen at the back of the house had a refrigerator, several free-standing cupboards, a large wooden table and chairs, and a one-burner propane "cooktop" (which we'd call a camping or patio stove in the States). Along one wall Niu stored the weed eaters (called "whipper snippers," which made me smile), a wheelbarrow, tools, and paint buckets. The "kitchen" faucet and sink were outside behind the house, covered by a wide eave. Village water was pumped from a near-by spring and unheated. It shut down from 8:00 PM until 5:00 AM and stopped occasionally during the day for short periods. As PC recommended, I boiled my drinking water.

Most of the cooking was done behind the house in the umukuka. A Samoan cookhouse was a small fale behind the main house with a corrugated metal roof and open sides. Food was wrapped in banana leaves or plaited coconut fronds and placed on the rocks of the *umu*, an above-ground oven of red-hot lava rocks covered with banana leaves and fala mats. It was remarkably efficient; they could cook a small pig in about an hour along with taro and breadfruit. For quicker cooking, there was also a fire pit fed with wood or the outer husks of coconuts.

Housing in every village and in Samoa in general was exceedingly varied. In contrast to my family's house, on the other end of the spectrum would have been a family of several people living in a conventional Samoan fale—a thatched roof supported by eight-inch-diameter poles with a plastic tarp pulled down on the sides at night or when the weather threatened. Shelves, boxes, tins, plastic buckets, and small cupboards held belongings. Clothes were usually kept in suitcases. Probably a single light bulb and a TV illuminated the family at night and the toilet and shower were out back near the umukuka. Laundry was washed in a bucket and hung up to dry or laid on the rocks. It was kind of like camping out for your whole life. Most village homes were somewhere between these two extremes. The first step to an "upgrade" was a metal roof, and then closing in all or part of the open fale walls with wooden siding or eventually concrete blocks.

One of my biggest challenges was that I was in a place where I knew no one including the people whose home I shared. Saina and the girls were in Āpia from Monday morning until Saturday. Niu left early every weekday morning to go to the national park and 'Ofisa walked from her family fale at the end of the beach road to do chores and care for Fetū, Tamamasui, and me. After school, Fetū ran around the village playing with his friends, Tamamasui smoked and talked with the other old men in the shade, and I was left on my own. That was what I wanted, wasn't it?

Each morning I sat at the fale 'i tai and made a plan for the day. I had to devise a plan because as a Village-Based Development volunteer, my actual job didn't yet exist. The Samoa Peace Corps handbook dryly said that my job was to "enable villagers to build upon their capacity to assess, plan, develop, and connect resources, programs, and services resulting in an increased ability to meet the developmental needs of their villages." As daunting as that sounds, we'd been taught how to complete a Village Situational Analysis (VSA) consisting of an environmental overview, economic and agricultural assessment, health and school review, and community resources summary. This data would help me figure out not only what the village needed or wanted but which projects were feasible. Our task as PCVs was to help the Samoan people help themselves and leave behind sustainable projects that would continue after we left, and my specific mission for the next few months was to get to know the village in order to do that.

To include comprehensive population statistics, we were instructed by PC to conduct a detailed house-to-house survey. I began that questioning in earnest a few weeks later, after I'd settled in a bit. I was expected to present my VSA in English and Samoan in six months at Group 78's early service conference. Over time I went to the public library for historical research, to the Division of Internal Affairs for assistance, visited the local schools and the medical clinic, and attended village meetings and church services.

However, on that first afternoon while I'd shared Cokes at the Women's Committee house, Tumema had invited me to go with her on the upcoming village inspection. Tumema was a strong, tall woman, my age, with short, graying hair. I don't think I ever stopped by her house when I didn't find her working—in the garden, doing laundry, sweeping, or cooking. She spoke limited English, but we got by and she became a good friend.

Every village had a Women's Committee that was responsible for village health matters and cleanliness. The wives of the highest village chiefs headed up the committee and at the Committee House the village women wove fala mats, painted *siapo* (bark cloth paintings), played cards, gossiped, and napped. Tumema was the committee member designated to conduct the monthly inspection, called the *asiasiga*, which literally means "visit," but in a village context meant a particular recurring monthly visit on the fourth Saturday. Tumema checked each family compound for general tidiness, to make sure the grass was cut, the litter picked up, and the umukuka clean—as clean as you can keep an outdoor cooking shed.

Occasionally, attention was called to a safety or health issue. For example, we saw a pit covered by old pieces of corrugated metal that the family had been told to fill in, and at another house they were told to relocate their outhouse to the rear of the property instead of the front. If a family didn't maintain a tidy area, they paid a fine to the village. Each December, there was a more detailed inspection that assessed the quality and the quantity of the linens, dishes, and other facets of the family's living conditions.

Tumema on the asiasiga inspecting a cookhouse.

Leaf and grass litter weren't allowed to accumulate around the houses. Each day on my morning walk, I saw children picking up the large breadfruit leaves around their homes. They also started the school day doing the same on the school grounds. The fallen leaves and the shorn grass cut with large machetes, often by the children, were swept up with rakes made of coconut frond spines, then burned or tossed into the ocean.

However, on this volcanic island, the area immediately surrounding most houses was covered with small smooth black *ili'ili* stones, not grass, which was mainly along the roads or in open areas such as the malae and schoolyard. Between the 'ili'ili, or in the blackish sand if the village was close to the sea, grew small weeds and grass which were pulled by hand by the women and old men until nothing but pebbles or clean sand was left. Tamamasui spent a significant part of each morning and afternoon in front of our house cleaning out these small green intruders.

And yet, some Samoans littered carelessly, tossing candy wrappers on the ground or out the bus windows, and homes were often cited for a pile of household rubbish in back. Another PCV said she saw her family pick up the litter around the fale in buckets for the asiasiga, then throw it out afterwards and do it all over again the next month.

As time passed, I didn't accompany Tumema on these monthly visits, but for the first few months she and I trudged in the heat from fale to fale. As she walked briskly along, I struggled to keep up. She briefly introduced me to whoever was home and I dutifully wrote down the names of each family as she patiently repeated and spelled for me.

These walkabouts were invaluable to create my village map. I learned that there were approximately fifty-five "homes" or "family compounds." The number of actual structures in each family compound varied. Some were small, with only the main living quarters, an outhouse, and a cookhouse. Others had extended family living together in a main home, more relatives living in several smaller fale, a large fale serving as a meeting house and gathering space, and the usual outbuildings. Nearly fifty family members from great-grandmother to tiny babies lived in one village family compound, the largest by far.

*I worked on my village map all morning. Time to be fa'aSāmoa and mālōlō. Here at the fale 'i tai the breeze and shade make the temperature manageable. Here everything is beautiful and peaceful. I forget about any turmoil or worry in my life, or the world at large. It's my cocoon, where for a little while I'm in my own time and space, and the rest of the world does not exist.*

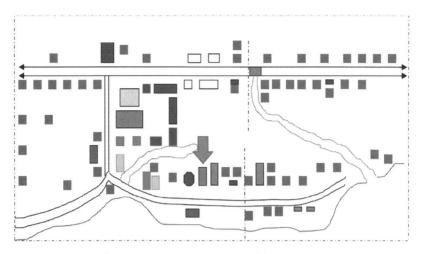

The arrow center front points to our house; the fale 'i tai is across the road. The three large buildings on the ocean side are the two churches and the church hall. (Not to scale!)

## *Food is Everything We Are*

Chef Anthony Bourdain said, "Food is everything we are. It's an extension of nationalist feeling, ethnic feeling, your personal history, your province, your region, your tribe, your grandma."

My real experience with Samoan food didn't begin until I moved to Poutasi. Even though I'd lived with a family in Manunu to learn and acclimate to the culture, staying with Roma and Wilma didn't prepare me for a typical Samoan daily diet. Yes, they ate the same foods, but there were two key differences both attributable to the fact that Roma was a Congregational pastor. Although they're not chiefs and play no formal role in village governance, the deference to and authority of a Congregational pastor in a Samoan village is impressive. Every Sunday morning before church, young people from families throughout the village came to the back of the house, were invited in, knelt with bowed heads before Roma seated on a chair, and presented prodigious gifts of food. They always brought something I liked such as heaping bowls of scrambled eggs, fried chicken or roasted pork, and taro and breadfruit baked in the umu. In addition, because as pastor he had more money, the family had spoiled me, buying my favorite blackberry jam, apples, oranges, juice, and occasionally Coke. And, while in training, they'd bought a mini fridge for me to use where I kept these goodies. Other than Manunu, I'd had about three meals in a Samoan village, so when I arrived in Poutasi I had my first regular diet of ordinary Samoan food.

Samoans, like most Polynesians, ate a lot of taro (*talo*), a root crop the consistency of a sweet potato, but without the sweet. They fried, mashed, boiled, baked, or roasted it. (They didn't make *poi* from it though—that's a Hawaiian thing.) Breadfruit and taro were especially tasty when baked in the rock oven, leaving slightly singed edges, smoky flavor, and firmer texture, but I never grew to like green bananas.

Papayas, mangoes, avocados, pineapples, and other fresh fruit grew in abundance, including more "exotic" fruits such as star fruit and rambutan. And coconuts were everywhere! You could order a *niu* from the drinks section of a local menu and you'd be given a fresh chilled coconut with a straw in the cut-off top. *Masi popo* was my favorite coconut biscuit (like a large shortbread cookie), *panipopo* were simple bread buns resting in a sweet coconut cream sauce, *palusami* (taro leaves stuffed with seasoned coconut cream sauce baked in the umu) was an indispensable accompaniment with taro, and of course I could nibble fresh coconut any time. And that's not even close to an exhaustive list of coconut delights!

A characteristic meal included taro, breadfruit, or green bananas and chicken soup—the broth containing watercress (which grew in the streams), cabbage, cucumber, or cherry tomatoes, with the chicken served separately. It seems silly now, but I'd never thought of cooking cucumbers, having always eaten them raw. A squash shaped like a small green pumpkin was also common. Vegetables weren't served as side dishes by themselves.

*I bought fresh veggies in Āpia at the market yesterday but forgot to buy salad dressing. So this morning I walked the half mile to the general store for mayonnaise and catsup for makeshift Thousand Island. At lunchtime, ʻOfisa, Hemara, Tia, and Fetū watched the apparently fascinating process of chopping tomatoes and green peppers and tearing lettuce into bite-size pieces. The kids wanted a taste so I gave them small bites. I don't think any of them swallowed it. The vegetables here (on the rare occasions when we have them at mealtime) are cooked to mush.*

Every family had a few free-range chickens, so eggs were plentiful—scrambled or fried. We ate egg sandwiches with white bread from the family bakery, a thick slice of which was a snack by itself, sometimes sprinkled with salt, which was added generously to everything.

A serving of meat with every meal wasn't the norm. Intermittently, we had chicken, pork, fresh fish, lamb (from New Zealand), or canned fish (slippery, smelly, briny tinned jack mackerel or herring). I read a wonderful online article by Aaron Gilbreath[4] about how "Americans will shove just about anything in our mouths, from e-cigarettes to dirty dollar bills at strip clubs, along with all the processed crap that passes for food in our country, yet we treat canned fish as the oceanic equivalent of potted mystery meats like SPAM, more fit for cats than humans. How come? The gag reflex is clearly culturally transmitted, one we're taught or simply mirror by example. It isn't inborn." And I was one of those Americans who just couldn't eat the tinned fish.

Most commonly, meat was the ubiquitous canned corned beef, which deserves its own paragraph. One of the first canned foods to come to Samoa was pea soup, so the Samoans created a word for it—*pisupo*. When canned corned beef came, it was also called pisupo, which for some reason eventually came to mean only the corn beef. It was often cooked with cabbage and onions, with spaghetti, or sometimes eaten

---

4 https://www.thesmartset.com/ode-to-canned-fish/

right out of the can. To me it was strangely pink and very fatty. This, of course, was an American opinion about the fat—Samoans savored fat or grease of any kind and it would have been wasteful not to. When I cut the fat off a piece of meat and set it on

the edge of my plate, someone in the family ate it. One of my fellow volunteers told me that she boiled, skinned, and deboned some chicken thighs, setting aside the skin, fat, and bones to toss away. Some kids asked if they could have them and ate nearly every morsel down to the bone marrow. How wasteful we Americans are! But there was no avoiding the fat in pisupo, and I never became accustomed to this Samoan staple which also played an important cultural role. Gifts of cases of pisupo were a must for weddings, funerals, special birthdays, or celebrations of any kind, to be reciprocated on an appropriate future occasion. My family had stacks of boxes with cans of pisupo ready for when the occasion demanded it. I sometimes wondered how many times the cases changed hands without being opened!

*So far, the food has been difficult to swallow—literally. Tonight we had boiled taro, boiled Chinese cabbage mixed with canned jack mackerel, and soup with rice and lupe (wild pigeon). I'm not opposed to eating game birds but the thing was boiled whole (with the head). 'Ofisa cut it at the table and gave me the bottom half. Maybe that was an honor, but I couldn't eat the poor little brown bird with tiny feathers still sticking out of its boiled skin here and there, its puckered little asshole winking up at me, and its curled-up claws lying in the bottom of my bowl.*

*So I ate a half cup of the broth and a few bits of taro and cabbage.*
*I tried to avoid the jack mackerel, spread it around on the plate,*
*and snuck a few pieces to the cat. I said I wasn't hungry, gave the*
*lupe to Tamamasui, and was glad I had an orange left in my room.*
*I suspect I'll never again think so much about food.*

It's true that much of it wasn't, and still isn't, to my liking, such as
one of Niu's favorites—sea cucumber innards marinated in lime juice.
Although I must confess that I didn't taste it, *thetraveltart.com* describes
it as "salty snot with a hint of citrus."[5] I don't want to know. However,
looking back I'm somewhat chagrinned by seeming ungrateful and un-
willing to try more Samoan food.

I'd never thought of myself as a picky eater. I ate roast guinea pig
in Peru, seviche in Veracruz, turtle soup in New Orleans, sashimi in
Hawai'i . . . so I was surprised that it was such a big deal for me. Of
course it wasn't so much about the grease or the guts or the bony fish,
but more about my identity and lack of comfort food. American jour-
nalist Jennifer Lee said, "Our comfort foods map who we are, where we
come from, and what happened to us along the way. What you cook
and eat is an accumulation, a function of your experiences—the people you've dated, what you've learned, where you've gone. There may
be inbound elements from other cultures, but you'll always eat things
that mean something to you."

Indeed, I married a man from Texas and I still love grits and authentic Tex-Mex food. Growing up in the 1950s in land-locked Nebraska,
it's not surprising that I don't care for most seafood, but I love shrimp.
Is it a coincidence that the first time I ate crunchy deep-fried shrimp I
was on a date with my high school boyfriend? Would I like pucker-pro-
ducing rhubarb cobbler if my grandmother hadn't made it?

Since my host family was expected to provide meals for me, that

---

5 https://www.thetraveltart.com/seafood-recipes-raw-sea-cucumber-guts-marinat-
ed-in-lime-juice-samoa/

meant eating together. So I faced a double dilemma: I was living with a family when I'd hoped to live alone, and I wasn't able to cook my own food. From the beginning, I was determined to fix my own breakfast and lunch and retain a bit of autonomy. Even that was challenging since I had only an electric tea pot which I used to boil drinking water and a toaster that Saina had given me. Using the one-burner propane cooktop with an attached tank in the kitchen wasn't an option. There was often a pot of soup or other dinner fare bubbling away, I was afraid it would run out of propane (which happened often), and, I'll admit it, I didn't want to share if I used the cooktop, but it wouldn't have been fa'aSāmoa not to. I was zealous in retaining my American self-sufficiency and sense of personal space and I relinquished it grudgingly. So, I had only the most minimum tools to prepare even two meals a day.

Samoans didn't eat breakfast or sit down to a lunch meal at home but instead grabbed some leftover taro, a couple of thick slices of bread, or whatever they could find. At first, 'Ofisa cooked eggs or soup for me in the middle of the day but gradually I convinced her that I'd take care of myself. When Niu came home from work, she served dinner to the four of us. I was very sensitive to what it might look like if I declined to eat with the family.

*I usually try to eat a passable amount of food for dinner, but to-night we had cold boiled taro chunks and mashed squash mixed with canned mackerel. It's all I can do to eat it. A couple nights I've begged off and said I wasn't hungry. I don't know how to politely get out of sharing the evening meal, and I don't think I can stand it for two years. Niu asked me today what kind of food they can buy for me. He said that since I'm part of the family I should eat with them and let them know what to cook for me. Even if I gave him a list of foods to buy it wouldn't be what I need. I must figure out some way to preserve this one little piece of me.*

I struggled with food challenges during my entire PC experience but eventually two things saved me—an electric skillet and a tiny, borrowed refrigerator. After two months of worrying and going away from the dinner table hungry many nights, circumstances helped solve my dilemma.

> *I told Saina that I'm going to buy an electric skillet to cook my own food and she can borrow it sometimes. The conversation went better than I anticipated, partly because she knew that for dinner the last two nights we ate leftover boiled taro, unheated canned spaghetti, and pisupo right out of the can. I nibbled and spread some around on my plate to look like I was eating something last night, and the night before I said that I wasn't hungry. 'Ofisa hasn't been here all week. Despite my complaints, her cooking beats Niu's! At least she usually makes some soup I can eat.*

That electric skillet gave me back some control of my life and my daily routine. In one corner of my room designated as my "kitchen," I began to cook an evening meal for myself, joining the family on weekends when Saina and the girls were home. On a borrowed three-foot by three-foot table, I put my three appliances, dishes, and a cutting board. Covered by lengths of colorful cloth hanging to the floor it also provided needed storage space underneath.

On Sundays, I tried to help Saina prepare the midday meal called *to'ona'i*, but she always shooed me away saying, "Mālōlō!" So I'd change out of my church clothes and relax until one of the kids came knocking on my bedroom door. We sat at the wooden kitchen table, although many Samoan families ate in the traditional manner seated on mats on the floor. We used plates, bowls, and tablespoons, although more often just our hands. They always gave me a fork and knife too, yet I rarely used them. I was always served first as a gesture of respect to my age and status, followed by the other adults. After the meal, the children brought each of us a small basin of water and a hand towel to wash up, then the children ate what was left.

*We had a yummy Sunday dinner today—rack of lamb and taro baked in the umu, chicken soup, coleslaw with pineapple and carrots because Saina knows it's one of my favorites. But best of all were the green beans from the Āpia market which Saina steamed for me with nothing added. They tasted so good! Saina's mother, Paugata, sent me an orange and a Snickers bar. It seems silly to write about food in such detail, but it's more important than I ever knew.*

Later that afternoon I wrote:

*A reality check on the food—tonight I ate burned rice and left-over soup. I declined the fried canned herring. Oh well, I had a good Sunday dinner.*

A helpful quote from the PC handbook: "The host family or one of the neighbors might have a refrigerator that the PCV can use. Eating with the family, or learning to make simple, quick dishes on a daily rather than several-day basis, helps volunteers to adapt without this luxury."

I was fortunate that my Poutasi family had a refrigerator when I arrived (although a few months later it died and wasn't replaced). But whatever I put into the refrigerator was considered fair game for the family. Samoan families bought or harvested food day-to-day and didn't keep many items on hand in a stocked pantry except for pisupo, canned fish, or boxed milk from New Zealand (the only milk we had). Even inside the refrigerator there were only a few essentials like butter and catsup. There was rarely leftover food—if you didn't eat all that was on your plate, someone else would. So for several months, I reluctantly shared the family refrigerator, not knowing if what I bought yesterday would still be there today.

Eventually I nervously asked Roma and Wilma if I could borrow the small refrigerator that they'd bought for me to use in Manunu.

"Yes, of course!" they said, and about a month later they brought it to Poutasi. Peace Corps now provides small refrigerators to all volunteers in Samoa!

*A good food day. Slightly stale Frosted Flakes for breakfast, grilled cheese with Fritos for lunch, potatoes and cabbage for dinner—but the best of all was a box of Jell-O butterscotch pudding Mom sent from the States. Since I now have cold milk (that no one else can use) I can make instant pudding! I also had ICED tea!*

Even with the mini fridge it was a challenge to keep more than a few days' worth of food on hand and it got tiresome.

*I just ate cucumber, tomato, and onion salad with cheese and crackers for lunch for the third time this week. It's still tasty, but I can't do it again. I put the rest in the refrigerator for the family.*

In Āpia, I shopped for fruit and vegetables at the open air Fugalei Market—a jumble of stalls under a huge tent with produce piled high on low tables smelling of ripeness and the earth. On the edges tumbled stacks of taro and coconuts. Vendors from the villages brought produce and crafts, such as *salu lima* (hand brooms) made from coconut midribs, fala mats, or coconut shell jewelry. In addition to the market, I went to several small shops to get what I needed at the best prices such as cheese at Lucky Foodtown and canned goods at Chan Mow. Sometimes if I was feeling rich, I'd go to one of two "specialty" stores that carried pālagi food.

*I bought a few treats—one Hormel chili, one Van Camp's pork and beans, two kinds of Campbell's soup, a box of macaroni and green peas to make pasta salad, and for dinner tonight—one plump, boneless, skinless, chicken thigh ($2.75 USD for just the piece of chicken). The peas are dried, but the package says they'll taste fresh*

*when cooked; we'll see. I also brought home a bottle of liquid soap*
*for the bathroom (if I leave bar soap it disappears, but the liq-*
*uid stays), a four-pack of toilet paper (which I keep in my room*
*and take with me each time, otherwise it's likely there'll be none),*
*a small tube of toothpaste, a package of cheese, and four Cokes.*
*Altogether today's groceries cost $85 tala—about $35 USD. With*
*lunch, bus and taxi fare, and a snack at Pacific Express, I spent*
*$135 tala in Āpia, which isn't much, but it's thirteen percent of*
*my monthly Peace Corps allowance gone in one day. I'm fortunate*
*to have another source of income if I need it; most of the younger*
*volunteers don't.*

In every village there were stores ranging from small to tiny.
Fa'afetai & Karolina's F&K Store on the government road sold cigarettes, cold drinks, snacks, random vegetables, and necessities such as
disposable diapers, boxed milk, or small plastic bags filled with sugar
or flour. On the other side of the Congregational church was Uiti and
Feonu'u's tiny store. Close friends of Niu and Saina, their two girls also
went to St. Mary's and sometimes rode to town with us. Uiti taught
school in a neighboring village and was a church deacon and Sunday
School teacher. Feonu'u ran a store the size of a walk-in closet with
snacks and a few staples on shelves to the ceiling. The store was a family
operation, often closed, but if the large wooden shutters on the front
were open but no one was there, I'd just shout to the house in the back.
There were two other stores like this in Poutasi and one or more in all
villages. I usually went first to Feonu'u to buy a Coke, but she was often out. Indeed, occasionally the whole island would be Cokeless while
we waited for a boat to come.

Feonu'u at her tiny (but well stocked) store in Poutasi.

*I just finished a delicious lunch of pancakes made with Betty Crocker blueberry muffin mix that was marked down at Chan Mow, probably because it's pālagi food. No syrup, but good with butter. I can still smell the sugary blueberry aroma! Now I'm hot and sweaty after cooking in 85° without a fan. I can't have the fan and the skillet on at the same time because it'll overpower the electrical circuit. Oh, to cook in a real kitchen again, with a range, oven, sink, and a real refrigerator! And a grocery store with everything you could ever want to buy just a few minutes away!*

### Riding Emotional Waves

The entire time I was there, it seemed as if I never knew when I'd wake up feeling exhilarated at my good fortune living on a South Pacific beach, or overwhelmed with the size of the task before me, or just tired of trying so hard to fit in and adapt.

*This is so damn hard! So many things are confusing and complicated. Last week I went with the mayor to his auntie's eightieth birthday party in Sāleilua. He said I should go because it'd be culturally interesting. It was, and I enjoyed meeting new people, but then I wondered if I'd been on a date when one of our PC trainers told me the mayor had told him that he'd be married to me in two years! Yikes!*

*And the language. All the protocol and appropriate behavior. The intricate web of Samoan courtesies and customs. I feel like I'm always on the verge of doing something wrong and it's easy to slip into feeling sorry for myself. Every day has its ups and downs, but today I'm the melancholiest since I first arrived.*

*I'm expected to do something meaningful here. Probably something significant. Can I do that? I have no idea. I'm not supposed to rush into anything; I've only been here three weeks. I'm doing my job by getting to know the people and the village.*

*I had odd dreams last night. I was reading to the village children (who were dressed up like cowboys and cowgirls with straw hats, red kerchiefs around their necks, blue jeans, and boots!) and I lost my place in the story. I couldn't find the page again, so everyone had to go home.*

*I didn't go on my usual early morning walk today. Instead, I was trying to balance a cup of hot tea, a plate with toast and jam, my journal, and my cell phone, to come to the fale 'i tai to write. I dropped the plate, it broke, and tears welled up in my eyes. That, like the dreams, sums up the whole situation. Everything is juggling and balancing right now.*

And then, unpredictably, the world looked rosy again.

*A few days ago I was miserable, and now I'm calm and confident. They warned us it would be like this. I'll have another nosedive again no doubt, but maybe each one will be less daunting. There's a haze of smoke in the still air as families start their umu fires for Sunday dinner. I'm drinking my tea in the early morning, looking out to sea, smelling the lingering fragrance of wet earth. It rained overnight, as it often does, and the village is fresh and clean. Leftover raindrops sparkle on the palm fronds as the early morning sun hits them, stirred by the light breeze. Last night we celebrated Hemara's eleventh birthday at the house with family, neighbors, and a flock of giggling girls. I ate so much potato salad, fried chicken, and birthday cake that I was stuffed—the first I've felt like that for weeks.*

Despite my desire to get started on a project, or schedule or plan, I followed PC protocol, gathering information for my Village Situational Analysis and chipping away at learning about Poutasi. That meant that each day much of my time was spent reading, writing, and hanging out at the fale 'i tai, interspersed with small daily missions "getting to know the village" such as attending a Women's Committee meeting or going to visit the village school.

The school in the village was a district secondary school with approximately two hundred students from Poutasi and surrounding villages. (The primary children went to the school in Sāleilua.) From the road I could see that the school consisted of three small, clapboard buildings with peeling and faded sky-blue paint. On the day that I visited, I noted the signs marking the office, shop and home economics buildings, and a long building with seven small classrooms, all with piles of flip flops outside each door.

"Tālofa!" I greeted the principal, who was expecting me. At her invitation I sat directly in front of her desk, in that spot that always makes you feel like you're about to be chastised no matter how old you are. She told me that there were two classes each of levels 9 to 11 and one class of level 12 students. They had eight teachers, including the principal, the deputy principal, and a JICA (Japan International

Cooperation Agency) volunteer who taught Design Technology (shop class). There had been eleven teachers, but three of them including the math teacher had recently left, so the students studied their math books in the classroom without a teacher.

As she and I walked around the school, I saw that they needed so much. There weren't enough desks so some students sat on laufala mats on the floor. They had very few reference books and no computers. In the home economics classroom (for thirty girls), there were only two hand-operated sewing machines and one two-burner kerosene cook top. The gardens desperately needed fencing to keep out the pigs.

Samoan kids started learning English in primary school in Level 4, and by Levels 7 and 8 the teaching was supposed to be mostly in English. In Level 8 all students took national examinations—in English—and were placed in a secondary school based upon their scores. Some didn't go beyond Level 8. The Ministry of Education strongly believed that if the students didn't know English well, they'd have a harder time getting career-oriented jobs. However, one of our Peace Corps trainers actually said to us when we grumbled about the number of drop-out students: "It doesn't matter because there aren't enough local jobs for them anyway." Like many other underdeveloped nations, Samoa suffered from a "brain drain" when the best and brightest "had" to leave the country to succeed in a career or find well-paying work (and send remittances home). Nonetheless, regardless of the level of education, subsistence living "employed" family members who were needed to work the taro plantations and gardens, raise pigs, fish, and maintain a household.

Level 12 students who wanted a university education had to pass an English national examination in order to be approved to progress to a University Preparatory Year, and then pass an international examination developed and maintained by the countries that participated (Samoa, Tonga, Vanuatu, Cook Islands, Solomon Islands, and Kiribati). Most attended the National University of Samoa in Āpia; others received scholarships and were able to go to the University of the South Pacific in Fiji or to universities in New Zealand, Australia, or the United States.

Facts, figures, and new information continued to bombard me every day. I was constantly memorizing new words, making lists, listening, and learning. I looked forward to the days when life in the village would get easier and it would be smoother sailing.

*I took a book from the PC library that I didn't return—*Eat, Pray, Love *by Elizabeth Gilbert. It's a tale of adventure, discovery, searching, and finding as she travels and lives in Italy, India, and Indonesia for a year. No matter that it's one woman's story—we're all on a similar journey, just a different cast of characters, different time, different place. As the critics might say, every tale of life's adventures is a "formulaic" story. Sometimes it's a clumsy melodrama with heart-tugging sentimentality, sometimes a fall-on-the-floor-laughing comedy, sometimes an action-adventure that we can hardly believe was part of our life, or sometimes a drama that bores into our very soul, making us wonder with awe. And of course, most of our lives are all of the above, in bits and pieces, over decades (if we're lucky), with a lot of just plain living in between.*

*Sometimes we consciously think about it; sometimes we can't afford to. Sometimes we think about it a lot, especially at transition times in our lives—when we've graduated from college, after marriage, or a divorce, on certain birthdays, mourning the loss of a loved one, after the retirement party at work, or while serving in the Peace Corps in a foreign country.*

*I'm astonishingly bored this afternoon. I've done some writing, played solitaire, listened to Radio Australia, and read an old* New Yorker *magazine someone left at the PC office from cover to cover. At least I'm outside and there's a nice breeze instead of in the house where it's too hot and there's not enough air circulation. Finally heard a temperature on the radio—29°C (84.2°F) this morning in Āpia. Ah, springtime in Samoa.*

*I haven't been feeling blue today, but I'm continually surprised how much it cheers me to be here by the ocean. It never fails to make me feel better than I was feeling.*

## Radio Australia and Other Windows to the Outside World

"It's 5:00 AM in Honiara, 6:00 AM in Suva, and 18 hours universal time." So went my morning salutation for the 7:00 AM news on Radio Australia, my main connection to the world. I relied on it to entertain me, inform me, keep me company, lull me to sleep, and greet me in the morning. When it was unaccountably off-air in Samoa for a couple of days or a couple of weeks, I missed it significantly.

At night in the dark house, a light breeze wafted through the louvered windows as I'd lie in bed listening to the surf break on the reef, occasional muted voices, no vehicles, and dogs barking here and there. Then I'd plug in my earpiece, close my eyes, turn on my radio and travel the world.

*I've discovered Radio Australia, like National Public Radio in the States. I was delighted yesterday to hear a speech given in South Australia by Robert Reich, from Clinton's cabinet, talking about the challenges of globalization and technology, immigration, and the population imbalance created by the baby boom generation. Fascinating! He's written a book titled* Supercapitalism. *This morning I listened to a captivating interview with two men who've written about species extinction.*

In addition to international and Australian news, I heard reporting and music from the more than ten thousand islands in Oceania.

"*Pacific Beat*" was one of my favorite programs—"interviews with leaders, newsmakers, and people who make the Pacific beat"—with stories about rescued adrift fishermen, reverberations of the 2006 Fijian coup, or women starting small businesses in Vanuatu.

*I finished reading* In a Sunburned Country *by Bill Bryson today. At the end he says, "It seemed a particularly melancholy notion to me that life would go on in Australia and I would hear almost nothing of it." I'll feel that way when I leave here—not only about Samoa, but about Australia, New Zealand, and the whole South Pacific. Listening to Radio Australia everyday has put me in closer touch with what's happening there than what's happening in America. I get reports of only the biggest news events from the States, but I know exhaustive details about the drought in Australia, the upcoming election in Nauru, the controversy over the Kokoda Track in Papua New Guinea, and much more.*

But sometimes, even Radio Australia failed me.

*Cricket is on RA tonight. I know the sportscasters are speaking English because I recognize the individual words, but they're strung together in that odd lingo of a cricket match. I have no idea what they're talking about. They might as well be speaking Martian. Bored, bored, bored.*

Every other month a huge box arrived in the Peace Corps office from *Newsweek* with dozens of copies of back-issues. I'd excitedly dig in, pulling out a couple months' worth, and binge-read them cover to cover. Near the end of my Peace Corps service, *Newsweek* stopped sending them—because of the cost we were told—and I lost that important link to America.

Mom sent me awesome packages on a regular basis replete with M&M's, cashews, granola bars, or delicious foil packets of ready-to-heat salmon or ahi tuna filets. Sometimes she'd include random surprises, like a small fabric Jack-o-lantern at Halloween. I tried to explain the holiday and trick-or-treating to Hemara, Tia, and Fetū, but in the telling it sounded so weird to my ears that I gave up, imagining how it must sound to them. Mom always included clippings from her local Colorado paper, and whenever boxes arrived from the States with wadded up newspapers for stuffing, I spread them out and read every sheet.

*I've been reading a Wall Street Journal I flattened from a box from the States. Delightful, yet frustrating when an article about the Denver Broncos was continued on page W-12, and no page W-12. There's a lot of gloom and doom about the economy and a good review of WALL-E, a new movie.*

We had a television like most Samoans, but there were only two channels with mostly local programming. Every Sunday a church service was filmed somewhere in the country, broadcast live, and then repeated several times during the week. Many school activities were televised, and any festival in Āpia would be rebroadcast over and over as well. In a small country everyone seemed to end up on TV sooner or later, as I was at least a half dozen times for some village or Peace Corps-related event.

There was a lot of televised rugby, both local and international. It was a hugely popular sport and every village had a team. Samoans were serious about rugby. The national professional team, *Manu Samoa*, consistently ranked in the top twenty in the world—impressive considering that they came from a speck of land in the middle of the Pacific with less than two hundred thousand people.

Other programming consisted of old American re-runs like *I Love Lucy* or the *Brady Bunch*, dated American movies and cartoons, and Filipino soap operas with subtitles. Each evening the local Samoan news was broadcast in both English and Samoan, followed by the New Zealand news.

However, I rarely watched TV. Besides the barely interesting programming, the last thing I would've wanted was for someone to discover me glued to the tube during the day. Somehow sitting by the sea reading a book seemed a more acceptable and less profligate use of my time. On weekends when Saina and the girls were home, the TV was on much of the time. Every now and then I'd lay on the bed in the center room and watch a movie with the kids or stop and watch the Samoan or New Zealand news broadcasts as I walked through. But in the evenings during the week, I felt awkward hanging out in front of the TV with the three guys, Tamamasui, Niu, and Fetū. Seventy-year-old Tamamasui didn't speak English, Niu was always quiet, and Fetū was a bouncy seven-year old just beginning to learn English, so there was no conversation happening, and they were usually watching a program I wasn't interested in. So I'd retreat to my room and Radio Australia.

I experienced the entire Obama/Clinton presidential campaign through Australian eyes, weeks-old Newsweek magazines, or the occasional Associated Press article in the *Samoan Observer*. It's a peculiar gap in my recollection and it seems odd that I have absolutely no experiential memory of those momentous times. Every now and then someone will mention some news event I don't remember, and I'll discover that it happened in 2007 or 2008.

In addition to communication from the world outside Samoa, above all I needed to be in touch with the people in my life in the States. Their love and support made an immeasurable difference. Fortunately cell phones came to Samoa six months before we did, so our group was the first with the option to get one upon arrival. There was only one mobile carrier, Digicel, which sold cards with phone credit codes—one of the seven or eight stops I scurried to each time I went to Āpia.

My little black phone was tiny by today's standards, making it laborious to text, and texts and calls to the States were prohibitively expensive—about a dollar a minute—so I rationed carefully. I talked to family and a couple of dear friends about once a month. That seemed like scant time compared to the frequent texting and calling I was accustomed to, so those minutes became even more precious. I'd sit at the fale 'i tai in the shade of the metal roof, the trade winds blowing lightly, relieving the oppressive heat of the day. In my wide wooden chair with a picket-fence back, resting on floral-print cushions, I'd look out to sea, watch the clouds float above the horizon, smell the salt air, prop my feet on a matching chair, and spend Sunday afternoons with my loved ones far away.

My other contact with the world was online. Internet connectivity was also relatively new to the country. Social networking was in its infancy, upload time was painfully slow, and smart phones were years away. As PCVs we had free access to two computers in the Peace Corp office resource room where we'd hang out laughing, networking, and commiserating, while waiting for our turn on the sign-up sheet. I also went online at bustling internet cafes for $5 USD per hour. But since I was typically in Āpia only once a week with a long list of errands to run, I didn't surf the net or read stories online. At times we'd inexplicably have no internet on the entire island.

The uplifting and supportive responses to my periodic email updates to family and friends kept me going.

Elizabeth R
Wed 9/5/2007, 12:25 PM

Dear Donna,

I want to thank you for your e-mails of your fascinating experiences. I will be candid; I don't envy you, but I do greatly admire you. I hope that you are saving all your e-mails. I'm serious about urging you to publish your experiences when you get back. You write so vividly. I'm particularly fascinated by your psychological revelations. I'm not surprised that you are experiencing what might be considered culture shock. I am well aware of what a strong person you are, and I am pleased that you are willing to be so frank with some of your "downers." I'm looking forward to your next e-mail. Take care.

Betty

Connie H
Sun 6/1/2008, 8:59 PM

Hi Donna,

I am always blessed by your emails, but this one just really touched my heart. What an awesome feeling to have had a part in accomplishing something that will make a difference not only now, but for generations. My thoughts are always with you!

A hui hou,
Connie

Uncle Bob wasn't a long-talk-on-the-phone-person. He was much more voluble face to face. On the phone, after a while he'd say, "Well, nice talkin' to ya." So over the years we wrote long letters and then email, especially while I was in Samoa.

RE: October 17, 2007 - Update from Samoa
harold bailey
Thu 10/18/2007, 9:39 AM


Tālofa , Donna!


I read and printed your new letter and will pass it around.
I've discovered by intuition and dream that all is foreordained and will flow as it will flow. Our job is to just go with the flow and embrace events and accept them.
Our life seems to go through phases: first, experience; then, analysis and patience and wisdom; and finally acceptance—an important one—it's assimilation, sort of like a dog settling into "its place," and becoming a part of it. Once we have acceptance, we have control, and once we have control, we can find contentment. Life is about contentment: some seek happiness—I seek contentment.

Love,
Uncle Bob


Even though I didn't read Uncle Bob's message until a few days later when I went to Āpia, on the same day that he emailed me, I wrote in my journal:

*Poutasi is a beautiful village. The people are kind and interesting. I have a pleasant room, in a lovely house, with a caring family. I have the fale ʻi tai, the sea at my back door, a beautiful sunrise over the mountains each morning, and an equally gorgeous sunset over the ocean each evening. I'll have challenging projects, which may not happen, but some that I can foresee being successful. It's coming together and will be whatever it's meant to be.*

### The Promise of Romance Tempts Me Again

I'd been in the village for a couple of months when I got a message from Jackson. He said he'd been thinking about our time together before I left for Peace Corps and how much he missed me.

*He signed the email with the "L" word for the first time. I should be thrilled, and I'm pleased, just wary. But still, there's something different coming from him. So because I do want to be loved and love in return, I haven't much to lose by giving it a go.*

With some analysis of where we'd been and why in a series of emails, we agreed to resume our path toward some sort of a future together when I got back. Like everything else in my life at that moment my reaction was filled with ambivalence, but I began to look forward to his emails on my weekly trips to Āpia. We talked when we could, though like all phone calls they were brief and a poor substitute for being together.

The truth was, I didn't know what to think. We'd been down this road for so long without going anywhere. Jackson had always been as ambivalent as I was. When it was great, it was great! And then we'd call it off.

# Chapter 4

# Beginning to See Beneath the Surface

*O le malie ma le tu'u malie*
*"Every shark has his price"*
*Every act receives its reward.*

What might be called a sarong in other parts of the world was a *lāvalava* in Samoa—the four feet of colorful cloth wrapped round the body, tied or tucked at the waist or under the armpits, depicted on a stunning Polynesian beauty on the beach, with her dark hair blowing in the breeze. I observed that portrayal, but the lāvalava was much more than that, and was part of one's dress every day in variations.

Due to the strong Christian influence, clothing styles were very modest. In the village, women wore a t-shirt (not a tank top) and a lightweight tropical-printed lāvalava coming somewhere between the ankles and knees. Men wore the same for casual wear and working in the village, either with a t-shirt or shirtless. Young men constructed elaborate knots in the front whose interpretation needed little imagination.

"Inside the fale" I could wear long shorts and a tank top. I use the quotation marks because often "inside the fale" was the space surrounded by four non-existent walls. For a culture that had lived for centuries in close proximity in open houses, the custom evolved to respect that space. Before the missionaries came, women lived bare breasted and when I was there it was still okay to go topless "inside the fale." Breast feeding was the norm whether at home or in public and very young children often ran about naked.

In Āpia dress was more western. Even so, a Samoan woman wouldn't have worn shorts or a skirt above the knees. One day I walked behind two middle-aged local women following a family of tourists with two blond, scantily clad teenage girls and heard their "tsk tsk tsk" as they observed with disapproval. Although men always wore shirts in town, most people wore what they'd wear in their village.

Clothing at church depended on the denomination. At the Congregational church we dressed in white every Sunday. The women donned fancy, broad-brimmed, white hats and a white *puletasi*. A puletasi was a well-fitted top with short sleeves, no collar, hip-length with a matching lāvalava underneath worn to the ankles. Men wore a white or dark lāvalava to the knees made of suit-weight fabric with pockets and a belt, a white dress shirt, and sometimes a tie and matching jacket. Our pastor always wore a white suit and tie with the bottom half being a lāvalava instead of pants.

A puletasi in a colorful fabric was the typical business or formal wear for women as well, and at a fiafia or party they might don an off-the-shoulder top or spaghetti straps. Men put on a dark lāvalava and a locally made aloha shirt for work or special occasions. Everyone, with rare exception, wore rubber flip flops or went barefoot. Women usually kept their hair long, but outside the fale they always pulled it back in a bun or a braid, and men cut their hair short. Both sexes often tucked a flower behind an ear.

One could buy a lāvalava at every store and at the markets in Āpia in an array of colorful designs, preprinted, hand painted, or wood-block printed. Ready-made clothes were sold at stores in town, some imported, some locally sewn, and used t-shirts and other clothing were plentiful at the large local thrift store (overseas donations). However, most clothing was sewn at home or purchased from a seamstress in the village or in Āpia. When I needed a new puletasi I crept up the rickety stairs to the small shop of Saina's favorite seamstress in Āpia to be fitted.

For someone who'd always bought off-the-rack, it felt rather decadent to have a dress custom made for me, and delightful to have one that fit so well.

As Peace Corps volunteers we were expected to dress according to local customs and rules, which differed for each village. Facial hair was prohibited in Poutasi and most other villages. Two guys in Group 78 had to shave when they arrived at their assignments. I always wore a lāvalava and t-shirt out of the house, and a puletasi when appropriate. All women swam in long, baggy shorts or a lāvalava and t-shirt. I wouldn't dare have sported a swimsuit, no matter how modest! A lāvalava and t-shirt were comfortable and I quickly got used to it. I sometimes wore a long, modest sundress or Capri-length shorts with a tank top to Āpia, but even then I changed or wrapped a lāvalava around the shorts coming and going on the bus to the village.

# ODE TO A LĀVALAVA

skirt, pants, sarong, swimsuit

curtain, tablecloth, sheet, towel

shawl, turban, hat, scarf

pillow, hot pad, napkin

shower curtain

upholstery

room divider

bundle, basket, baby wrap

bandage, sling, tourniquet

sun shelter, beach blanket

mosquito net, umbrella

weapon to fend off dogs

foothold for climbing a coconut tree

rope for a drowning person

life saver

## *O Le Pupu-Puʻe National Park*

It was about this time that Niu invited me to a meeting at the park he supervised, O Le Pupu-Puʻe National Park, about five miles from Poutasi. Near the entrance, the cascading Togitogiga Waterfall and its bubbling pool were said to be visited by the great warriors of Samoaʼs past. The Coastal Walk to the sea rewarded hikers with spectacular views, and lava caves were home to the *peʻapeʻa* bird (white-rumped swiftlet). This was not only the first national park established in Samoa in 1978, but also the first in the South Pacific. There had been a visitor center until it blew down in Cyclone Ofa in 1990 and Niu was supervising reconstruction of the structure with help from Japanese volunteers.

In addition, he had another important goal—for people in neighboring villages to learn about and get involved with the park, hopefully spreading the word.

*Niu said that local people donʼt appreciate or even fully understand the concept of a national park and most have never been there. I told him about the Friends of the Park volunteer group in the States and he said that Samoan people always ask for money. They donʼt want to volunteer for anything—even if you ask them to help pick up litter, they want to be paid. I wonder what thatʼs about . . . because it doesnʼt directly benefit their family, village, or church?*

On the day of the scheduled neighborhood meeting, one of Niuʼs co-workers pulled up in front of our house in his black Mazda pickup. It had no seat belts and like many Iʼd encountered, it had been shipped from New Zealand or Australia because it was right-hand drive (on a roadway meant for left-hand drive vehicles). Along the way we picked up three people walking along the road. In Samoa you just started walking toward your destination and someone, probably somebody you knew, offered you a ride.

Although the park headquarters was inland, surrounded by forest except for the cleared area around the administrative buildings and workshops, there was a refreshing steady breeze. About twenty village and park representatives gathered in a large open fale next to Niu's office on folding chairs—a mixture of women and men from three of the villages closest to the park. A cappella voices joined in an opening hymn followed by a prayer. After formalities and a brief introduction about the park, it was time for tea, which was koko Samoa, sandwiches of canned tuna and cucumber slices, and chunky breadfruit pudding served on small "trays" woven from palm fronds.

Following tea, Niu and his colleagues presented an overview of the history, geology, and natural environment of the park. Then it was time for lunch. We were each given two Styrofoam hinged-lid containers stuffed full of food—a portion of baked chicken, a hearty scoop of pisupo, a pasta dish with chunks of lamb, a sausage, three one-inch thick slices of taro, a small fried fish, a chunk of pork, and a coconut to drink. I chatted with the ladies from Poutasi as I ate the chicken, a half slice of the taro with palusami, the pasta (it had a few canned mixed veggies in it), and a couple bites of sausage. I usually would've eaten the pork but the piece I got still had hair on it and I had plenty to eat without it.

After lunch, we broke into three groups and brainstormed about how to get locals to interact with the national park, such as guided hikes for kids or clean-up days. Niu graciously introduced me at the beginning of the meeting and encouraged me to participate, although my knowledge of the park was limited at that time. Afterwards, dignitaries from the villages planted trees in front of the building. In addition to closing with a hymn and a prayer, several of the village leaders made the usual impromptu ceremonial speeches of thanks and farewell. At the end, each attendee got leftover food to take home and an envelope with $20 tala.

*I thought it was very well presented and effective. I'll be interested to hear what Niu thinks. Some of them probably came only for the money but the message about the value of the national park is spreading. It was all in Samoan, but I was amazed and pleased at how much I understood—maybe half. It helps when I know the subject matter so that I can pick up words contextually.*

In addition to information about the park and the copious food, opportunities such as this gave me valuable time with Niu to talk professionally about matters in which he was an expert and which were appealing and interesting to me, such as the goals of the Samoan government to preserve the biodiversity of the islands and eradicate invasive species.

### Samoan Church Resurrects Old Conflicts

*It'll be time for church again soon. Today is the first day I don't feel like going. I've had a relaxing lazy afternoon and don't want to break the spell. I don't have a choice; it's part of my job.*

My relationship with church in Samoa was as complicated as my history and perspective on religion in general. In *Eat, Pray, Love*, Elizabeth Gilbert used the term "culturally Christian." I certainly grew up culturally and theologically Christian. I was surrounded by Christianity and I was a believer.

Mom's father was a Conservative Baptist minister. And that's not a redundancy—even though it's an especially fundamentalist, evangelical faith. All Baptist churches are independent, however ours was affiliated with the Conservative Baptist Association. When they were newly married, my grandparents applied to the board of missions and planned to go to Africa. Those plans were dashed when Grandpa's asthma wouldn't allow them to make the journey. Grandma was perfectly suited to life as a preacher's wife—compassionate and outgoing, and she lived her life by the Golden Rule.

I have fond memories of getting up early on Sunday morning, smelling the pot roast Mom had put into the oven for our big meal after church, getting dressed in patent leather Mary Janes and one of my nicest dresses, hoping my two brothers tumbling about in the back seat wouldn't get it dirty before we got there. Our church was a classic, white, clapboard rectangle with a pointed steeple above the bell tower. My other grandmother was the church pianist. She got a degree in music, taught at a one-room country school, met my grandfather, raised five boys, and gave piano lessons to me and I don't know how many other kids. Their farmland was adjacent to the church yard and small cemetery. In the valley below, the tilled fields, two-story white ginger-breaded house and red barn made an idyllic tableau.

The children sat in curtained-off "rooms" in the basement for an hour-long Sunday School, while the adults did the same upstairs, then all went to the main service for an hour. I can still hear Grandpa's strong voice delivering his sermon behind the wooden pulpit, teaching the meaning of the scriptures. Sometimes there was a potluck afterward with rotating variations of casseroles and Jell-O salads, oven-fried chicken, potato salad, deviled eggs, homemade pickles, and fresh bread, along with mouth-watering brownies, pies, and cakes. If there wasn't a meal at the church, we'd go home to the pot roast and vegetables. Often on Sunday afternoon we'd join aunts, uncles, and cousins at Dad's family homestead. We kids romped in the hayloft and cedar woods until we dropped. Later on Sunday evening we attended the Youth Group meeting, followed by an hour of evening service. There also were Wednesday night prayer meetings and Thursday night choir practices. Prayer and Bible readings at home were part of everyday life and memorizing Bible verses was my special talent.

Church families made up much of my social life as well. Drinking, smoking, playing cards, and dancing were forbidden, and movies were suspect, but there were fun outings—summer picnics, Halloween parties, hayrides, sledding, and playing games all night in the church basement on New Year's Eve. Although I did beg, plead, and lie to go to my high school sophomore homecoming dance, saying it was "really just a big party" and that I wouldn't dance. Of course I did!

I didn't question my faith until I was a teenager. One Saturday afternoon my girlfriend Sue and I were laughing and talking, sprawled on our backs on her bed with the white frilly coverlet that I still remember. Our chatter somehow turned to religion and I was surprised to find that Catholics believed almost the same as we did—the same God, Jesus, resurrection, heaven and hell. From what I discerned at that point, the only major differences were the saints, the elevation of Mary to a quasi-deity, and priests, which according to our religion came between you and God. When I next saw Grandma, I recalled the conversation and said, "They believe the same thing we do." She was dismayed, hurried to correct me, and said that they weren't "Christians." According to her, only those who had personally confessed their sins in prayer to Jesus, asked him to forgive and save them, were Christians, and thus "saved" from hell and welcomed to everlasting life in heaven. You couldn't be saved by being baptized as a baby when you didn't know what you were doing. I'd been saved at the age of seven and recommitted my life to Christ at thirteen when I was baptized in a lake. Nonetheless, I didn't doubt my faith; I was only surprised to find that Catholics weren't complete infidels even though Grandma thought they were.

I chose to attend a small Lutheran university because it was affordable and only a twenty-minute drive from home. There I took a required religion class that covered the history of Christianity and a smattering introduction to other spiritual traditions. With more recognition of the world of possibilities beyond my religious beliefs, I still stayed steadfast.

In 1969 everything changed. It was a tumultuous year for me at twenty, as well as for America—Woodstock, the Stonewall Riots, the Manson Murders, Richard Nixon's election, and that one starlit summer evening we watched, enraptured, as Neil Armstrong walked on the moon. Earlier that year, Mom and Dad had reconciled after being separated for three years. They'd nearly divorced after Dad had an affair with a woman *from church*—yeah, add that into the mix! When they and my two brothers moved from Nebraska to Colorado that year, I stopped going to church. I began to stray from my faith. I had my first drink, began a ten-year cigarette smoking habit, lost my virginity, and had a painful break up with the sports editor I was "supposed" to marry. I went "home" to Colorado to a house I'd never lived in, still hurt and angry with my dad. Bit by bit I forgave him, and he and Mom remained together until he passed away after their 58th anniversary. I was deeply unhappy and despondent. Joining the Air Force was admittedly running away from my problems, but it worked.

I still have my military dog tags that say SO BAPT—for Southern Baptist because it was the closest they had to Conservative Baptist. No momentous revelation occurred when I stopped believing. I considered myself a Christian when James and I met the next year. I remember his shock when I said that Catholics weren't Christians. He'd grown up in a loosely Christian faith, not as fundamentalist or consistent as mine, but when we met he was an agnostic, my first nonacademic exposure to the possibility of no faith at all. To my family I paid lip-service to Christianity, never spoke of my disbelief and kept up the pretense, although they knew I didn't go to church. Over the years I became an agnostic and finally an atheist. I'm comfortable with that. Science and nature won out in the end.

Then I went to Samoa and ... bam! Right back to the religion of my youth and an integral part of their culture. My beliefs didn't change, but surprisingly the church was comforting when I was alone and feeling vulnerable, especially in those first months in their country. I didn't pray, but I found a forced meditation with the rhythms and ritual of prayers and hymns, the soaring voices of the choir, the way the sunlight played in and out of the open windows, and the sudden babble of voices after the dismissal by the pastor. I didn't think or worry; I was just there.

Growing up as I did, I understand what it's like to believe thoroughly and totally, to *know* that you are correct and true to your faith. I understand how it becomes a part of you and frames and guides how you interact with the world around you, as it does for the Samoans. It was easy to blend into their Christian culture; I knew the Bible lessons and verses from my youth. I don't have bad memories about my childhood religion, on the contrary, generally positive ones. It's just that at some point I no longer believed what I'd been told was the truth. Again, I paid lip-service to the Samoans' similar Congregational faith, not wanting to hurt anyone's feelings or make them think that I needed to be saved.

I grew up caring a lot about what other people think. I was raised by a mother who was a "preacher's kid," who had the burden in her youth to be an exemplar of the faith. And that was passed on to me. It was important to be seen as a "good" person, not bring shame on the family and to always be *in control* of how the world perceived you. As a preacher's kid, Uncle Bob also carried expectational baggage, but he dared to take another path and eventually evolved into an agnostic.

I know that Conservative Baptist culture is even now a fundamental component of who I am. Writing "I am an atheist" feels a bit like "coming out." I've asked myself over and over why this public admission is so difficult for me and why I couldn't reveal that part of me in Samoa . . . and the answers are as complicated as my religious experience. I still don't want to disappoint anyone—and I worried about that while I lived there—because I know how much their faith means to them and saying that I have none is antithetical to the core of their beliefs. I felt like I ran the risk of losing the high regard of my real family and my Samoan families, and that seemed too costly. Now I feel as if I was a hypocrite, and for that I am sorry. As Elizabeth Gilbert said about Christianity, "To those who do speak (and think) strictly, all I can do here is offer my regrets for any hurt feelings and now excuse myself from their business."

While I was in Samoa, their census reported that the country was 99.9 percent Christian with the most prevalent being the Congregational Christian Church of Samoa. Over the world, specific Congregational doctrines vary widely, from theologically conservative to liberal and Unitarian. The church in Samoa was on the conservative side, established by John Williams. an English missionary active in the South Pacific. There were also Catholics, Methodists, Mormons, Seventh-day Adventists, and about three thousand Baha'i, including King Malietoa Tanumafili II (who died just a month before I arrived). The open-air Baha'i worship space in Āpia with its fabulously landscaped grounds is the Mother Temple for the Pacific Islands, one of only ten in the world. Regardless of denomination, God was part of everyday life for everyone.

Throughout Samoa at 6:00 PM every weekday, a church bell rang in each village signaling people to return to their homes for evening prayers and hymns. During this time, no one was allowed to work or walk about in the village. If you didn't return to your home, you were expected to sit quietly wherever you were until *sā* was over. In some villages there were enforcers who sat watch to make sure everyone complied. After about fifteen minutes, another ringing of the bell indicated that *sā* was ended. Because most of my family was away at this time of day, we only had evening prayers when everyone was at home.

*Religion in Samoa is similar to what I envision in Islamic nations. Not the theology of course, but the pervasiveness of it. It's not something people do. It's who they are. It isn't a place they go on Sundays, but an integral part of life every day. Every public event includes a prayer to Atua (God). Nearly every article in the newspaper references Atua, even on the sports page. Everyday conversation and every meeting of any kind includes Atua. To eat a meal anywhere without a prayer of thanks is unthinkable. The country's motto is "Samoa is founded on God." And it clearly is.*

## Adjust Your Behavior Accordingly

The Samoa Peace Corps handbook sent when I accepted my invitation to serve said:

> [E]ach village has its own rules of conduct. You will need to be aware of these rules and follow the norms and behaviors expected. This includes respecting times of prayer and religious observances by attending services or at least refraining from activities that are not considered proper by the village on Sundays and other religious holidays. Christianity is the prevalent religion, and Volunteers will need to adjust their behaviors accordingly.

I was both strangely comforted by a religion that I'd forsaken and frustrated to death with the mandate to attend once I began to realize how much church time there'd be. Even if affiliated with a similar faith, the requirement seems anomalous to Americans with freedom of religion at the top of our list. But if this is what everyone is doing, then you do it too. If you refused it might impact your effectiveness, and there'd be *so much* about the culture and the village that you'd miss. Beliefs aside, church in Samoa was entertaining, inspiring, educational, and informative. The singing was uplifting and mesmerizing, services were perpetual opportunities to learn the language, and the announcements (when I understood them correctly) told of upcoming events that everyone needed to know about.

*Sunday afternoon church started at 4:00 PM and lasted for about two hours. It was longer than usual because members of the congregation read from the Bible and several men spoke instead of a sermon by the pastor, although of course he had a few words to say too. This is always particularly tedious because it strains my language translation skills. Afterward we had a brief choir practice. Saina stayed for a meeting of the Women's Fellowship, which I sometimes go to, but I'd had enough church for the day.*

So even with my ambivalence, I knew it was an important part of understanding the village and integrating as much I could, so I joined the church choir. I have an ordinary alto voice but I love to sing and so do Samoans! Robert Louis Stevenson once said that the Samoans composed a song for every trivial occasion. Whether traditional melodies, Caribbean reggae, or church hymns, they sang with gusto and effortless harmony.

The choir's twenty women sat on five wooden benches on the right, facing the pulpit along with the rest of the congregation, altos in front with the sopranos behind and an equal number of tenors and basses on the left. Our choir director was a strict task master. We practiced each song over and over accompanied by our pianist, a college student with curly black hair who played energetically on an electric piano. The choir made up about half of the attending adults in the church, with the remainder scattered throughout and those with babies in the back. The children sat on the far left with the pastor's wife who kept them in line, properly shushed and listening. We all faced a fading, red Plexiglas cross that took up most of the back wall of the sanctuary, and through which the sunlight cast a warm glow on Sunday mornings. Each week, women from the congregation decorated the front of the church with displays of anthuriums, pink and red ginger (*teuila*—Samoa's national flower), palm branches, or croton leaves until it looked like a small floral shop.

The Poutasi Congregational Church ready for Sunday morning.

After the bell rang every Sunday morning, I'd walk the fifty feet from our front door to the six wide steps of the church. Small kids ran back and forth in the sandy church yard, mothers ran after them, the men talked in small groups, and old women sitting on the benches next to the front door clucked over the babies and admired new hats.

"*Tālofa Donna! O a mai 'oe?*" (Greetings Donna. How are you?)

"*Tālofa! Manuia, fa'afetai. O a mai 'oe?*" (Greetings! Fine, thank you. How are you?) I replied, as I put $20 tala in the basket on the table in front where Valasi sat with the offering book. My contribution was duly recorded by my name so it could be announced with everyone else's following the service. This still seems shocking to me but it's very Samoan. These offerings were indicative of commitment, wealth, and status, and were discussed in the village and beyond. Often Samoans were expected to give more than they could afford. Education took third place after family and church. Sometimes families contributed half of their income, leaving parents without enough money for school uniforms or modest school fees.

I'd find my seat in the choir section two rows back, and on cue from the piano we all rose and sang the doxology. The church was filled with praise and joy as the sopranos soared, the basses boomed deep and loud, and the altos and tenors blended smoothly. Occasionally several congregations gathered on Sunday morning in a neighboring village. In addition to the songs that everyone sang together, the choir from each church sang an individual song accompanied by our own pianist. We'd practice a new and difficult song for weeks and, although only obliquely acknowledged, it was quite competitive and I was proud of our choir.

The mayor, Luafutu (left) and Meleisea Seti after church; the fale 'i tai is behind them.

The front of the church with Niu and Valasi at the table with the offering book.

Poutasi Congregational Church choir
(Mataomanu is in the second row, third from the left).

There were other church activities during the week including bingo on Friday nights, deacon's meetings, and Women's Fellowship endeavors. One afternoon Saina came home unexpectedly and said that it was the day of the annual offering to the pastor and his wife. Our pastor, Letone Uili, had a compelling voice, softly raspy like Muhammad Ali, and his cadence was evenly paced even when he wasn't preaching. Logo his wife was cute, plump, and petite. In my "getting to know the village" rounds I'd stopped at their house next to the church hall and been warmly welcomed.

I'd heard talk of this event but didn't know much more. Saina and I walked to the hall where for three hours the Women's Fellowship presented laufala mats and other household items to Letone and Logo seated at the front. Each woman brought three kinds of mats—two sizes and grades of the more utilitarian seating mats (*papa laufala*) and also finer mats used for floor covering with colorful strands of dangling yarn trim and designs in the weave. All told, there were fifty-four of one kind of the papa laufala, seventy of the other, and sixty-three of the finer floor mats. Most were made by the women; Saina and a few others purchased their gift mats. Other offerings included a large tea kettle, miscellaneous kitchen items, a coffee table, and bedding. Saina bought a bedspread with pillow shams for me to give since I didn't plan for it and needed to bring something.

Then each of the finer mats was brandished aloft in the hall, displayed by a woman holding up each end and carried in a final presentation to Letone and Logo, along with speeches, prayers, singing, and of course, food.

After I'd been in the village for a while, if I persisted I was allowed to help with other church events. Insistence was necessary since my status as a Peace Corps volunteer and my maturity normally excluded me from such activities. One such day I helped when sixty pastors, their wives, deacons, and other church leaders met in Poutasi for an island-wide annual Congregational church meeting.

When my alarm went off in the dark at 6:00, I told myself (out loud actually), "This is part of your Samoan experience. This is what you signed up for." Several women, including Saina, had stayed up all night, decorating the church, and getting food ready. The assignment they gave me was usually a job for the young women but since it was a weekday, they were short on young women. We set up long buffet tables at Logo and Letone's house and then served breakfast to the pastors, and after they were finished, to their wives. While they were eating, we fanned the food with laufala fans, kept offering more food, and afterward took away plates.

*Because it's Samoa it can't ever be a light meal. There was a buffet of waffles and pālagi pancakes with syrup and blueberry fruit topping, two huge platters of cut fruit, flying saucers, hard fried eggs, toast, triangles of toast with sliced hardboiled egg, koko esi (cocoa and papaya), and hot dogs in buns with mayonnaise, mustard, and ketchup. We ate after we served everyone. Although the pastors and their wives only nibbled at them, the waffles and pancakes were my favorite so I brought some home along with topping and some fruit. After the breakfast, we made up foil packets of leftovers for each of the pastors' wives. Of course we served a huge lunch about three hours later, so I have some of that left too. Saina told me that after church last Sunday each family was told to bring roast pigs, along with the usual special event fare, but the women objected and wanted to keep it simple. Good for them! Each Styrofoam container at lunchtime had hearty helpings of beef stir fry, two slices of umu-cooked taro and palusami, a piece of chicken, cabbage salad (chopped cabbage with mayonnaise), and potato salad (boiled potatoes with mayonnaise). It was all food I liked for a change, and I still feel full. It's now 1:00 PM and I've done my "work" for the day. The women are still doing dishes and cleaning up. I didn't offer to help, but they wouldn't have let me anyway.*

It was logical that I'd attend the Congregational church regularly since my family went there and it was next door to my house. However, to be successfully integrated, it was important to demonstrate that I was the Peace Corps volunteer for the whole village by going to services at both churches. So every few weeks, I made the short walk along the beach road to the Catholic church. Slightly more than half of the villagers were Catholic and two of my women friends, Tumema and Soloao, went there as well.

Sunday mass was always a pleasant change. I was comfortable there since I'd learned the rites and rituals when I was Director of Real Estate for the Archdiocese of Denver prior to my retirement job with the State of Colorado. For eight years, in conjunction with the job, I'd attended Catholic services occasionally (including a mass with Pope John Paul). As a former Conservative Baptist, I was still allured by the aura of mystery and magic in the burning incense and repetitive incantations so unfamiliar to my own simple church upbringing. I was always welcomed warmly, often with a lei of sweet smelling moso'oi flowers.

Mary in her niche in front of the Catholic Church.

*After mass Eseta (Esther) invited me to Sunday dinner. Theirs is the last fale in the village going east. To get there we had to either walk across the river on a log bridge about fifty feet long (one big coconut tree flattened on the topside) or walk through shin-deep water along the beach at low tide. The family said that their great-grandfather was German and worked on ships. He married their Samoan great-grandmother and had a cacao and coconut plantation. They told me "black people who worked for him are buried somewhere on the property." Their house is a quaint, pitched-roof, European-style building, with a mottled stucco exterior and white plaster inside. The faded, sky-blue ceiling is vaulted with an intricate curlicue design painted in gold on the center beam and rafters. It must have been exquisite when it was new. It's showing its age but Eseta said they "won't fix it, it's an antique and we'll let it fall down when the time comes." What an amazing anachronism in the middle of the jungle.*

The coconut log bridge across the river.

Over time I began to fit in at both churches.

*I'm at lotu pope (Catholic church) just before the service is to begin. They're still always pleased to see me but at least I've been here often enough that it's not a big deal now, and I feel more at ease. The seats are more comfortable, real church pews, not just wooden benches. I like that everyone comes inside to pray or meditate before the service instead of talking out front like they do at our church. Of course, much of that's my lack of comfort with and overload of Samoan small talk. And not being in choir gives me the opportunity to sit in the back, observe, and write like this. There's a baptism of a baby this morning using an 'ava bowl.*

I kept going to church as part of my PC job, despite feeling like it was one more time when I didn't have control of my time and individual desires, which in a Samoan family is normal but doesn't come naturally to an American pālagi. I went twice on Sunday, sang my part, and did the other things expected of me while spending most of my days at the fale ʻi tai.

## Walking Gives Me Perspective

*I'm at my place by the sea where I can regroup, unwind, relax, and let the breeze and the waves smooth out any rough edges of the day. How amazing that I've been in Samoa for four months! I feel like I've experienced so much already, and yet I'm just getting started. I'm feeling positive and upbeat. I wonder if the ups and downs, or cycles of whatever emotions, will continue for two years. I suspect so.*

Those "ups and downs" were devastating sometimes when I was depressed and longing for home, and yet like a bipolar episode, the next day I'd be so in love with Samoa that I'd fantasize about staying beyond my service. I began to establish a routine of sorts, although there was never a day that was the same. In the October springtime, as dawn was breaking in the eastern sky, I woke to roosters crowing raucously all over the village and birds cheeping in the bushes outside my open window. The family was often still asleep in the center room—the girls, Hemara and Tia, on the bed, Niu, Saina, and Fetū on the floor, and Tamamasui on his cot. I'd tiptoe over and around the sleeping family to the bathroom.

The fale 'i tai and Rocky from my front door.

Next, I'd take a walk to the edge of Sāleilua in the cool 77⁰ F morn-ing, one of my favorite times of the day. When I stepped outside facing Mataomanu and Meleisea's family compound a hundred feet away, the ocean and the fale 'i tai were to my left.

I'd walk across the sandy open space to the narrow road along the sea, past the church hall next to Logo and Letone's house, to the fork in the road. My friend Soloao and her family lived there. She was my age, a teacher at the primary school in Vaovai, and I'd sometimes see her bustling about and return her wave. I'd walk on toward Sāleilua with the government road and F&K store at the end of the fork to the right.

Next, on the mountain side of the road was the family compound of Samu and Lupe, close friends of Niu and Saina.

L ro r: 'Ofisa, Saina, Uiti, Feonu'u and Lupe in our kitchen.

Samu, who worked at the park with Niu, was a Sunday School teacher and church deacon and Lupe taught at the primary school in Sāleilua. Along with Uiti and Feonu'u, they spent a lot of time at our house with Niu and Saina, preparing bingo sheets, counting the church offering, or just hanging out having fun, laughing, smoking, and talking.

A beach fale on my morning walk to Sāleilua.

When I turned around to walk home, Nuʻusafeʻe Island and the fringing reef were on my right, a view I never tired of. A hen and her fuzzy chicks often scampered into Soloao's taro patch, fishermen floated in their canoes, and kids in their green and yellow uniforms began the one-mile walk to school. Everyone I met along the way greeted me with the respectful and customary *"Ke alu i fea?"* ("Where are you going?") I answered with my usual response *"Savalivali."* ("Going for a walk.")

*On my morning walk I was thinking that one of the reasons it's sometimes difficult to see the needs of the people here in Samoa is because of the overwhelming beauty of the place. If it was dry and barren instead of lush vegetation with flowers growing profusely everywhere, the picturesque little huts tucked in amongst the breadfruit trees and palms at the edge of the ocean wouldn't seem so quaint.*

*It's interesting to observe how we're lulled into complacency by the presence of greenery and natural beauty. I saw women washing clothes in a clear, spring-fed pool surrounded by a rock wall at the edge of the ocean. The view from there is spectacular, looking out to sea, behind us the forest-covered mountains brushed with early morning clouds. If it had been women washing their clothes in a dirty river in Africa at the edge of a dusty plain it would've seemed much different.*

*I'm at the fale ʻi tai with a cup of tea. After my walk, I went into the ocean for a short swim. I love being able to jump into the calm, shallow water for a quick dip anytime. Someone's blowing a conch shell. Everyone who needs to know is aware of something happening this morning, and this is the notice that it will happen soon.*

*The last muted hues of sunrise are gone now, and the day is brightening. Earlier there was a brief shower—looks like there may be more coming. There are rain clouds on the horizon. The roar of the breakers on the reef accompanies the gentle lapping of the waves. The air smells of wet earth, roosters crow, an occasional vehicle rolls by on the sandy road, and women talk and laugh.*

### Samoa From the Bus Window

In 2017 when interviewed by the *Samoan Observer* for an article about the 50th anniversary of Peace Corps in Samoa, I was asked for a vivid memory. I said, "The bus rides. Sometimes it felt like I spent half of my Peace Corps service bouncing along on a hard, wooden bus seat." It wasn't far from the truth. Some days I spent four hours traveling to and from Āpia to shop, go to the Peace Corps office or project meetings, do email, and catch the last bus back to the village by early afternoon.

Peace Corps volunteers weren't allowed to drive due to liability concerns, unless we took a vacation day. But more importantly, we were supposed to live modestly at the same standard as the local people. Per my house-to-house survey, less than half of the families in the village owned a vehicle. But I missed driving! I learned to drive a tractor at ten and a car by fourteen. I grew up in the West where our nearest neighbor was as far away as the next village in Samoa, and where driving was fundamental and brought freedom to go when and where we wanted. But Samoan buses weren't just transportation; they were integral to the culture. Unless you lived in Āpia or your family was wealthy enough to have a vehicle, you rode the bus from the time you were a baby.

The buses were a unique riot of color. Mountain scenes and seascapes, or portraits of American rock stars or cartoon characters were hand-painted on the sides and back of the bus body of flamboyant red, blue, green, or stunning yellow. They were shaped like a classic American school bus with a stubby nose, their wood frames covered with metal sheeting. The hard, wooden bus seats bumped against my backbone in an uncomfortable place just below my shoulder blades. The doorway and windows were open spaces, although a two-inch board midway across the window offered some bit of safety. If it rained, a piece of scratched, formerly translucent Plexiglass with a wooden handle could be pulled up between two grooves. It usually stayed in place from the pressure since none of the openings were square anymore. Each driver had a CD player that blasted Samoan pop music over and over from the same disc for the whole ride.

Everyone knew and followed a seating etiquette. Young men went to the rear, followed by young women. On the morning ride, teenagers in red, blue, or green uniforms depending on their school, sat in the back, flirted discreetly with their eyes, and passed notes, since passengers didn't talk. Old men and women sat in the front, and everyone else in between. If someone was seated toward the front and an older person got on, there was a spontaneous shifting to make room for the elder. At times the bus was so packed that people literally stacked up since passengers were expected to sit on one another's laps if it was full. The young people (thirty or under) started first, girls seated on girls, boys on boys, and small kids could sit anywhere.

When I left Āpia for Poutasi, I always tried to get on board early to get a good seat, preferably by a window. Once, I hurried to get there by 3:00 PM because it was a holiday weekend and there wouldn't be another run until Tuesday. I'd just pulled out my book and my journal, and the bus was instantly filled with sweaty people with their holiday shopping, as we waited for the usual 4:30 departure.

*I couldn't count how many people were on the ride home. Once before I counted sixty-seven, which seemed startling at the time since there are only twenty-nine seats, but more than that today! Back to front in the aisle, there was no need to hang on since the bulk of their bodies held them upright. Passengers were seated on one another's laps and at least a half-dozen guys crammed in up front, on the steps, hanging out the doorway. The police stopped us, didn't write a ticket, but made four guys get off. They walked to Pacific Express store, got back on the bus there, and six more people got on along the way! Everyone was squished up against someone else; I had a boy of about eight on my lap.*

In Āpia, taxis buzzed about ubiquitously and I could go anywhere for $3-5 tala ($1-2 USD). To catch a bus back to the village, I walked or took a taxi to the *fili māketi* (flea market), a long, wooden, open-sided building with a metal roof, populated with dozens of stalls selling flowers, t-shirts, handmade clothing or handicrafts, interspersed with tiny cafes. It burned in a massive fire in 2016, probably as a result of an open cooking flame. Next door was the fish market with anything from freshly caught yellowfin tuna to octopus, crabs, or eels, at unbelievably low prices. The men went to sea in the wee hours of the morning and the women sat at the market and sold the catch wrapped in newspaper. Next to these markets was an enormous field, dusty or muddy depending on the weather, where buses from all over the island gathered in no particular order or pattern, pointed in all directions. They were usually in the same vicinity each day, but you could always spot yours because it was painted differently from the rest.

The first time I rode a Samoan bus by myself was back during training when each of us spent two days with an experienced volunteer, in my case to go to Jordan's village. One of the "lessons" of our volunteer visit was to figure out how to get there by bus or ferry. I hailed a taxi from the street in front of the Peace Corps office for the five-minute ride to the flea market. On Beach Road, with the ocean on my right, we whizzed past shops, restaurants, and famous buildings—Aggie Grey's hotel[6], the Immaculate Conception Cathedral, the Parliament Building designed in 1975 with assistance by a Peace Corp architect,

---

6 Aggie Grey's is one of the most storied hotels in the South Pacific and its eponymous owner was said to be the model for Bloody Mary in James Michener's *Tales of the South Pacific*.

the traffic circle in front of Chan Mow store with the clock tower in the middle. Alighting from the taxi, I'd caught a hint of the fish stalls as I looked about uneasily for the right bus.

This wasn't my first time on a Samoan bus, however all other trips had been "chartered" by Peace Corps to take us various places as a group. This was the first time I'd left the confines of town alone without other Peace Corps volunteers or staff in this still-baffling foreign country. There was the possibility that I might get lost or stranded in a place where I knew no one, with only the most rudimentary grasp of the language, and only intermittent reception on my mobile phone. I was still constantly unsure if I was being charged the correct amount for goods and services, I had to remember to take an appropriate food gift for Jordan's host family, and I was sure I probably wouldn't know when to get off and might go past her village. I breathed a sigh of relief when I immediately spotted the bus, since Jordan had told me to look for Iosefa's (Joseph's) vividly turquoise bus. I relaxed as we left the city and began to enjoy the new scenery.

On the cross-island road we were coming down the mountain after crossing 2,500-foot Tiavi Pass. Downslope, I saw glimpses of the southern coastline and the sea beyond. Most of the vegetation was lush, dense, and dark green, but here and there were open grassy pastures under towering coconut palms planted neatly into rows during colonial days. Just past the crest, Iosefa stopped on the side of the road. "Now what?" I thought. Everyone sat quietly while Iosefa set the emergency brake, then reached down to get one of the three large, white, plastic jugs from the floor beside him. On previous rides I'd seen drivers stop and use similar jugs to fill the radiator, so I hoped it was no more than this. As Iosefa walked to the front of the bus, he put a large nipple on the plastic jug and crossed the road to feed a small brown and white calf that had started running along the fence line as soon as it saw our bus. After the calf drained the milk, Iosefa started up and we were on our way.

Soon I could smell the ocean and the road was more sandy than rocky. After a young man got off, I was the last passenger, so I had the bright idea to move forward to the front seat behind the door. Just as I placed my carry-on suitcase on the floor, the bus started with a jolt. The bag flew out the non-existent door, and the bus ran over it. Simultaneously, the cucumbers, cabbage, and peppers from the basket I'd brought for Jordan's family bounced down the aisle to the back of the bus. It was an "I Love Lucy-esque" moment—this blond white lady, dressed in a black t-shirt, red Samoan lāvalava, and flip-flops, shouting, *"Tāofi fa'amolemole!"* (Stop please!), while scrambling down the aisle with her butt up in the air, retrieving vegetables under the seats.

When Iosefa braked to a halt, the young man who'd gotten off ran up with my bag. Apparently the tire caught just the edge and unbelievably nothing inside was damaged. Later, I beat the bottom and side back into place . . . sort of. It would've made a great advertisement for Pierre Cardin.

A few minutes later, Iosefa pulled up in front of Jordan's family compound; she'd told him I was coming. He played the clown, recounting to Jordan's family the story of my bouncing produce. As I sheepishly handed the basket of certainly bruised vegetables to her host mother, I tried to remember the appropriate and respectful words of greeting that the trainers had taught us.

When I'd moved to Poutasi, I was delighted to learn that a bus went to town every weekday, driven by my neighbor 'Afakasi (Mataomanu and Meleisea's son) who lived next door with his wife, children, and other relatives. 'Afakasi's bus was lipstick red with a huge advertisement on the back and sides for Digicel and an American flag across the back window. America was well-liked in Samoa so it wasn't unusual to see American flags here and there. He drove to Āpia the long way, around the eastern tip of the island, an hour longer than the cross-island route. But the extra time was worth it, not only for the convenience, since I only had to walk about a hundred feet out my front door to get on, but because it was comfortable! The bus was newer, with vinyl seats instead of wooden benches.

'Afakasi's bus.

'Afakasi left in the early morning and returned late afternoon, with an intermittent midday run. If I needed to return to the village sooner, two other buses—the green or the yellow one—would bring me as far as F&K store on the government road. However, the half-mile walk to my house from there was especially tedious when I returned with heavy bags or walked home in the pouring rain or blistering heat. In addition, when I'd first arrived in Poutasi, Niu told me sternly, "Never ride the yellow bus because it isn't safe," and another PCV told me she'd seen one of the drivers drinking beer behind the wheel. There were three yellow buses, operated by a company called *Laumoso'oi Breeze*. I tried not to ride them, but sometimes it was the only option to or from Āpia. A few months after I moved to the village, I wrote:

*Niu and Saina just told me that one of the Laumoso'oi buses crashed today on the cross-island road on the way from Āpia. Three people were killed. As we discussed it, Niu said that the official at the ministry responsible for issuing operating licenses for the buses was given a red pickup truck by the owner, then the licenses were granted even though the buses are unsafe. I was supposed to go to a meeting at the Peace Corps office this morning but decided not to at the last minute. I would've been on that bus if I 'd gone, since it's the last to leave Āpia for Poutasi on Saturdays.*

Article from *Newsline Samoa* online newspaper:

The driver of the bus that killed three people in a road accident at the weekend could serve up to 5 years in jail for negligence driving causing death. He is being charged on three counts of negligence for the two women and a boy who were killed when the bus rolled over at the Tiavi Cross Island Road. A further 12 counts of negligence causing injuries have been filed as well for the court to rule on.

The accident reportedly occurred when the bus lost control as the road leveled off, after a downhill run from the steepest part of the road. It was while passing another bus gearing up for the uphill drive that the driver lost control and rolled over. The bus frame shattered on impact and was scattered all over the road.

Speeding is blamed as the official cause.

The rollover accident is the worst so far this year. The death toll is reportedly second only to another bus accident in 1988 where 5 people died and all the passengers injured.

And then there was the waiting! People wait in Samoa all the time and everywhere, but waiting and Samoan buses are like taro and palusami—they just go together. Not only did they run late but it was ridiculously difficult to discern the bus schedules. There wasn't an app to pull up on your phone and I don't think I ever saw a printed bus schedule the entire time I was there. You just asked someone, and hoped they were right. But in its own way, the waiting became a good thing. It slowed me down when I needed to learn how to do that. So I read books, wrote in my journal, frequently found someone from my village to talk with, and watched Samoa around me.

*I've been waiting and waiting for the green bus. I don't like this part of the Samoan experience. The waiting is okay; I can handle that. It's the not knowing when or if it will come. I stayed in town last night and Saina told me there was a bus at 8:00 AM. I thought there was one at 8:30. Either way, I missed it, or it's not come yet at 8:45, so I decided to take one of the two remaining yellow buses and we're supposed to leave at 9:30. I'm reluctant to be on it after the accident. Statistically not logical, but still . . . at least I'm on a bus.*

*Later . . . just a few minutes ago, as we were parked at the gas pump on the drive home, a water truck backed into the bus and dented the side opposite where I'm sitting. A big jolt. Everyone gasped and jumped. Unnerving after my trepidation of being on this bus. The two drivers are talking. It's not much damage—there'll probably just be some money paid.*

Group 78 had been in the country for only three months when we were involved in a frightening, near-miss accident. We'd stayed for a few final days at Āpia Central Hotel, busy with last minute preparations to move to our new villages. On the way to Manunu for our swearing-in ceremony we bounced along in a bus hired by Peace Corps, talking to one another, having a good time. Without warning, the brakes went out as we approached another bus parked half on and half off our side of the narrow two-lane road. Meanwhile, a black pickup approached in the oncoming lane! Somehow, our driver managed to squeeze between the two with only inches to spare. At that point we would've been only shaken, but it happened just as we hit a wide speed bump with no brakes. Except for those in the front who could see ahead, we had no idea what was coming. Everyone bounced up, and back down—hard! Cameras, backpacks, and anything that wasn't fastened down flew everywhere. Those of us in the rear got the biggest jolt. I was seated over the wheels, and I doubt there were shocks left on any of the buses. As soon as the bus rolled to a stop we bolted off.

If the driver hadn't managed to keep those few inches between the vehicles, it would've been serious. There was only one real injury—one of the young men, Christian, bruised and cut his leg badly. Of course, in America they'd have called 911 and we would've each been checked for injuries. But in Samoa, our Peace Corps Medical Officer Teuila tended to his leg while we waited by the side of the road for another bus to continue on to Manunu. My back and neck hurt for a day or two, but I was okay.

Neither the crash of the Laumoso'oi Breeze nor our almost-accident were near-death experiences for me by any means, but it made me reflect on the fragility of life, and how easily it was risked on a Samoan bus. With some exceptions, they were often mechanically unsafe, the drivers weren't professionally trained, there were numerous distractions inside and outside the buses, and they were usually overloaded with people and goods. Two weeks after the fatal crash on the cross-island road, the government acted on the unsafe bus situation and I wasn't at all happy about it.

*The government (either the Prime Minister or the Minister of Transportation) decided—and that's what it is, just a decision by one person, no hearing or public input—to ban buses from the cross-island road. So effective Monday, all buses to the south side go the longer two-hour way. It doesn't make sense since there are dangerous curves and hills on that road too. Even though I usually ride this way on 'Afakasi's bus, at least I had an alternative for an earlier and slightly faster trip home from town. And any added time sitting on those narrow wooden seats is dreadful.*

A couple of months later they resumed the usual routes.

*I'm thinking of going to Āpia today . . . if 'Afakasi's bus comes at noon I'll let that make the decision for me.*

*Later . . . I saw 'Afakasi's bus from my window earlier than expected, threw my stuff together, and quickly walked over. It wasn't a regular run, but he gave me a ride anyway. The bus was chockfull of glass soda bottles in plastic crates, stacked on every seat and in the aisles, which he was taking for recycling. I sat in my usual front seat with his two-year-old son, Nonu, sleeping on my lap as we clinkety-clinked our way to town.*

And you never knew what you might encounter:

*I missed photographing a fantastic sunset tonight. The bus was late getting home, I had to pee desperately, and by then it was too late for the photo. I was going to go at Pacific Express, but there was no toilet paper and feces-stained paper towels strewn all over the ground and on the floor of the outhouse. A not-so-subtle reminder of the vast range of services and living conditions in this country.*

Or as I wrote one day after an especially noteworthy bus ride:

*The bus ride to Poutasi was interesting today. A young mother was going home from the hospital with her three-day-old baby. Such a beautiful little girl! The young mother, and her mother, sat in the two front seats across from me. And there was a pigeon on the bus. It had a string tied to its leg and was perched placidly on a young man's backpack on the dash of the bus next to 'Afakasi. I can only think of three reasons why someone would bring a pigeon on the bus—1) he was dinner; 2) he was a pet; or 3) he was breeding stock. I don't know the answer.*

Later, I learned that catching wild pigeons had a time-honored history in Samoa. Tamed pigeons were trained to fly around and around in a clearing on strings up to thirty feet long, while men crouched concealed under a covering of brushwood. Every man flew his pigeon, and soon the area looked like a place where pigeons were flocking for food or water. Wild pigeons attracted to the spot were caught with nets attached to long bamboo poles. Some were baked or boiled and others tamed for future hunting.

*And then we had a flat tire near Satalo. Thankfully, the young mother got off at the village just before. There was no spare, so since the flat was on the left front wheel, they took one of the tires off the dual wheels in the back and put it on the front. The young guys from the bus who helped Kasi change the tire seemed to enjoy the adventure. Watching out the window, it was a comedy of errors. I heard Kasi say "Shit!" more than once (a favorite Samoan expletive—even among children). No one on the bus was upset or agitated (like I'm sure they would've been in the States). So, it turned out to be a three-hour bus ride home, which meant I spent five hours on the bus today.*

Yet, when I rode on 'Afakasi's bus in my favorite seat with no one sitting on my lap, I loved the ride. I had a sense of contentment and connection with Samoa in a way I didn't at any other time. There was something about watching people live out their normal everyday lives as I passed by day after day, week after week. I watched the new church steeple rise taller and taller, knew that a village was expecting an upcoming festive event as they decorated with palm fronds and teuila, and noticed the taro grow. I smelled the ever-changing ocean and sensed the splendor and strength of the land and the people. I was an observer, yet part of it too, like a living Venn diagram. It became a sort of meditation where all I saw was the passing scene before me.

What I observed was reflected in one of my updates to friends and family back home:

----- Original Message -----
Sent: Monday, March 19, 2008 2:26 PM
Subject: Update from Samoa

It's still dark and I'm groggy when my alarm clock chirps at 5:15. There's no water from the tap yet, so I use some from my storage bottles to wash my face and brush my teeth in front of the house, tossing the remainder from the small basin into the bushes. I check off everything for the day in town—umbrella, cell phone, money, paperwork, books to return to the PC office, something to read on the bus, my journal, flash drive, and camera. A little before 6:00 I start to watch out my window for 'Afakasi to start the bus. The roar of the engine tells me it's time to go, so I gather my things and walk the short distance between our family compounds. Settled into my favorite seat behind Kasi, on the left by the window, we drive into the sunrise with shades of intermingled pink and orange and blue on the horizon.

A dozen or more people get on in Poutasi as we drive through the village, often with large bags of taro or squash to sell at the market, stowed in the luggage compartment until it's full, then up front by Kasi. We stop at every village along the way and in between until we get to Salani. To catch a ride, you don't need to wait at a bus stop, you just stand on the road and the bus will stop for you.

At Salani we cease traveling along the southeastern coast, passing Sopo'aga Falls as we ride along the Mulivaifagatolo River to climb the road to the pass. As the bus labors up the mountain it creaks and groans and Kasi downshifts and urges it along. From the 1,000-foot summit, a stunning view is revealed as the canyon walls drop sharply to the valley below where the Falefa river courses to the ocean visible seven miles away. The chasm and the surrounding hillsides are lush with twenty-foot-tall tree ferns, coconut palms, towering banyan trees snaking roots to the ground, and an understory of vines and ferns. In the sunshine everything is vibrantly green with brilliantly blue sky and white puffy clouds. Wayward, wispy clouds wind their way through the valley below as if looking for a way out.

Scattered homes pop up here and there along the mountain road, but no villages. After we descend from the pass, we drive through coastal villages again all the way to Āpia. We pass Falefa Falls and drive beside the roaring river. Now we're on the north side of the island. Waves crash close to shore and the white foam of the breakers sprays onto the black lava rocks beside the road. About 8:00 AM we reach Āpia and I lean forward and tell Kasi, *"Tāofi i le 'Ofisa Pisikoa fa'amolemole."* ("Stop at the Peace Corps office please.")

After email, shopping, other Āpia errands, and lunch in a restaurant (an extravagance!), I rush to be early enough to get a good seat on the ride home. The last time that I was late I sat four seats back, wedged between a very large man sitting by the window with a crying child on his lap and another very large man standing in the aisle next to me, smoking (Yes, people smoke on Samoan buses!). The bus was totally full when I got there so someone gave up that seat to me.

Yesterday, Mataomanu sat by me on the ride home with her four-year old grandson Sam on her lap. She's 'Afakasi's mother and also my next-door neighbor, president of the village Women's Committee, and a third-grade teacher at the primary school.

We begin the journey home. A couple of miles out of town we stop at Pacific Express general store where most people get off for drinks, snacks, and a few last-minute groceries while 'Afakasi fills up with fuel. Everyone returns to the same seats and it finally begins to cool off with the wind blowing in the open window. A CD plays loud Samoan music, the air is wet, and the colors intense from the rain shower just past. The sea and the coconut palms rush by on my left; the forest is a vivid green blur on my right, with houses, churches, and small stores interspersed as we pass through villages. We drive by men trimming bushes with machetes and teenagers playing volleyball in the mud. Waves crash on the reef offshore. We pass a procession of twenty people walking along the road, led by a priest carrying a three-foot high cross upright in front of him—everyone is dressed in white. Two young boys run alongside, racing the bus as it goes by. Multicolored laundry is spread on rocks in front of the houses to dry. Bananas, cacao, taro, mango, breadfruit, and papayas grow everywhere. Young men going to Āpia crowd into the back of an old, blue pickup truck, others hang out in front of the tiny village stores. Young girls walk down the road holding hands. Old women pull weeds from between the small rocks in front of their houses. There are ever-present flowers of pink, red, yellow, orange, and white. Dogs, chickens, and sometimes pigs, scurry to get out of the way. Women wash cooking pots at the water tap in the front yard. A boy on a bike wobbles carrying coconut frond baskets filled with garden produce on each side of the handlebars. Children clean up the yard picking up large leaves and placing them in woven baskets. I smell the smoke of cooking fires. There are people everywhere. Families gather at the end of the day.

As we pass Falefa Falls, leaving the villages and beginning the climb to the pass, mud hens frequently dart across the road. Soft clouds brush the mountaintops. Three-foot-high bundles of coconuts are stacked by the road to be picked up by the buyer. Cattle graze in the valley below in between the palms. We cross the summit at Lemafa with its spectacular view all the way to the sea, more waterfalls, and roadside stands selling produce. Now we drive through the villages on the south side of the island. A mother sits on her front step nursing her baby. Strips of laufala dry in front yards to weave into mats. Naked little boys run across the grass. A beautiful young woman stands in front of her house with a huge hibiscus flower in her long, black, shiny-wet hair, wearing a bright pink and blue lāvalava wrapped around her sarong-style. We pass the still, clear water of the mangrove lagoon in Vaovai. Horses are tethered at the side of the road eating grass. We slow for the bumpy drive into Poutasi. Children splash and play in the sea. The sun sinks into the ocean in a blaze of red and gold. It's 6:30 PM. Home sweet home.

Toe feiloai (till we meet again),
Donna

Girls from Poutasi on the yellow bus.

'Afakasi getting ready to drive to Poutasi from the fili maketi.

# Chapter 5

# At Home in Poutasi

*Se'i lua'i lou le 'ulu taumamao*
*"First pick the breadfruit on the highest branches"*
*Do the most difficult task first.*

Not long after I arrived, Niu got a promotion in the Forestry Division and started working in Āpia instead of at the national park just down the road. That meant that I could catch rides to and from town more often. We'd go for miles without speaking with only the voices of the perky morning radio DJ talking with callers. When we did converse, it was about PC or proposals, not social chat. But when Saina was home for the weekend, the three of us sometimes passed the time in the shade alongside the house as they smoked their Rothmans cigarettes in the fading light of the day.

*We talked about Fiji, where Niu went to university, and where the family lived for a time; evolution, which they don't believe in; Polynesian migrations; how they first met (in high school, although they didn't begin dating until after they'd graduated); and Indian food, which is too spicy for them. For once there weren't other people around.*

I could now also spend more time with Saina since she began staying in Poutasi during the day on Mondays. Although Niu almost always returned to the village on weekday evenings, sometimes he and Fetū slept at Saina's mother's house in Āpia with the rest of the extended family. As time went on, if I wanted to stay in town after the last bus home, I too often stayed in the big rambling house. Sometimes I met Saina at Mari's for lunch, then we'd shop, window-shop, or run errands together, like picking up a new puletasi from the seamstress or buying produce at Fugalei Market. Saina was the life of every party, with an infectious laugh. When the women got together to work on church or village projects, she'd often dance a playful impromptu siva to cheers and whistles. I remember one day seated at Mari's Cafe, how I chortled and nearly inhaled my Coke as I was telling her about living in Texas and she asked, "What do you call a Samoan with a cowboy hat? A Western Samoan!"

Saina was an incredibly hard worker. All Samoan women were! If not family obligations, it was church stuff or village requirements. The demands on the women to organize, cook for, and clean up after family, church, and village affairs were immense.

On weekends, school breaks, and holidays, the kids were home in Poutasi. Samoan kids got three months of school break, scattered throughout the year, including a month off in the middle of the Samoan winter and five weeks at Christmastime. In addition, there were numerous national holidays, like the four-day Easter weekend and the three-day weekends for Mother's Day, Father's Day, and Children's Day.

At six and seven, Tia and Fetū were curious and precocious, asking questions, touching everything, eating my food, and pulling stuff out. It seemed like I was always saying, *"Aua! Leai se tago!"* ("Don't! No touching!"). I'd brought colored paper, crayons, scissors, stickers, and other crafty stuff with me from the States and they'd sprawl on my floor coloring or drawing. I helped them with their homework, read them books from the public library in Āpia, and we had lots of silly fun. They'd hang out in my room until I needed quiet time and shooed them out. But they also brought laughter and energy to my little space.

Fetū and Tia drawing pictures in my room.

Tia and Hemara posing.

Hemara was just shy of her eleventh birthday when I got there, but she always seemed older to me. She was tall for her age, like I was, and I suppose she reminded me of my younger self in other ways. She liked school and reading and languages and discovery. While the younger two were still learning English, Hemara spoke it fluently and she was already reading English chapter books. We talked in both languages and she (and the little ones) taught me Samoan. Since she was older, and therefore needed less supervision and could be reasoned with, she spent more time in my room. But we also just enjoyed hanging out together. My bed was also my sofa and my desk, with the help of stacked pillows for a backrest and a folding bed tray that I'd brought with me. Hemara would sprawl on the bed and we'd chat about her week at school or my life in Hawai'i as I organized photos or did PC paperwork on my laptop and she did homework. During school breaks, Saina still stayed in town to work during the week and Niu was at his office, so Tamamasui and 'Ofisa were responsible for the kids during the day, although like all Samoan children they were literally raised by the village.

*School's out. Hemara got the prize for being first in her class and Tia was second in hers! Last night and this morning they were hanging out in my room. I kicked them out to write and work; I'll probably let them back in later.*

### Musing From the Fale i Tai

*From my usual place by the sea I've been watching several young men fishing. There are seven of them, in their twenties, bare to the waist with their lāvalava tied shorter than usual to give them more agility in the water. The bay is so shallow that you can walk nearly all the way to the fringing reef in water that's about waist deep at low tide. It's crystal clear—like a huge swimming pool with no deep end.*

Two of the young men held the net—a rectangle about twenty feet long and six feet wide. Another paddled in a traditional dugout outrigger canoe painted a bright turquoise—a brilliant compliment to the pale, blue-green sea. The others walked along in the water looking intently, two with spears and the others carrying sticks. As they spotted fish, they pointed in that direction and the men with the net began to ease up toward the school. When they were in position, the others ran forward, beating the water with their hands and the sticks, shouting, chasing the fish toward the net. Occasionally an exuberant young man leapt out of the water and dove forward, face down into the water, arms outstretched, scaring the fish toward the net. Then they all charged in to spear the fish or hit them with the sticks to stun them and tossed them into the canoe. In between, as they walked along, they pushed each other into the water, or threw their sticks high into the air and tried to catch them on the way down, just like young men everywhere. Two young boys about ten or twelve years old floated on chunks of salvaged wood a short distance away, watching and learning.

*They'll divide the catch amongst themselves, and maybe share with other families depending upon the success of the day. I also watched a mother and her children looking for sea cucumbers, clams, or other shellfish, bending and reaching into the water when they spotted one. Her seven- or eight-year-old boy alternately pulled along or floated on a white plastic bucket in which they placed their catch. When I first saw them go out, I thought it'd be interesting and maybe fun to go with them, but they were in the water for about two hours in the direct overhead sun. It is, after all, dinner not amusement.*

## Figuring Out My Job

When I walked the village with Tumema, she always made sure to tell me the full name of the matai of the family we were visiting, which I dutifully wrote down. The social structure of Samoa was based on the matai system, intertwined with the basic unit of Samoan society, the 'āiga, or family. A matai was the chief of the 'āiga and families formed the village community. Except for a few royal titles, every matai title belonged to a specific village differing in degrees of importance within the village and within the country. The Samoan national government was a parliamentary system with a head of state (a monarch/king). However, the government only had jurisdiction over nationwide affairs, other matters were handled in the villages governed by the matai.

It was important to know the names and status of the chiefs since the village was a microcosm of Samoa's complex and pervasive stratified social structure. Everyone had a designated status and was greeted and spoken to according to their title, occupation, or family rank. As a Peace Corps volunteer, I automatically had a higher status. For example, whenever Letone mentioned me in church he referred to me as *"Samalaulu pisikoa 'o Donna."* In ancient times, Samalaulu was a rival for the throne and the name had come to refer to high-ranking Samoan women. I'd smile from my pew—for the longest time I thought he was referring to my blond hair—*sāmasama lau ulu!* When I addressed certain people—high chiefs, orators, pastors or priests—there were differing honorific words, which weren't even the same for a pastor and a priest. The respect was observed not only in the language but also in actions. An untitled person speaking to a seated matai always knelt or sat on the floor while doing so.

In Poutasi the chiefs met every Monday morning regarding village matters, deciding by consensus. Every village had one or more high chiefs, but one was the highest, and could sway a decision, or in some cases "direct" the outcome. Some matai were orators— "talking chiefs." The orators' duty was to understand history and tradition, and be able to speak a special variation of the Samoan language used only on formal occasions, filled with ancient stories and proverbs.

Apart from obligations to the village, the most important duty of every matai was to look after his 'āiga(which always included dozens of people). Even those living away from the village (including in other countries) were expected to make contributions of food or money for church or family functions back home. He controlled customary family land and allocated its use. Family members provided for the matai by cultivating crops and cooking food, and in turn, they received food, lodging, and sometimes money.

Although the system resembled feudal barons who gave serfs protection in return for their services, it differed in one important respect. Family members decided who became the matai. Usually, direct heirs were the first to be considered, but they weren't always chosen. The decision to bestow the title was made on a consensual basis and was sometimes difficult to reach. Saina's father had been the village high chief, and she told me that after he died it took the family nine years to decide on a new matai. It was unusual for a woman to be given the title, although it did happen. Not all chiefs lived up to the standards set by the system. Members of the family could express dissatisfaction and seek removal of the title, but it was rare. Like positions of leadership worldwide, some were active leaders, some were active followers, and some were along just for the ride.

I'd visited previously just to observe, but in October, two months after I'd arrived in the village, I was directed to attend the Matai Council meeting to discuss village projects. The chiefs, bare chested wearing colorful lāvalava, sat cross-legged on mats on the concrete floor of the large open fale designated for the weekly meetings. The early birds found a post to lean on (there were about two dozen matai titles in Poutasi, although they were rarely all in attendance), but there were also designated seating arrangements. The high chief and any important guests, like me, sat at the end, and centered along one side sat the highest orators. The rest were seated along the other side. All looked intently at me.

I started my presentation (in Samoan):

*Greetings to you respected chiefs of our village. To be in your presence is a great privilege. May you be honored like the great chiefs of your ancestors. I'm grateful that the kindness and love of God has brought us to together today in happiness and good health. Thank you for the opportunity. Thank you for your support. Thank you for your patience.*

I told them that although I hadn't completed my assessment, possible projects identified by the villagers thus far were to improve the water system; reduce erosion with plantings along the seashore, the river, and the spring; increase the water flow under the bridge from the inland lagoon to the sea; and create a homework center.

*They directed me to work on several projects: (1) improve the water system; (2) build a new primary school building; (3) build a seawall; (4) replace the culverts under the bridge; and (5) create a homework center for the kids. Yikes! That's about a five-year plan! A lot will depend upon getting grants or loans, with matching contributions from the village.*

*The most immediately possible project is the homework center. I'll see what I can do on all of them, but that one I might actually see before I leave. It could look something like this: a secure room, like the empty storeroom in back of the church hall that Niu told me about, to be used by young people after school and in the evenings to do homework and study, with supervision and assistance by adult volunteers. If we could get a few computers, printer, and small copier, that equipment could be available to everyone in the village for a reasonable fee to pay expenses, with dial-up internet eventually. I could ask friends and family on the mainland to send reference books like dictionaries and encyclopedia.*

It would take another couple of months to eventually define my projects. Peace Corps recommended six months, so I guess I was ahead of the game, although it sure didn't feel like it. In the meantime, those first weeks dragged by, while I practiced to increase my fluency, gathered statistics and analyzed data for my Village Situational Analysis, talked to the villagers on my house-to-house survey, walked with Tumena on the monthly inspections, attended services at both churches, chatted at the Women's Committee House, went to Matai Council meetings, learned from the women about sewing or other small business projects, and visited the schools.

Although I sometimes complained about the unstructured nature of my job in Poutasi, I'm grateful it worked out that way. I needed that time to gestate ideas, reflect on the past and future, and it was a gift to be able to relax and unwind at the fale 'i tai as I pondered. If I'd been assigned to teach at a school or work at a government ministry with a nine-to-five job, it would've been easier in some ways, but also a continuation of my former work life, not a transition to what's next. However, I also had to figure out the "What's next?" for my PC job.

I eventually had a PC committee to help me. After a village was assigned a volunteer, they were to form a PC committee. At the meeting in Āpia when only the mayor showed up with no committee, I'd felt disheartened, especially after being dumped off in the village to fend for myself on my first visit. After I moved to Poutasi, there was still no PC *Komiti*. Although my job initially was to get to know the village and work on my VSA, as a person who craves organization, I felt I needed a PC committee to connect, network, tell me what to do, and what not to do. I asked the Peace Corps office if I could go ahead on my own and set up a committee and they encouraged me to do that.

The good news about not having a PC Komiti was that I was able to choose who was on it: Niu and Saina of course; the mayor; Meleisea

Seti, our neighbor and a village high chief; Valasi, a young woman who taught at Meghan's school in Si'umu; and Vaeila, a matai and Congregational church deacon. Later, as the homework center evolved in the church hall, Pastor Letone was added.

One month after I'd arrived, we'd held our first meeting in the front room of Niu and Saina's house. Not everyone was there, but the attendees were enthusiastic and supportive. We continued to meet monthly, although timing and attendance were always problematic and rarely all attended.

*We had an excellent Komiti Pisikoa meeting last night at the open fale behind the church hall. All the regular committee members were there along with Letone. I had to keep from laughing at one point. Logo and some other village women decided it was a good time to* vele le vao *(pull weeds and grass from between the 'ili'ili in front of the fale). I had no problem with it—it's a good way to disseminate information—and they so obviously wanted to know what was going on. It was probably more my idea than the rest of the committee's to end the meeting—Samoans can, and do, sit and talk for hours, stretching discussions out to astonishing lengths. Finally, I said, "Vela le fala," a Samoan saying literally translated as "the mat is getting hot," but figuratively means, "we've sat here long enough."*

### Peace Corps is a Family

We were "warned" in training about going to Āpia too often. In other words, we should stay in our villages most of the time and not hang out in town. Of course it was necessary, and part of my job to go there. Later, I went more often for project tasks and recreation but in the beginning it was usually once a week.

I started my Āpia days when 'Afakasi or Niu dropped me off at the Peace Corps office in the mornings. The weakly air-conditioned rooms smelled of old paper, sweat, and food. Floor-to-ceiling shelves snaked along the hallway walls stacked with donated books to borrow and return. Sometimes piles of "FREE" stuff left by home-bound volunteers would greet me just inside the door. I checked my mailbox hoping for something from the States in the twice-weekly delivery, said "Tālofa!" to staff in the kitchen/lunchroom (someone was always eating or preparing food), and visited the PCV Resource Room with its shelves of reference books and DVDs, comfy furniture to lounge in, and the two computers for volunteers' use. In the Resource Room we relaxed, regrouped, networked, gossiped, practiced our Samoan, and supported one another. I waited my turn to use a computer to check email, do banking, or print PC-related documents.

Then I dropped off my laundry across the street. My family had offered to wash my clothes with theirs in five-gallon buckets in the shower then hung on the line. But I opted for the luxury of Nellie's Laundromat, where for $19 tala she'd have it washed, dried, and neatly folded at the end of the day, smelling of fabric softener. From the PC office I walked or took a cab to the town center bustling with taxis, buses, cars, trucks, and people. I often ate breakfast at McDonalds, Āpia's only American fast-food restaurant. The choices were mostly the same as in the States, but my favorite breakfast wasn't on American menus—pie with New Zealand apples (baked, not fried), and a Coke float. I sat at a table by the glass store front, surrounded by the familiar red and yellow, while I people-watched, wrote in my journal, and planned my day—Digicel to buy phone credit, the bank to get cash, the post office to send mail, and stops at stores along the way.

While a trip to Āpia was time-consuming, tedious, hot, and tiring, it was a welcome respite to the smallness of village life. It was also an important connection point to PC staff, potential donor agencies, the Division of Internal Affairs for advice and information, and to other volunteers.

I think that *"'O a'u o le Pisikoa"* ("I am a Peace Corps volunteer") was one of the first phrases I learned. Peace Corps was well respected and nearly everyone in the country had a family member who'd been taught by a volunteer or had a Peace Corps story themselves. The earliest volunteers were famous for the *fale pisikoa* (Peace Corps houses), the name given to outhouses with water seal toilets introduced to replace squatting over the ocean via long piers. In 2007 there were forty PCVs in Samoa on three islands. Half were teachers, and half, like our group, were Village-Based Development volunteers.

The fortieth anniversary of Peace Corps in Samoa was celebrated in October 2007, including a reunion of the first two groups who came in 1967 and 1968. Just after dawn on an already muggy Friday morning, the returning volunteers, current PCVs, PC staff, and Group 79 (who'd just arrived) met at the Peace Corps office. Together we marched five abreast down Beach Road to the government building, led by our 40th anniversary banner and the Royal Samoa Police Band playing briskly. The Samoan flag was raised as we sang the Samoan national anthem, followed by the necessary speeches, including a lengthy and gracious oration by the Samoan Prime Minister who thanked Peace Corps for all its years of service. When I got back to Poutasi, the kids said they saw our little parade on TV.

Like the in-country volunteers did for us when we came, that night we welcomed Group 79 with a fiafia. All the PCVs did a Samoan sasa (seated dance with lots of clapping), the women danced a siva, and the men stomped and chanted a fierce haka. Because of the 40th anniversary, additional guests included the returning volunteers, distinguished dignitaries, and even the Head of State—His Highness, Tui Atua Tupua Tamasese Efi!

The next morning, in a large open fale (on chairs rather than mats) I attended a symposium with panel discussions by the returning volunteers, current volunteers who were leaving soon, and Samoans, about the effect that Peace Corps had on their lives. In a moving speech, a local woman who was personally guided and motivated by one of the returning volunteers credited her successful career as a secondary school principal to him and his wife. I jotted down pertinent points that I wanted to remember.

*The U.S. Chargé d'affair said, "You are the face of America to Samoa." We heard similar statements in training, and I try to remember that every day. Talking about what he'd learned, one of the alumni volunteers said, "I cherish the American way of life, but it's not the only way of life. It's a good life, but not the only good life." And another, "You are a citizen of the world; don't be afraid to change it."*

I was astonished to discover that one of the returning volunteers from Group 2 had been a teacher in Poutasi and lived with my family when Saina was four years old! She came to the anniversary with her husband, also a volunteer from that time. And then I learned that they lived on the Big Island of Hawai'i! We've become good friends, always sharing any news we have of Poutasi.

Although Peace Corps was highly thought of in Samoa, there was a noteworthy consequence that our trainers called the "fishbowl effect," which meant that as a pālagi and a pisikoa, everything I did was watched, scrutinized, and most certainly discussed. "You went to Āpia yesterday?" "Who was that man who came to visit you?" "You weren't in church on Sunday." It seemed as if everyone in the village knew when I came and went and everything that I did that wasn't behind closed doors. And even then, I'd sometimes see a curious young face peering into my bedroom window when the curtains weren't drawn. I knew that people would know what I purchased from the village store, so I was cautious about how many Cokes and Snickers I bought so they wouldn't talk about how much money I had. I'm not rich in America, but by Samoan standards I am. This was sometimes a real concern for volunteers. I lived with a generous family who could afford to send their children to private school in Āpia. Another Group 78 volunteer lived with a needy family with eight kids. They were always asking him for money, which became a real dilemma for him.

I didn't know until I came back to the States and talked to other returned Peace Corp volunteers that the sixteen of us in Samoa's Group 78 were a small cadre. Some volunteers from other countries went through training with twenty-five, or forty, or one hundred others! While I feel a bond with PCVs who served anywhere in the world, it's my group for which I hold the most affection.

Safiya was in her late twenties from a large Jamaican family in Brooklyn, NY, where she worked at a food bank and community center. She had a big heart and loved working with children, so she was excited to hear that her village on Savai'i wanted to build a preschool. She sang a soulful and moving version of Marley's "No Woman, No Cry."

Justin was from Tennessee, twenty-something, with a degree in Environmental Health Science, and he lived in a large village near Āpia. He wore glasses and had dark hair, a wide smile, and a quirky sense of humor. It was Justin who'd had a chicken lay an egg at the end of his bed when we trained in Manunu. Although he was a bit shy, he was kind and good with kids.

Minnesotans Nick and Mary were both tall and fair and in their early sixties. Mary raised kids and did volunteer work and Nick retired as a small business owner right before coming to Samoa. Their village on Savai'i built a Samoan style fale for them and at first Nick wanted to live totally local style with no refrigerator, fan, or TV. But Mary prevailed. Nick was our Group 78 unofficial "orator."

The other married couple were Renee and Paul from Oregon. She was in her forties, a prematurely gray office manager who had been a Peace Corps volunteer in Senegal in her youth. He was a red-headed, freckled, poetic carpenter in his fifties. Paul had difficulty with the language; I'm not sure they would've let him stay if he wasn't with Renee, who spoke it well. Their village was one of several nestled along the shores of Fagaloa Bay on 'Upolu encircled by a sheer mountainous backdrop, cascading waterfalls, and spectacular views—one of the oldest settlements in Samoa and on the UNESCO World Heritage Tentative List.

Mark from Tennessee was tall with short blond hair and a lopsided smile, and he was introspective and compassionate. He went to a small college on a tennis scholarship, was in his early twenties, and wanted to be a foreign service officer. He lived on the south side of 'Upolu, a few villages beyond the end of the cross-island road at Si'umu—too far to get together often, but he sometimes called me for advice.

Crystal, a sales manager for a hotel chain in San Antonio, was twenty-nine, very pretty with black hair, dark eyes, and beautiful brown skin. She spoke the language well enough, but besides her hatred of bugs, one of her challenges was when local people mistook her for Samoan and began talking a mile a minute in the K-language. She lived in a room in the Women's Committee House in her village near Āpia.

Kaitlen was my orientation roommate in LA and thus the first member of our group that I met. She was in her late twenties, from New Jersey, sharp-witted, buxom, blond, and blue-eyed. She told me that first day that she wanted a Samoan boyfriend, and she dated several, but nothing serious came of it. She intended to complete her Masters in Agriculture when she went back to the States.

From West Virginia, Benj was tall, thin, and wiry with short blond hair, in his mid-twenties, with a degree in Economics. He was bright, considerate, charming, and one of our best haka dancers. He lived on Savai'i working on a water project and had a Samoan girlfriend in his village.

Jacob from Denver was twenty-five, with a distinctive shaved head, physically fit, and he'd graduated with a degree in Management. Sa'u had asked us to bring a new Samoan word to share in class each day and Jacob always brought something to do with death or destruction (along with a knowing smirk).

Shane was from Sacramento, California, in his mid-twenties with buzzcut blond hair. He had a great sense of humor and was full of energy. One day during training, because the best of the meager phone reception was in the middle of the malae in Manunu, he knelt there crying and pleading with his fiancée in front of God and everybody. They were engaged just before he left and soon after we arrived she called, angry and weeping, saying she couldn't believe he'd leave her for two years, blah, blah, blah, even though they'd agreed. She visited a few months later and they broke up.

Christian was an Inter-Coastal Management volunteer, twenty-something, pudgy but not overweight, from Oregon, with an undergraduate degree in Biology. He smiled so much that it seemed like he was always laughing. He worked at a nonprofit in Āpia but lived in a village close to Manunu. He planned to go to Thailand and beyond after PC, paying his way as a dive instructor before pursuing his Masters.

The volunteers I became closest to were Hannah from California and Erin from Maryland. They were also Inter-Coastal Management volunteers specializing in marine biology, and they shared a simple wooden house in Āpia provided by the Division of Internal Affairs.

Hannah was in her early twenties, a bubbly, bright, and curious brunette. She'd traveled extensively (to thirteen countries) and picked up languages easily, including Samoan. She studied Marine and Freshwater Biology at Ohio University and worked in Āpia at the same nonprofit as Christian. We got along well but had another connection as well since she was dating Leleiga who lived with my Samoan family in Manunu.

*She's one of my favorite group members and we've laughed that I'm her "mother" here in Samoa. She has an irresistible smile and is a talented singer and dancer, thus she's become the de facto social director for our group. I think she'll do well here.*

Erin was twenty-three, wore her brunette hair pulled back most of the time, and occasionally wore glasses. She'd traveled in Europe, lived in Germany since her parents were both nurses in the military, and went to Trinity College in Dublin for her degree in Zoology. She worked at the Department of Fisheries in Āpia.

*She's kind of geeky and I like her—another of my "children." She seems fragile occasionally, but I think she'll stick it out for the two years. She has an exceptional work ethic and she walks incredibly fast!*

Later I changed into a matching puletasi aftet my solo dance at the fiafia.

Other volunteers provided invaluable support. We were occasionally able to meet for lunch in town or go to a movie, although most often we'd catch up at the PC office, but it was always fleeting. In my village, even with my Samoan families, I continually carried the small burden to represent Peace Corps well, to be fa'aSāmoa, to speak properly, and not to offend. But with other PCVs, we could relax, talk about world politics and bits of news from home, gossip, worry, bitch, console, and give each other pep talks.

## Sharing My Village on White Sunday

*I'm at the fale 'i tai—my favorite place in the world (at least in <u>my</u> world at <u>this</u> moment), reflecting on a very pleasant White Sunday weekend. One of the village women just paddled by. I shouted, "Ke alu 'i fea?" She replied that she's going to Soloao's fale. I'm in a good mood and I hope it lasts for a few days.*

The second Sunday in October was Children's Day, a religious holiday dedicated to the children of Samoa and also called White Sunday. It may have been a Christian adaptation of pre-contact celebrations of planting and harvesting seasons, but the most common narrative was that it was established to commemorate Samoans who succumbed to the influenza epidemic of 1919, which took the lives of at least one-fourth of the Samoan population, many of them children, in only two months.

It was known as White Sunday because children wore white, the girls in frilly dresses and the boys in shirts and ties, trying to stay clean for a change. However, that was somewhat of a misnomer, because at the Congregational church everyone wore white every Sunday, even the kids. Nonetheless, they were all in their newest finery as the children of the congregation came marching and singing from the church hall, down the sea-front road. Fetū led the way, his knees raised high. They marched past the white, painted lava rock wall and concrete pillars surrounding the churchyard and up the steps into the church.

On this day, kids got out of doing their daily chores and were served their favorite foods, before the adults ate. It was more anticipated than Christmas! Their new clothes were usually sewn at home, although also available in stores in Āpia. Saina and Niu gave Hemara and Tia matching faux pearl necklaces and bracelets and Fetū sported a white bow tie! They also got new shoes, school supplies, and ice cream!

Hemara, Tia, and Fetū on White Sunday in their finery.

Once we were seated inside, the young people conducted the church service, including the Bible reading and prayers. Then each Sunday School class sang, danced, and did skits enacting Bible stories or other religiously themed plays. They'd practiced for weeks to memorize their lines, the songs, and the coordinated dance movements. One of the performances included an 'ava ceremony with the boys playing the roles of the chiefs; it was also practice for life in a Samoan village. The morning service was three hours, and two more hours in the afternoon.

That was a lot of church in one day, but the kids were delightful. Plus, I had company to share it with since Erin rode the last bus to Poutasi on Saturday morning to visit for the three-day weekend. We walked about the village, watched a movie on my laptop, did cross-word puzzles, ate with the family, and just hung out.

> *It was nice to have someone pālagi to talk to and she's easy to be with. I shared "my" village with her and felt proud of it. I had a lovely swim in the ocean, now I'm going to escape with* Pop Goes the Weasel *by James Patterson and then see what's going on at the house.*

A couple of weeks later, I was invited to a Saturday meeting at the Women's Committee House where we sat on fala mats in a circle to discuss the nationwide tsunami drill scheduled for the coming Monday. The church bell was to be rung, and we were supposed to run to higher ground.

> *It's Saturday afternoon at the fale 'i tai. I'm still feeling very positive—in a good mood. They told us in training that there'd be a point in about six weeks or two months in the village that would be like this—searching for a metaphor—hump, plateau, hurdle, when we'd settle in, and those who get to that point would most likely make it for the two years.*

And then on Monday, we didn't do the tsunami drill. Saina and I were relaxing, talking, ready to do it, but the bell never rang. The drill went off as planned in Āpia and that evening on the TV news we saw people running from stores and office buildings.

Later that week, I continued my house-to-house survey with

Tumema's help, asking questions in Samoan such as: how many members in the family, where do the kids go to school, do you have electricity, do you own a vehicle, how do you make a living, and how many pigs do you have? I was hesitant and nervous, but Tumema bolstered my confidence. Even though I didn't say so, in the beginning I wanted to quit after a few houses, but she just kept going, and it got easier. I was grateful to have her with me!

The weeks started blending into months, my frustrations were minor, and the biggest national news was when the Samoan Prime Minister said the government officials who refused to take part in the official fasting program didn't deserve to keep their jobs. They weren't supposed to eat anything before noon in observance of prayer and fasting for safety for the upcoming cyclone season. He acknowledged that the mid-morning tea prepared for visitors was especially tempting.

> *Although I know it's fa'aSāmoa to take my time, I want to start working on projects now, yet nothing happens. This week Tumema can't go on the house-to-house survey with me, so hopefully that's happening next week. And it's so frustrating not to know what's going on. The Sunday morning service last weekend was at Sāleilua and nobody told me till the last minute. Maybe I don't hear about it because I'm not fluent yet, but they all know these things through the coconut wireless (what we in the States call the "grapevine"), and I wish they'd tell me. How ironic since everyone knows what I'm doing!*

### My First Trip Back to Manunu

In November, I went back to Manunu for my first visit since training. I took the bus to Āpia on Friday morning and stayed the night at the family house in town so that I could catch the early, and only, bus to Manunu on Saturday morning. I was a little anxious about the visit and wondered if it would feel the same as it had back then. Even though it had only been three months, it felt like much longer since I'd been there. But of course, everything was the same. Roma, Wilma, and all the kids rushed out of the house to greet me with hugs and kisses, ushered me to a comfortable chair, and offered a cup of tea. My namesake, Little Donna, was now seven months old. She'd mastered the rollover and was trying to crawl, but not quite. Babbling to herself, she scooted and skittered about on the fala mats in the front room as I wrote in my journal. Her brothers played with plastic cars on the floor, and in Samoan style people came and went. I slept in my old room with the fancy bed, mirrored dresser, and carved wooden wardrobe, listening to the youth band practice in the fale next door as I fell asleep.

*Last night after a fabulous meal of fried chicken, shrimp, bread-fruit, rice, and fresh sliced cucumbers, Roma and I talked and watched TV news. They bought my favorite jam, and we had toast, papaya, bananas, and fresh coconut for breakfast. I feel so comfortable here. I've lived in Poutasi for eleven weeks while I lived here for only seven, and yet I feel more "at home" here. Surely part of the closeness I feel to this family is because we PCVs came to Manunu as very impressionable newbies and needed this home away from home. It's not that my Poutasi family isn't welcoming and compatible, but this relationship is unique.*

*And ironically, even though I sometimes still wish that I lived alone, I'm lonely some of the time in Poutasi. It's not a big issue, just there. While my family is kind and I get along well with them, they don't feel like friends (yet?). Saina's in Āpia most of the time and when she's home on the weekends, she's super busy, and needs to rest and spend time with Niu and the children, so I don't want to get in the way. Or they have friends over in the evening and it feels awkward. So then I feel stuck inside my room's four walls. That sounds whiny, even to me.*

As I reflected on my continuing ambivalence, I wrote:

*Advantages of living with a family:*
*Safety*
*Don't have to clean house*
*Don't have to cook if I don't want to*
*Better connections in village*
*Get rides to/from Āpia*
*Have company when I want it.*

*Disadvantages:*
*Little privacy*
*No kitchen*
*My food gets eaten*
*Costs $200 tala/month donation to family*
*Children sometimes exasperating.*

Back in Poutasi, I continued my rounds with Tumema, went to church, and spent a lot of time at the fale 'i tai, reading, studying gagana Samoa, and watching village life revolve around me.

*I haven't been going on my morning walks. I was trying to talk myself into it this morning and it started raining. It sounds like I'm feeling down, but I'm not really. At least not overtly—maybe a little withdrawn, which is probably a symptom of some emotional phase. I'm not worrying over it though, just going with the flow. I remember they told us in training that it'll usually be between six months and a year before anything starts happening. I sound like I'm trying to justify staying in my cocoon, and I am.*

However, things were about to change significantly after I had my first official conversation with Tuatagaloa Joe, the matai of my Samoan family and high chief of Poutasi, and his wife Tui.

# Chapter 6

## Unexpected Benefits and Losses

*'Ā 'ua sala uta, ia tonu tai*
*"Inland mistakes are resolved at the coast"*
**All problems can be resolved by asking or action.**

I'd exchanged greetings with both Tuatagaloa Joe and Tui after church, spoken briefly with them at the Matai Council and the Women's Committee meetings, but they didn't (yet) live in Poutasi and they'd been travelling overseas. So, we hadn't talked about village projects or gotten to know one another. I was fortunate to have an alternate version to my village Peace Corps life largely because of my relationship with the Tuatagaloa family.

The Tuatagaloa chiefly title was the highest in Poutasi, and one of the uppermost on the south side of 'Upolu, so it carried traditional weight and influence. Saina's father, and his father, and his father, held this title for generations. Their elaborate, black lava rock graves were outside my bedroom window.

When I lived in the village, the Tuatagaloa was Saina's cousin, Joe Annandale. Tuatagaloa Joe's grandfather, Bethune Annandale, emigrated from Scotland at the turn of the twentieth century and married a Samoan woman with Tuatagaloa and Malietoa connections. The last notable King of Samoa was a Malietoa. In addition, Tuatagaloa Joe's mother was the daughter of Ta'isi O. F. Nelson, the son of a Swedish settler and a Samoan mother. Nelson was one of Samoa's most successful businessmen of his time and a great supporter for Samoan independence. Thus, Tuatagaloa Joe was the inheritor of extraordinary rank in a status-conscious society. He knew everyone with power or influence.

I lived in the home where Saina's father and mother, Tuatagaloa Fetū and Paugata Lee Hang, lived and raised their ten children. Saina was the only one of the ten who still lived in the village. (Paugata was half-Chinese, hence her daughter's name, "Saina," which means "China" in Samoan.) Saina had sisters and brothers and aunties and uncles and cousins all over Samoa and overseas. Her sister Mari's cafe, bakery, and small grocery store in the heart of Āpia employed numerous family members. Paugata, long-since widowed, sat at *her* table at the back entrance of the store, presiding over all like a good matriarch should. From that same table Saina worked till 2:00 AM in the small portion of the store well known for staying open late for fresh-baked bread, beer, cigarettes, and other necessities in a town where everyplace else was closed.

Their cafe was about three blocks from the Peace Corps office. Frequently after checking email and doing PC business, I'd walk there over the Vaisigano River bridge, which smelled briny and a little foul where it emptied into the harbor. I'd get a cinnamon roll, warm from the bakery, and some *masi popo* (coconut biscuits) to take home. I rarely paid for anything. Their generosity was remarkable, and I was treated as family. The cafe/store was also a regular rendezvous point where I met Niu to ride home to Poutasi or Saina to taxi to her mother's house.

Although he'd grown up on 'Upolu, Niu's matai title was from his ancestral village on Savai'i, so he wasn't part of the Matai Council in Poutasi. However, he was a respected leader in the village and at the Ministry of Natural Resources and Environment.

How lucky I was to be placed in the home of this high-ranking and significant family!

Finally in November, I met with Tuatagaloa Joe and Tui at Sinalei Resort and Spa a few miles from Poutasi. We sat at an oceanside table in the open-air restaurant, a mid-afternoon breeze blowing across the white sand beach and through the plumeria blossoms. Both were tall, about my age, and educated in New Zealand. Tuatagaloa Joe had a commanding presence and his shaved bald head glistened in the slanted sunlight. Tui had fine features, short, graying hair and had been the first Miss Samoa. As we began to talk over plates of fresh fruit and cold drinks, I liked them both immediately.

Tuatagaloa Joe and Tui had opened Sinalei in 1996, named for Tuatagaloa Joe's mother, Sina. A one-lane road wound through the middle of a coconut palm-dotted golf course to a porte cochere surrounded by abundant ferns and palms. After walking over a tiny bridge spanning a lotus pond, you were graciously greeted at the open-air reception desk. A covered walkway continued to the bar and restaurant in a huge, round, traditional fale, with detailed carving and intricately tied coconut cordage lashing together the curved supporting beams overhead. Adjacent was an infinity pool and scattered about were lovingly appointed villas. The service was superb, the food was scrumptious, and the ambiance truly divine.

A decade before, Tuatagaloa Joe and Tui had lived for two years in an open fale on the property with no running water and cooked over an open fire. They cleared the property, began building a few beach huts for rent, and eventually achieved their dream, supported by people from the surrounding villages for whom the resort provided jobs.

When we met that day, Tuatagaloa Joe had just returned from a trip to China, and had also recently gone to New Zealand to arrange for young men from Poutasi to pick apples there seasonally. They didn't yet live in the village but it was at that meeting that I learned they were planning to build a small house across the road from ours, next to the fale 'i tai, for themselves and Tui's wheelchair-bound mother, Anna.

Tuatagaloa Joe at the pier restaurant at Sinalei.
(Photo courtesy of pacific.scoop.co.nz.)

Perhaps those earlier weeks would've been easier if I'd met with them sooner. Their input was invaluable, and their support, guidance, and friendship made it possible to accomplish our projects. On the other hand, I had needed those three months to begin to discover the village, the people, the politics, the culture, and the personal tools that I needed for the challenges ahead—all assets in developing a relationship with these two influential people.

The month before, I'd gone to the Matai Council meeting where they told me to make improvements to the water system and bridge, build a seawall, create a homework center, and build a new primary school. There had been a primary school in the village, and at that time the children from Sāleilua came to Poutasi. The structure still stood in ruin near the present secondary school. I'd heard through the coconut wireless that the village/matai/Poutasi school committee/whoever hadn't acted several years earlier to construct a much-needed new building, so Sāleilua took the initiative and built a new school. Now Sāleilua wanted $30,000 tala from Poutasi to help pay for it since the

Poutasi children now walked about a mile down the government road to the new school.

The thought of building a new primary school as one of my projects felt like way more than I'd bargained for and too close to what I'd done in my career life. But regardless of any personal hesitancy, there were pro and con factions among the villagers, so I'd heard it from both sides. Even though the kids had to walk to Sāleilua rain or shine, which wasn't good, it didn't seem justified with the new school nearby and only sixty students from Poutasi attending. There was a nationwide teacher shortage to take into consideration and the commitment of matching funds if the village was able to get funding from a donor agency.

To my relief, Tuatagaloa Joe (who hadn't been at that matai meeting) told me that the primary school building needed to be discussed further by the Matai Council and not to take any specific action right away, so I happily put it on the back burner. The topic came up from time to time, including more than once from one particular matai. I told him, "Tuatagaloa Joe said to wait until the matai talked about it further."

He replied, "The matai talked about it, but Joe wasn't at the meeting, and all the matai want to build a new school in the village."

I just kept ignoring the pressure, putting it off and relying on Tuatagaloa Joe to guide me. We didn't proceed any further with a new primary school while I was there.

Ever since I'd come to the village I'd heard, "We need to improve the water system." True, it was frustrating not to have water certain times of the day and the skinny PVC pipes laid atop lava rock connecting between homes broke regularly. I'd often see a fountain in someone's front yard. However, what I heard from Tuatagaloa Joe and Tui was also critically important before moving forward.

I learned that the previous year the village had applied to the United Nations (UN) to fund a more reliable water source for the village, but was turned down because there was a government funded district-wide water project planned. However, the United Nations told them that grant money was still available if the project was amended to encompass a marine component, including a Marine Protected Area (MPA). I came away with a stack of paperwork to read and information on who to contact at the UN.

Tuatagaloa Joe and Tui were totally supportive of a homework center. So my mandate from the Matai Council was whittled down to that and the proposal to the United Nations for a marine project that would include a seawall and improved bridge.

### I Enjoy the Privileges of Status

That day they told me that I could come to Sinalei anytime I wanted to get away or have a change of pace. It was an adults-only boutique resort and most of the guests came for a holiday from New Zealand and Australia. Not long after that, Tui told me it was the slow season so I could stay (free, of course) for the weekend.

> Life is sooo good right now! Who would've ever thought that this would be part of my Peace Corps experience? I'm in the honeymoon fale, right by the ocean. Wooden louvers instead of windows, facing the sea, perfect air temperature, a nice breeze. I went for a swim in the pool before lunch and maybe I'll go snorkeling this afternoon. Until then, I'll read and write and relax in the hammock on my private deck. I hope to come back often.

In the coming months when I went to town with Tuatagaloa Joe or Tui for village project meetings or just catching a ride, we'd often stop by Sinalei for breakfast or dinner. Sometimes, if I timed it right and there was room, I'd get a ride from Āpia to Sinalei in the air-conditioned van when it shuttled guests to and from town for shopping and sightseeing. Then I'd shed my bags and my stresses and hang out by the terraced, lushly landscaped pool until I could catch a ride to the village.

*Here I am, beside the lovely pool at Sinalei, feeling totally and wonderfully decadent. I just went for a short swim and I'll relax with* Stones from the River *by Ursula Hegi and margarita until I can ride with Tuatagaloa Joe back to Poutasi.*

Several weeks after our Sinalei meeting, Tui invited me to join the local chapter of the Pan Pacific and South East Asia Women's Association (PPSEAWA). Its mission was to "strengthen the bonds of peace by promoting better understanding and fostering friendship among all women of the Pacific and Southeast Asia and to initiate and promote cooperation among the women of these regions for the study and improvement of social, economic, and cultural conditions." On a sunny Saturday afternoon, Tui drove us to a PPSEAWA garden party fundraiser for scholarships for girls at the home of the New Zealand High Commissioner, Caroline Wilke. I wore a red puletasi with a hand-painted gold design (a gift from Saina that was one of my favorites) and borrowed a straw hat from Tui with yellow flowers on the brim, since all I had were white church hats. It was such a pleasant change from village life to dress up and drink tea on the balcony overlooking the exquisitely manicured grounds.

Fiame Naomi Mata'afa, the keynote speaker and one of very few women in parliament, spoke compellingly about the importance of education for young women. Fiame is the daughter of Samoa's first post-independence prime minister, and in May 2021 she herself was elected to that esteemed position in a controversial election.

With Fiame Naomi Mata'afa at the PPSEAWA garden party.

The party officially ended at 5:00, but Tui and I, along with Caroline, Fiame, and a half-dozen others, stayed and relaxed with a glass of wine on the veranda. Many of the women active with groups like this were expats from New Zealand, Australia, or the USA. There were a few local women there whom I'd met before, including Tuatagaloa Joe's sister, a physician in Āpia, and his cousin, a newspaper reporter. We laughed and talked, and as usual I took lots of photos. One exquisitely lovely seventy-year-old told stories of acting with Gary Cooper as a seventeen-year-old in the 1953 movie *Return to Paradise* that was filmed in Samoa.

*It was such an honor and a treat to be part of that esteemed group. This is another example of how my PC experience is different from others, but that's just what it is—different. And it suits me.*

Tui (front) and our mutual friend, Hilda.

This part of my Peace Corps life was carefree, I could speak English, I was accepted as a peer, there was no need to figure out status, and I relaxed. They were interested in what I was doing in the village, and what I'd done before I came to Samoa. These women were like those I'd been used to associating with back home and we had different conversations than I had with PCVs, PC staff, or villagers. I was there because of Tui, and I was grateful that she saw that I'd fit in, enjoy their company, and want to contribute to their cause.

*Sometimes I feel "guilty" about living an atypical, more "luxurious" lifestyle some of the time, with good fortune like Sinalei, connections, free food from the cafe and store, and a place to stay in Āpia. But this is where I've been placed, and it doesn't mean that I can't make a difference. It certainly makes life more pleasant while I'm here, and that's worth a lot. It's good to see another side of life in Samoa sometimes.*

It's interesting to observe my "guilt" and justifications regarding the advantages and benefits provided to me through my Samoan families. Although it didn't seem like an "authentic" part of the Peace Corps experience at times, I was fortunate by virtue of these privileges to see the full picture of the country's economy, education gaps, attitudes, and lifestyle, and I learned an equal measure about Samoan life and culture through these opportunities.

### Blending Holiday Traditions

With November came plans to go to Colorado for Christmas. I'd gone home for the holidays every year since I'd moved back to Hawai'i, so I was continuing that tradition, but of course I was also anxious and excited to see Jackson. Since we'd reconnected, we continued our once or twice a week emails and talked when we could. I looked forward to being held in his strong arms.

*The last couple of evenings, I've been hearing the Samoan version of fireworks "because it's getting close to Christmas." The "fireworks" are muffled booms—well, not so muffled if you're up close. From our house, it sounds like the launching sound at a fireworks show echoing from about half a football field away, behind the big mango tree by Meleisea's pig pens. I went to see what was going on and watched three boys about ten years old having fun with fire.*

*Here's how they do it. On the ground they lay a stalk of dried bamboo about five feet long and four to six inches wide with a one-inch diameter hole in the top near one end. They pour in a small amount of kerosene from a nearby soda bottle and blow into the hole to activate the fumes. Then they light the gas from the top with a small flaming stick kept in a coconut husk fire nearby and jump back. Poof! Bang! A flame shoots up a couple of feet in the air and a burst of smoke comes out of the end of the bamboo. Again, and again, with a small explosion every few seconds. It takes practice to make the loudest bang. It's called a "bamboo cannon," and ironically the children use it as an alternative to commercial, "dangerous" fireworks, which are illegal.*

A bamboo cannon.

Thanksgiving is a uniquely American holiday not observed in Samoa, so all the PC volunteers were again invited by the Chargé d'affair to celebrate.

*I'm at the American Embassy listening to American music, soon to be eating an American feast on a gorgeous sunny Saturday in Samoa! Group 78 was in charge of Thanksgiving decorations so several of us came mid-morning to do our thing—a combination of traditional construction paper pumpkins and turkeys, and patriotic red, white and blue—it is after all an <u>American</u> holiday—with*

*Samoan greenery and flowers all around. I'm looking forward to*
*the food. Roast turkey and all the trimmings sound fantastic!*

As it turned out, the dinner was yummy, but I was disappointed that there were no mashed potatoes and gravy, sweet potatoes, or
pumpkin pie.

By the beginning of December, I'd finished my house-to-house survey and was working on my Village Situational Analysis. Next to the
fale 'i tai, work continued steadily on the construction of Tuatagaloa
Joe and Tui's house.

*On the drive to town for a United Nations meeting, Tuatagaloa*
*Joe told me about his childhood and his schooling in New Zealand.*
*One of the things he wants to do for the young people in Poutasi*
*is make it easier for them to stay in the village, with ideas like a*
*village-owned bus to and from Āpia with a subsidized fare so they*
*can come home from school or work at night, and creation of jobs*
*in the village.*

After I'd read the previous proposal and other materials Tuatagaloa
Joe gave me, I met with Malama in the Environment & Conservation
Division at MNRE (the Ministry of Natural Resources and
Environment), where Niu worked in a different division. To my delight
she told me that they were eager to help with a Marine Project. Later,
we'd also involve the Ministry of Agriculture and Fisheries, where my
PC friend Erin worked. Indeed, she was present at some of our vil-
lage meetings.

Our "Marine Project" was officially titled by the United Nations
as "The Poutasi Marine and Mangrove Conservation Project." In the
village we called it: *"'O le Atina'e mo le Fa'aleileiga ma le Puipuiga o*
*le Gātaifale"* (The Project for the Improvement and Protection of the
Coastal Waters).

A key part of the project was establishment of a Marine Protected

Area. MPAs around the globe protect ecosystems, preserve cultural resources and archaeological sites, or sustain fisheries production, and
they're established and managed by all levels of government. In our
case, the MPA in Poutasi's bay would be created by a lopsided circle
of plastic rope held up by floating buoys with concrete anchors. Inside
would be off limits to fishing or boating, thereby creating a fish nurs-
ery and allowing the coral to revive. Trespassers would pay a fine to
the village.

Malama gave me a sample proposal and other resources to read.
The revision was due on January 28th and we were required to have a
community meeting in the village before submission. It was now too
close to Christmas and Tuatagaloa Joe would be in New Zealand after
the holidays, so the meeting wasn't scheduled until January 25th after
he returned.

I was packing my bags and looking forward to my Colorado visit, but it didn't seem like Christmas without gift shopping, wrapping,
baking, parties, trimming the tree, and decorating the whole house.
There were some of those things in Samoa—I saw people bringing
home toys on the bus and the children practiced in the afternoons for
their program at church—but I wasn't part of it. However, the holiday
music was inescapable.

*Samoan Christmas music is playing non-stop on the buses and
in the stores. "Samoan Christmas music" is traditional American
Christmas music sung by Samoans with an island beat. I can't
imagine that they have any idea what "chestnuts roasting on an
open fire, jack frost nipping at your nose" really means. I'm sooo
sick of it already. On the bus I have to listen to the same CD over
and over every time I go to and from Āpia. Bah, humbug!*

*On a different note, Radio Australia played an Australian
Christmas song on the radio this morning. It was about the birds
singing in the blue ranges (mountains) on Christmas Day, and the*

*"golden weather" of Christmas time. I was struck by the realization that a significant part of the world has always celebrated when the weather is warm. How parochially we think so often!*

Mataomanu gave me a small "gift" before I left:

*I've complained about the procrastination and seemingly lackadaisical attitudes here, but Mataomanu told me today when we were discussing the Marine Project how much they appreciate me, and that they'd never get it done without me. I needed to hear that.*

### Christmas in Colorado

My two weeks in Colorado flew by. I was surrounded by familiar holiday rituals at Mom's house—the frosted cookies shaped like wreaths, stars, and Santa, the smell of evergreen boughs, and piles of presents beneath the angel-topped tree. The family gathered to open our gifts on a cold, snowy night as I endlessly snuggled with Jayden, my chubby, smiling, baby grandson.

*I've been eating like an absolute pig! I decided that there'll be no moderation for me this holiday. I've been uncomfortably full and delightfully so. At least a t-shirt and lāvalava will fit even if I gain ten pounds! And the hot showers! I just stand there. It's hard to imagine not taking a hot shower again for months. I updated my PC blog with the luxury of high-speed internet and I'm happy with it for the first time. I don't live with a lot of hardship in Poutasi, but these are things I miss and I'm thoroughly taking advantage of them.*

Jackson and I had scarcely any time together. He celebrated with his son and family, and I looked forward to spending time with my sons who were all in Colorado, together for the first time since the previous year. I rushed with last minute Christmas shopping, caught up with friends, and tended to unwelcome details, like replacing the dishwasher at my house and other matters that I'd postponed until I was back in the U.S. We saw each other when we could, and had a merry New Year's Eve with friends in front of the fireplace eating chili con carne that had never tasted so good. That night, and every time we were together, we talked and laughed and snuggled against the winter weather, and it was warm and comfy. But I wanted it to feel new, different, exhilarating, and not the same as always.

And it wasn't just Jackson. Even with all the joyful moments, the hustle and bustle, and the responsibilities, I felt oddly disconnected from it all. For the last six months, every day of my life had included an impactful moment and being back in America seemed vaguely anti-climactic. Yet, I enthusiastically shared about life in Poutasi and Samoa. Everyone marveled at my photos and was fascinated by the stories of my adventures thus far. I never hesitated about going back.

Despite my inner uncertainties, Jackson and I parted with words of love and intention. It had been seven months since we'd seen one another, and we knew that it would be at least another year until we were together again. When he took me to meet my returning Air New Zealand flight, we held each other close at the passenger drop-off, each enveloped in our own thoughts.

Back in Samoa, we sat in a circle in the center room as one by one I presented to the family the gifts I'd brought: a handheld Sudoku game for Niu; a fancy tank top and bracelet for Saina; an English dictionary, hair ties, and compact mirror for Hemara; for Tia, a storybook, barrettes, and compact mirror; and for Fetū, a Matchbox truck, coloring book and crayons, and Sponge Bob boxer shorts. For each of the kids I also bought plastic snow globes (at an after-Christmas sale for $.24 each) that turned out to be their favorite gifts. I got a pack of cigarette lighters for Tamamasui—what do you buy for an ancient Samoan man who has nothing yet needs nothing?

It felt good to be back in the village, the opposite reaction I'd had during my working life when I came back to the office with extra work to do after vacation. Here the respite was coming back to a more relaxed place and pace after rushing to holiday parties in snow and traffic, squeezing in lunches to catch up with friends, tending to business matters, and standing in long lines at huge stores packed with people. Back in Samoa nothing had changed since I'd left. Yes, there were projects to begin, but no overwhelming deadlines or tasks to be done immediately.

*At the fale 'i tai. It's a welcome relief after the bitter cold of Colorado. I was born to live in the tropics. I'm looking toward Nu'usafe'e, listening to the birds, the waves breaking on the reef, with music playing on the radio in someone's fale nearby. Some delicate muted shades in the sky tonight, but not a photo-worthy sunset. I've gotten quite picky. Home. For now.*

### Rain, Clouds, Ocean

I began to discern the subtleties of the rain, the clouds, and the sea in ways that I never had. At the fale 'i tai my view spanned from 'Ili'ili Point to the right, with Nu'usafe'e Island directly ahead, and the last houses of Poutasi on my left, where the river flowed into the sea. With Meleisea's boat bobbing in the foreground, I watched stunning sunsets unfold, metamorphose, and mesmerize. Sometimes it was almost too much to take in. I saw the water's surface change from glassy smooth, to choppy, to heaving swells. And how thrilling to hear a hammering downpour coming toward me through the rainforest!

Ah, the rain . . . it was misty, pounding, soothing, soaking, refreshing, and rhythmic, a manifestation of invisible convections and currents, a presence I looked for everyday in the sky. I often didn't want to deal with it, but I never hated it. It was just there.

Rain is a constant in the tropics. There's a wet season, when it rains more, and a dry season, when it rains less, but it always rains. It was warm, almost inviting, at least when it wasn't coming down in painful pelts. Little kids splashed about naked, and it was especially fun for them to run in and out of the small waterfall of a gushing downspout.

The rains filled the spring that provided water for the village, the cool brackish pool where the kids loved to play, and the lake whose dam generated electricity for the island. I was grateful for the watercress growing in the fresh streams and for taro, breadfruit, and coconut that depended on the rain to survive. I understood why early Polynesians chanted tributes of gratitude and supplication to their deities.

Studying the clouds, I learned how to distinguish an approaching shower from a squall or a downpour. Ah, the clouds . . .

*Windswept charcoal Rorschach blot unfolds on sky and sea*
*Downy bellies of avian giants reflect the golden light*
*Cumulus vessels float above and below*
*Feathery icy veils halo the sunlit island*
*Molten backlit ancient guardians linger on the horizon*
*Pearlescent overturned bowl of the sky glows warm*
*Swordfish and shark trail virga*
*Carmen swooshes mirror the water*
*Plowed altocumulus rows blot out the sun*
*Flames rise above silhouetted palms.*

With no modesty at all, I'll say that I took stunning photos of sunset after sunset over 'Ili'ili Point from the fale 'i tai. It wasn't my ability per se, but the magnificent combination of scenery, sun, and sea that made it happen. I looked forward to seeing what shapes and hues would appear each evening. Whether riotous color, muted pastel, or darkest gray with slivers of silvery backlight, it was always worth seeing. Anticipating, setting up, forming, changing, lingering, blending, fading—we see what we want to in the heavens, in the glints of light on the waves, and in the shapes of the tumbling clouds.

*As I sit at the fale 'i tai, it's pouring rain. As much as I adore this place in the brilliant sun of noon, or in the evening glow of sunset, I also love it in the rain. The air is warm, and I can sit here totally protected, watching water gush off the eaves of the roof where it's banging down.*

Hemara enjoying the warm "shower" off the eaves.

## The Bad Weather Continued

When I got back from Colorado, it was rainy for days and days with sporadic electric outages caused by passing weather fronts and a cyclone near Fiji. The atmosphere was conducive to working on my Village Situational Analysis, and I spent hours and hours on it while reviewing materials for proposals.

*The family's been in Āpia for the last couple of days. I'm enjoying the tranquility immensely. There's always the tradeoff of quiet time versus having company. All in all, it's a good fit. Most of the time, especially when school is in session, it's calm and I can do my own thing, yet when I need assistance and advice, I have that too. And it's nice to "have a family." Saina called earlier. She apologized for leaving me alone, was worried, wanted to make sure I was okay and had enough food. I assured her everything is fine. Today I finished reading* Treasure Box *by Orson Scott Card, reviewed a sample Marine Protected Area plan, and completed a draft of the Homework Center proposal.*

*I'm at the fale 'i tai. It's especially peaceful here right now, and pleasantly cool after a chilly night. I put on socks this morning and used a lāvalava as an extra cover along with the sheet last night. I hear snippets of conversations from women gathering seafood, with the ever-present muted roar of the surf in the background. Fishermen glide by in their canoes. The sky is gray. The water looks like liquid steel. I can see clearly to the bottom even from here, but no blue anywhere today. Out toward the island I just saw what looked like a shark, or maybe a turtle. An occasional—every few seconds—big fin, and a large dark shape under the water.*

In mid-January, I went to visit Roma and Wilma in Manunu. After waiting two hours in the muggy heat in Āpia for a bus, I learned there was no Manunu bus that Saturday morning. So, I took a taxi to the village. As always when I arrived, I was met with hugs, kisses and smiles. I usually visited on weekends so that I could be there to listen to Roma's sermon, sitting in the front pew beside Wilma.

*Donna La'itiiti, has grown a lot. There's a big difference between seven and nine months. She's been teething and running a fever, so as I write she's crying because she's getting a massage, and doesn't like it. The fōfō, or Samoan massage with coconut oil, is phase one for every medical problem. It doesn't hurt her, but I doubt that it helps for teething. And she doesn't understand why she's being held down and poked and prodded. My family in Poutasi also calls the*

*traditional healer for everything from a headache to the flu. I'm a*
*skeptic; it sometimes delays treatment for a more serious medical*
*condition, or might feel scary to a small child. Still, there's much to*
*be said for the power of touch.*

The next morning, I was stuck in Manunu. It had rained all night
and was still raining. The only road out of the village was flooded and
too dangerous to drive through. When it let up in the afternoon, I got
a ride to Āpia and took 'Afakasi's bus back to Poutasi. Although it was
passable, we still drove through water in places, the government road
had washed out here and there, and a large tree had been across the
road near the Pacific Express store.

The day of our important village meeting to present the Marine
Project started with intense rain. Representatives from MNRE were
supposed to come from Āpia and the roads were undoubtedly flooded,
so Tuatagaloa Joe and Meleisea Seti decided to postpone the meeting until the following week. The fragility of Samoa's infrastructure
was a constant challenge and frustration. Whenever there were heavy
rains, Āpia flooded, especially the main town area near the ocean, and
it was common to lose electric power. Samoa was gradually upgrad-
ing as it emerged from being a third-world country, but that status is
fraught with its own liabilities. It's like being one of the working poor
in America. You no longer qualify for aid, but you can hardly afford
necessities, let alone effectively deal with an emergency. So, in the case
of a nation, less foreign aid is available, yet the infrastructure is still
inadequate, and sometimes unsound.

The following week I had lunch in Āpia with fellow Group 78 volunteers, Paul and Renee. They told me that things weren't going well in
their village, and they were trying to find someplace else to be assigned,
or they would go home.

*Their village isn't welcoming and their mayor is difficult. I don't*
*know what I'd do under similar circumstances. I'm lucky I'm in*

*a friendly village with no problems so far, although I'm having a spate of boredom and loneliness right now. I'm writing to ease the loneliness. I could read, but that's more of a solution for boredom. There are subtle differences between these various emotional states. In the past I might have said I had the "blahs" or was "feeling down." Now I feel the difference between boredom, loneliness, frustration, or restlessness. There's another word too. Lonesome. Maybe lonesome just wants some companionship, and lonely is a little deeper. I'm not sure which this is. I think lonesome. I certainly have many moments of happiness and contentment here too.*

*Maybe the contrast upon returning from the States where there was constant activity and contact with friends and family had more effect than I thought. On the bus on Thursday I was reading* We Are All Welcome Here *by Elizabeth Berg and was moved to tears. Of course a good book will do that, but I kept crying, which was embarrassing. I wiped the tears, put on my sunglasses, and knew that the people who could see me weren't from Poutasi. Writing this I find tears in my eyes, which surprises me. Something is definitely going on. It's not as bad as it was when I first got to the village, but this is the most discontented I've felt for quite a while.*

The girls saw me tear up and told Saina on the phone. She called me to see if everything was ok, and I told her I was a little lonely.

*I don't think I can explain it, so I feel like I still have to fake it. I don't want them to be unduly concerned or hurt their feelings. Even though sometimes I still wish I lived by myself, maybe I'd feel too isolated and even more vulnerable during these down times, but it's trying to put up with other people when you really want to be alone—and yet I've just said that I'm lonely. It's so complicated!*

## *Safiya is Ripped From Her Village*

Group 78 had been in Samoa for eight months when we heard the disturbing news that Safiya was medevac'd to Hawai'i with amoebic dysentery. She'd been ill with gastro-intestinal issues for a couple of months before it was diagnosed. A week later Peace Corps ended her service and she left for New York directly from Hawai'i, so we didn't get to say goodbye.

*We knew one of us might go home early, but it's difficult to see it happen. I'm glad she'll get needed medical care, but it must be terribly disconcerting to abruptly leave her village, where I'd heard things were going well.*

Safiya's early separation shook all of us a bit, but little did we know that her departure was the first of more to come.

# Chapter 7

# Plodding Along, One Step at a Time

*"E pala le maʻa, a e le pala upu"*
*Even stones decay, but words last forever.*

Intentionally or not, PC prepared me gently for my village projects. Only a few weeks after arriving in Samoa, I'd stayed with Jordan in her village by the sea, about ten miles from Poutasi and within walking distance from Sinalei. We'd snorkeled at Palolo Deep Marine Reserve with its magnificent coral reef and sea life. My entertaining ride to her village wasn't my last time on the turquoise bus to Siʻumu where I'd visited Meghan's computer class the next day. I don't know if Jordan and Meghan knew where I'd be going and what I might do. I doubt it; I prefer to think that things unfolded with synchronicity.

During January, I focused on writing the proposals to fund the Marine Project and the Homework Center. The cutoff date for our Marine Project submission was only three days after the cancelled village meeting, and that meeting was a requirement. Fortunately, the United Nations agreed to accept the proposal before the rescheduled meeting with the endorsement of the Matai Council and the Peace Corps Committee. Although there had been general discussions at the matai meetings, I wasn't sure if most of them understood the proposed project yet, let alone the whole village, but Tuatagaloa Joe was willing to state that the Matai Council supported it. So early on the morning of the deadline, I dressed in my finest puletasi and accompanied Tuatagaloa Joe to Āpia to officially deliver our proposal. All conversations with UN, MNRE, and the Department of Fisheries had been encouraging and I felt optimistic about our chances. But it would be another month of waiting before we'd know, and $20,000 USD for the benefit of the village was on the line.

Two weeks later, I woke nervously anticipating the village meeting to present the project in detail in the church hall. One by one, the matai filed in and took their places on folding chairs in rows, with the best seats in front for guests and the highest titled chiefs. The younger untitled men sat in the back on laufala mats. The few women in attendance sat up front together, mostly members of the Women's Committee.

Since this was the first time that most of the villagers had heard the whole project in detail, there was much discussion, and of course the meeting started and ended with extended remarks, fa'aSāmoa. While I madly scribbled notes, half in Samoan and half in English, the planned goals and timeline were presented. There was some dissent when the men heard that fishing would be prohibited in the Marine Protected Area. The debate turned to mutters of "we'll see what happens" when it was explained that the diminished fish population could recover in this sheltered area, and then would provide more to catch when they grew and ventured out.

*We went at least an hour past the time when we planned to end. Of course, we didn't start on time; the MNRE staffers were late. I don't know exactly how late. I didn't look at my watch after it was a half hour past the time we were supposed to start, because it didn't matter. I was so tired when it was over that I came back to the house and slept for two hours! I greeted everyone at the beginning and then turned it over to Niu and the folks from MNRE and Fisheries for most of the program. I'll have him debrief me so that I make sure I understood all the comments and questions. Overall, I was very pleased with the meeting.*

Starting with a village-wide cleanup effort, and eventually teaching awareness of the marine environment in the local schools, the Marine Project was a year-long comprehensive undertaking with long-term objectives and involvement of many groups inside and outside the village. Indeed, it was meant to involve all the villagers, from picking up rubbish on the beach to planting trees or restocking giant clams.

### Envisioning a Homework Center

In the meantime, the Homework Center became my primary focus. The mayor had mentioned a "homework center" on my first brief visit. I didn't know exactly what that was, except what was obviously implied. From the beginning it was the one project everyone agreed upon. The construction and remodeling component nearly drained my patience reserves and I had to navigate occasionally troubled waters, but it became one of the most rewarding experiences of my life.

I began to envision our Homework Center as it eventually became—a place for kids to come after school two evenings each week for homework help, and a tiny computer center where I'd teach keyboarding and basic computer skills to adults and kids alike.

Soon after I'd arrived in the village, I'd started trying to figure out how to pay for it. Saina advised that I talk to her sister at the Ministry of Finance, who suggested the New Zealand High Commission. I picked up an application for a small grant, but it would take another month before I could start in earnest on a cost estimate since I couldn't get anyone to show me the locked room in the Congregational church hall that had been proposed for the center. I tried to wait patiently, but with only modest success. Finally, Niu took me to scope it out after I'd tried several times to peek in the one high, small window with frustration.

The hall was a large auditorium used for Sunday School classes, parties, and meetings, since it was the largest such structure in the village. It had a stage of raised concrete, two restrooms with adjacent showers, and a storeroom that would become the Homework Center. I immediately imagined what it could look like, even if it was only a dusty seven-by-ten-foot space with old lumber in a messy pile, a couple of broken whipper snippers leaning against the wall, and sandy grit underfoot. It'd be tight, but we could do it, with a long counter for the computers and a printer, and bookshelves on the far end. I drew a floor plan and made a materials list. We'd need lumber, paint, a new window, a wall-mounted fan, sheet vinyl for the floor, electrical and carpentry work, and a printer/copier. In February, I submitted the Homework Center proposal to the New Zealand High Commission asking for $5,000 tala ($2,000 USD).

And then we waited and waited . . . and I blithely moved forward with the demolition and construction as if we were going to get the money for the rest of the materials and equipment. The first thing to do was add a full-sized window and make the space three feet longer by taking out one of the shower stalls. That required some plumbing and concrete work which Tuatagaloa Joe donated. I remember briefly thinking, "What if we don't get the grant?" And replying to myself, "If we don't, I'm sure I can raise the money somehow."

I was also eagerly anticipating a response to my request for the donation of three computers. Three months earlier, Meghan had told me that the Mormon church gave away used school computers every two years, so I'd sent an email message to the church education administrator, Dr. Felix Wendt. And then we waited, and waited, and waited . . . and I learned.

At the end of November, Meghan had said that Dr. Wendt told her that someone would bring donated equipment for her school and for Poutasi to the Peace Corps office, but nothing arrived. I emailed, expressed our gratitude, gave him my phone number, and asked him to call me when the computers were available for pick up.

In December, I tried to call Dr. Wendt but learned he was in

America until January, so I was stalled again. I left a voicemail message and sent an email when I returned from Colorado but didn't hear back. Eventually, in February I told Tuatagaloa Joe about the problem. He said he'd check on it, and the next day he brought all three computers to the village! Who you know is more important than what you know all over the world.

When the concrete work was almost done, I asked about the Homework Center proposal at the High Commission. The clerk said the High Commissioner was out of the country for several days, so I should check back the second week in March. It'd be early April before I finally heard with gratitude and relief that they'd funded the project. Of course, they didn't call me after the decision-making meeting as promised, but I understood by then how those things worked, so I called the next day.

## *I Meet a German Engineer*

By now, Tuatagaloa Joe and Tui had settled into their compact, two-bedroom, concrete block house across the road from ours. When we needed to talk about PC projects, I'd often meet with them in the morning before they left for Sinalei or Āpia. and sometimes I'd eat toast, eggs, and fruit with them. Or, as was often the case, if Tuatagaloa Joe was talking with one of the villagers or was on the phone, Tui and I had a cup of tea and caught up while we waited. Since they'd begun staying in the village, Tui would sometimes swim in the bay with long, strong strokes when I was sitting at the fale 'i tai in the evenings.

I was delighted when the United Nations awarded a grant of $20,000 USD to Poutasi! The village had committed to contribute the equivalent of $16,400 USD in funding, materials, and labor as well. One morning, Tuatagaloa Joe and I were discussing the Marine Project and he asked if I'd been to the spring behind the Catholic church. Rebuilding the rock and concrete village spring reservoir for a backup water supply was part of the project. I hadn't been there because I didn't know exactly where it was. I'd heard that there was an old road behind the church, and I'd thought of trying to find it, but I was glad that I hadn't. We walked single file on a narrow path through shoulder-high grass and bush, and I wouldn't have had a clue which way to turn on my own. Tuatagaloa Joe said he thought it'd be a good idea to rebuild the former road for emergencies, such as tsunami or cyclones. Not long thereafter, he signed a letter that I drafted and delivered to the Ministry of Works, Transport, and Infrastructure requesting assessment of the drainage pipes which constituted the "bridge" at the fork, and the possibility of re-opening the previous alternative access road.

I took pictures of the spring to add to the project report, and then Tuatagaloa Joe headed off to Sinalei. I continued walking along the beach to the stilted mangroves where the river met the sea for more photos, wading through thigh-high water. Back on shore, I saw a pālagi man about my age photographing Nuʻusafeʻe Island from the village road by the fork, so I introduced myself. Hartmut was from Germany, and he had the most incredible, piercing blue eyes. We began talking about Poutasi, Samoa, his travels, and after an hour or more, I was getting hungry and thirsty so I suggested we have lunch at Sinalei. We hopped in his little red rental car and sped along the coast to the resort.

At the restaurant on the pier, we ate burgers and fries, drank a bottle of wine, and talked for four hours. He was a retired engineer with Siemens traveling the world and falling in love with the South Pacific. We laughed at the odd coincidence when he said he'd served in the German Air Force and was stationed in El Paso, Texas. He dropped me off at the house about 5:00 PM. The coconut wireless must have been buzzing!

I desperately needed a shower after tramping through the bush, sweating profusely, and wading in the ocean. Fortunately, the lāvalava and t-shirt I'd been trekking in had dried a bit by the time we'd started talking and I don't think I smelled. But I was tousled, and it was the "natural look" for sure.

Hartmut and I continue to exchange occasional email. He's now an award-winning photographer and lives in New Zealand. Would the spark between us have caught fire in a different time and place? Who knows? But of course, to complicate matters Jackson was continuing to woo me by email. He wrote, "I love you Donna. You knew that, even though I don't say it much."

*In the dozen years he's been in and out of my life, I've always loved him more than he loved me. And now he says he loves me. This morning I was lying in bed with closed eyes, realizing that I haven't paused to relish it enough. I don't fully trust that love yet, but nonetheless, I'll savor it and wrap it around me as if it were his arms I was nestled in.*

One morning soon after, Tia and Hemara came to my room with infected cuts. Tia had two small ones that didn't need more than a Band-Aid and salve, but she needed to be "doctored" too, especially since I was paying more attention to Hemara. She had a three-inch gash on top of her foot, filled with pus, red and swollen. She told me she fell on the weekend playing rugby and hit a chunk of cement. I helped her soak in a basin of boiled warm water, cleaned it with antiseptic from my PC medical kit, slathered on antibacterial salve, and taped on a gauze bandage.

As she sat on the bed and I knelt on the floor treating her wound, she told me about the death of her younger sister, Fa'asili. Hemara was still a toddler when five-year-old Fa'asili ran into the street and was hit by a truck in Āpia. She'd been walking with her sister Aileen, who was eight at the time.

*How dreadful that must have been for Niu and Saina! It makes my heart hurt to think of it. Her tiny grave with her photo is outside the back door where Saina often sits and smokes. On the radio I recently heard a survey by the UNICEF Alliance for Safe*

*Children that more children in developing countries die or are injured by accidents than disease.*

Although I saw now-teenage Aileen often when the extended family got together in town or in Poutasi, she lived in Āpia with Saina's sister Mari. Throughout Polynesia, children are still commonly entrusted to relatives. In America we associate foster parenting or adoption with something gone wrong. For Samoans, fosterage reflects love and kindness rather than pathology and misfortune. From their perspective, Americans, with our emphasis on the nuclear family, and exclusive rearing of children within one family, lack compassion. These transfers of children aren't absolute. They may last for years, but don't permanently separate them from their biological parents who have a deep and lasting commitment to their children. It's hard for Americans to understand, and likewise, the thought that we have orphanages appalls Samoans.

For a day or two, although the drainage in Hemara's foot lessened and she said it felt better, the red flush of infection spread and I feared she might need antibiotics, but finally it began to improve. Of course after that, Tia and Fetū constantly asked for Band-Aids for every little boo-boo. Sometimes I said, *"Leai se mana'omia."* ("No need.") When I did accede, they proudly wore their taped fingers or knees around the village.

### Paul Pulls Renee Toward Home

Then one day Renee called to say that she and Paul were going home. She said, "Paul just decided he'd had enough." Their ongoing issues in their village weren't any better and they hadn't been able to find other options. She'd told me previously that Paul couldn't stand not having something active to do all the time. That would definitely create additional challenges for a bored American pālagi in a small Samoan village!

*I'm sad that they're leaving. Now we're down by three. If they were unhappy, they shouldn't stay just because they felt they had to.*

Safiya had left suddenly with an illness. This leaving was different. It was by choice.

*At the fale 'i tai early in the morning, having a cup of tea and masi popo. I've been watching the water. Small schools of tiny fish about an inch and a half long were swimming close to shore. Now and then, larger fish enjoyed an easy breakfast. Now the tide is going out, and the little fish are beached here and there. A few make it back into the water when the right wave hits, but others don't— bird food. I've never had a chance to observe the ocean and marine life so closely. By the way, Niu thinks the "big fish" I saw not long ago was a reef shark and Tui's nephew told me a colony of sharks live by the island.*

Like the sharks lurking offshore, a bevy of emotions was always lying in wait beneath the surface. A few days later I wrote:

*I'm having a crying, blathering meltdown all out of proportion to what precipitated it. I had a nice talk with Saina today, one of the most relaxing times we've spent together. She told me that she and Niu were going to do some clearing this afternoon on land he's preparing by the government road for a fruit orchard. I told her I'd like to come and help, and she said she'd tell me when they were ready—and then they left without me, damn it! I was looking forward to doing some hands-on work. Why would she do that? I suppose a lot of pent-up emotions are coming out over this (duh!) but it's so emblematic. They tell me something, then don't follow through. I never feel a part of anything. I always feel like I'm in the way or interrupting something. Maybe they think I can't do physical work. Maybe they forgot, though that would be hurtful too. I want to be angry with her and tell her how it makes me feel. But it'd seem like I'm overreacting since much of this is coming from stuffing everything inside all the time and coping. But to say nothing would be to stuff it in once more. They have no idea how hard this is!*

I decided to fight saltwater with saltwater and wash away the tears as I floated in the warm sea. Because of the fringing reef the water was almost always calm in the small bay. There was a small pull toward the reef passage where the fishing boats went in and out. I could swim about fifty feet, then float in the slight current back to where I started and do it again in my very extraordinary endless pool.

*Next day . . . that was unexpected! No one can appreciate unless you've experienced it, how isolated you feel in a situation like this. I don't talk to Mom or the kids about it because I don't want them to worry. I try to tell Jackson what it's like, but I know he can't really understand. It's especially odd to say I feel "isolated" when there are people around all the time, but it's not home, and it's not the same.*

I told Saina I was disappointed that I didn't get to go and that I wanted to help next time. Firstly, she forgot. Then when she remembered, she thought I wouldn't have wanted to do that kind of physical work. I told her I was used to it and looking forward to it. Samoans seemed to think that a pālagi couldn't or wouldn't do strenuous physical labor. They'd say, *"Vāivai le tino o le pālagi,"* which means "Weak is the body of the pālagi." Other PCVs experienced the same thing. Or maybe it would have been shameful to have the elderly village pisikoa out hacking in the bush!

## *A Funeral*

I'd planned a visit to Manunu to see the family in March, but Roma called to tell me his mother had died. He asked me to come to the funeral set for ten days later.

I got up early and rode 'Afakasi's bus to Āpia. The custom for funeral attire was black and white, so I wore my white church puletasi top and a floor-length lāvalava of heavy-weight black fabric. Saina was a darling and met me at the fish market with a tuna sandwich for breakfast. She introduced me to her taxi driver cousin who would take me to Roma's parents' home in a small village on the other side of Āpia.

When I arrived, Roma asked me to sit by his father in front of the casket that was on a platform covered with expertly woven fine mats. It was overlaid with layers of white fabric, and a white lace canopy hung from the ceiling so that it resembled a four-poster bed. There in the open fale next to his parents' house, three dozen or more extended family, not counting children, prayed and sang tearfully together, led by the pastor and the choir of her church.

After the service, for more than two hours there was a formal presentation of gifts to the family from groups seated under a large tent outside—the women's fellowship from her church, a contingent from the church in the village where they'd lived before retiring (Roma's father was also a pastor), the congregation from Manunu, and others. With pomp and circumstance, his coconut sennit switch over his shoulder and talking stick firmly in hand, the orator from each group announced their presence, expressing gratitude, respect, and honor. A lengthy reply from the family orator followed as fine mats, money, cases of pisupo and canned herring, bolts of cloth, and flower arrangements were extravagantly displayed.

The flowers, with a couple of exceptions, were plastic—ironic in a place where lovely tropical flowers grew so profusely. I reasoned that they were preferred because they were still somewhat of a novelty, lasted longer, and maybe because they cost money, they had more value. In America we spend huge sums of money on fresh floral bouquets that wither on the cemetery ground within days and look with disdain on the entire wall of artificial flowers at the craft store that the same amount of money would buy.

The women of Manunu sang a hymn in harmony as they presented yards and yards of lacy white cloth from a mammoth bolt carried by ten women spaced several feet apart. That fabric and more was draped around the casket, mostly white lace and satin, but bright colors too. Each group left with mats and cases of corned beef or fish. After the exchange of gifts, the young men and women served us humongous plates of food. Then Roma's father opened the casket and the family gathered round to say good-bye with tears and kisses to her.

We walked to the village church where the two-hour service was much like a typical American Christian funeral with songs, a brief sermon, and eulogies from the family. When we returned, fine mats and intricately painted bark cloth (*siapo*) had been laid in the cement-lined grave alongside the house and the casket was wrapped with siapo. As her grandsons lowered the casket with ropes, the pastor said a few words, and the family sang a song ending with, "*Tōfā, tōfā, tōfā.*" ("Goodbye, goodbye, goodbye.")

After the burial, the remaining piles of fine mats, cases of cans, and a thick stack of cash were distributed amongst the family. Normally after such an event, the mats were rolled up and stored until the next funeral or wedding. I left at 2:30 via taxi while the distribution was still going on so I could catch the bus to Poutasi.

*All day I was treated as an honored guest. Although a certain amount of respect was due given my age, and my status as a pālagi and PCV, I wondered if I was an interloper at a sensitive time. I don't know if anyone saw me that way or if they were pleased with my presence. I hope the latter. I'm at the fale 'i tai in the cool of the evening. A little while ago I saw Mataomanu and asked how I can learn to weave mats. She said listen for the conch shell on Tuesdays.*

On the bus back home, I'd read an early 19th century poem by the Tongan poet and composer Falepapalangi in *The Girl in the Moon Circle* by Sia Figiel:

*If I give a mat it will rot,*
*If I give cloth it will be torn,*
*The poem is but bad, yet take it,*
*That it be to thee boat and house,*
*For thou art skilled in its taking,*
*And ever have I joyed*
*When the ignorant of heart have conned a poem*
*In companionship with the wise.*

The phrase, "*For thou art skilled in its taking*" intrigued me. Without trying to decipher any cultural implications or translation anomalies, how can someone be skilled in receipt of a poem? By listening, being attentive, letting it sink in and settle for a while, and then revisiting it again. By graciousness in the acceptance, knowing that the listener inevitably hears, at least at first, only the topmost layer of meaning. For what exposes our true self more than the writing of a poem and its sharing?

It often seemed as if I'd picked just the right book from the PC office shelves or the public library to find special resonance for me within those pages. I'm sure I was subconsciously looking for messages. Sometimes I found them.

### An Easter Promise

Good Friday started bright and early with church at 5:30. Each Sunday School class performed songs, dances, and Easter-themed skits. That afternoon, Hemara and I sat on my floor and rifled through stacks of old *Newsweek* magazines looking for pictures for her homework project. She made a booklet with stories about animals, and by the horse photo she wrote: "My brother likes to ride his horse to the plantation. The horse's name is Black Beauty. Black Beauty is 15 years old. He helps our family by carrying baskets and coconuts." She and I came from entirely different worlds, thousands of miles and forty-five years apart, but we'd both read *Black Beauty*.

On Easter morning, Hemara, Fetū, Tia, and Rocky tagged along on my usual walk along the ocean's edge, running ahead, dawdling, catching up. It rained lightly on us, followed by a spectacular rainbow arching over Nu'usafe'e Island. Niu and Saina had planned to take the family that afternoon to play on the wide beach at Tafatafa, two villages down the road. However, Letone reminded everyone in his sermon that we should take time to reflect on the significance of the day. So they decided it wouldn't be appropriate. Nonetheless, I felt in a celebratory mood, especially since Saina brought pizza from Āpia for dinner the night before, plus sour cream potato chips with dip and Coke!

The next morning, the women of the church cleaned up outside the pastor's house and the hall, trimming bushes, pulling weeds, cutting the grass, and raking with coconut frond spine brooms. I didn't ask; I just joined them. It was good language practice listening to the women talk among themselves and I caught up on the local gossip. They served food after, of course. I was hungry and ate two slices of taro and three barbequed chicken legs.

*The tide is coming in. I went for a swim and now I'm relaxed watching the last fading lemon-yellow glow in the west. A few lights in Sāleilua are twinkling in the trees. It's getting too dark to write. I'll sit for a while and enjoy the end of another day.*

Later, Hemara sat on my bed with pad and pencil in hand to write a poem about Easter for school the next morning. Together we came up with rhyming couplets that told about her weekend and the resurrection, with way too much giggling for "the significance of the day."

*She's so bright and capable. I promised her I'll buy her a ticket to Hawai'i when she graduates from the university. I have no doubt she'll do it. I can't wait to see her as a young woman.*

# Chapter 8

# Adjusting to Fa'aSāmoa

*'O le fuata ma lona lou*
*"Each harvest has its own tool"*
*Every problem has its own solution.*

Earlier that evening when I'd come in from the sea, I left my swim shorts outside the door to dry, and by the next morning someone had taken them. This was a common occurrence that I never got used to. For example:

*I walked to the store for some oranges and a Coke and the store was closed. So now I'm hot and sweaty after walking nearly a mile and I have nothing to show for my effort. Well, that's not quite true. On the way back I met two young boys who had my scrub sponge, which I'd put on the bench in front of the house to dry. You can't leave anything out here. I recently bought my fourth pair of flip flops. Two pairs mysteriously disappeared, although I probably left them by the door, which is like asking someone to take them. I left another pair in the hallway while I was in Colorado. When I came back and asked Hemara, she said she wore them to the beach. I never saw them again. I didn't make a big deal of it because it's the way it is. But you'd think you could leave a goddamn sponge in front of your door!*

The textbooks say that communal societies share their goods rather than valuing individual ownership. That's a fancy way of saying that it's no big deal if someone uses your stuff, and it's only stealing if they don't admit to taking it.

Although there was outright thievery. A month after I'd arrived in Poutasi, I was invited to observe the weekly matai meeting where they'd discussed a recent theft at length. Two young men from the village had stolen one of Niu's young steers pastured on the government road. They then tried to sell him in a neighboring village.

*As I write, I can hear him bellowing from where he's tied behind the house. I'm not sure if there will be any official government action. From what I've learned thus far, most of these matters are handled by the matai. Last evening the two young men sat cross-legged in front of our house for at least an hour, heads bowed, apologizing profusely. They'll also have to pay a fine to the village. Niu told me, "The rest is up to God."*

And there was inveterate pilferage. The first time that the Sāleilua primary school principal showed me around, he'd told me that a "sister school" in Australia had donated desks, chairs, computers, and sports equipment to the school when it was built two years earlier. When its construction was completed, several people "helped themselves" to some of the computers and the sports equipment.

Like many South Pacific island nations, Samoa was heavily dependent upon foreign aid that came with inherent corruption risks. In conversations with other Peace Corps volunteers, and even in Peace Corps training, we were cautioned that sometimes, "It's all about the money." The following hypothetical scenario was typical. A village might get funding for a construction project. If it would cost $100,000 tala to do it properly, the Matai Council would get a contractor (almost certainly family members of one of the chiefs) to build an inferior project for $75,000 tala, and they'd split the rest of the money amongst themselves. More and more, to help prevent that temptation, projects were funded with intermittent disbursements, like the periodic Marine

Project checks from the United Nations, written only when milestones in our plan were reached.

A Samoan friend told me a story about two New Zealand policemen visiting Āpia for a law enforcement conference. They were riding in a taxi with a Samoan policeman when the driver was pulled over for speeding. He turned to the Samoan policeman in the back and asked for $50 tala, which he handed to him. The driver gave it to the cop who stopped them, who then tore up the ticket. The Kiwis were astounded and asked the Samoan policeman if that happens all the time, and he said, "Of course!"

In addition to those rather petty offenses was the greater widespread bribery and corruption, from the village level to the upper echelons, in Samoa and throughout the South Pacific. Candidates for the Samoan parliament were expected to provide gifts of food and money to voters in an electoral system run entirely by one party. The Human Rights Protection Party (HRPP) had held office continuously since 1985 and the parliament wasn't much more than a convenient rubber stamp for the HRPP. The head of state was a ceremonial position; the actual power was held by the prime minister and the cabinet. Government positions were created frequently as political rewards, leading even to an increase in the size of the cabinet at one point as those at the top jockeyed for position and power.

Although not necessarily the result of corruption, government decision-making was often inexplicable. One of the biggest events to happen while I was there was the change from driving on the right side of the road to the left, and opposition had been brewing for months. In April 2008, Saina and I went to Āpia for a protest march against the change. PCVs were forbidden to participate in anything political, so I took photos from the sidelines on Beach Road as the line of marching men, women, and children stretched as I far as I could see in both directions. More than ten thousand marched according to the local news reports.

*Either the prime minister, or someone who suggested it to him, thought the change would be a good idea and so it was apparently introduced with little research or forethought. Now he'd lose face to change his mind. Or, there's some money involved under the table. Either or both are possible.*

*With the likelihood of increased accidents and exiting buses in the middle of the road (at least in the beginning), it would be dangerous. It's expensive for bus companies and taxis, many of whom are individuals, to replace or retrofit their vehicles. It will cost the government millions of tala when they could spend that money on other more important infrastructure or education. Some of the main reasons to purportedly justify it are questionable. They say that car dealers can then order directly from Korea and Japan. However, an article in the* Samoan Observer *said they already order directly from those countries. Another argument for it is that extended family in New Zealand and Australia can then send used cars and it'd be easier for them to drive here. I was talking to someone while waiting for the bus the other day and I said, "I just don't see what's in it for Samoa?" The response was, "There's obviously something in it for someone."*

*It'll probably pass in parliament, although two MPs have quit the HRPP in protest and others have threatened. The protest march made me proud of the democratic process and the Samoans. Nothing like this has ever happened here. There's definitely negative sentiment toward the Prime Minister. Even so, after the march they assembled at the government building and sang Happy Birthday to him.*

Eventually, the movement, People Against Switching Sides (PASS), sued all the way to the Supreme Court arguing it breached the constitution and would cause loss of life. But the court disagreed, saying it wasn't proven that more accidents would mean more road fatalities. PASS also asserted the change would harm the fragile local economy and estimated the retrofit to cost $2.5 million tala.

Nevertheless, a year and a half later in September 2009, with a two-day national holiday and a three-day ban on alcohol sales, Samoa became the first country in forty years to switch driving sides. Incredibly, at the time it was implemented, the Prime Minister stated per a newspaper article that the issue of buses with both doors and steering now on the wrong side had yet to be addressed.

There were already numerous right-hand-drive vehicles in Samoa—I rode in them many times—just on the "wrong" side of the road. At the time of the switch, cars with steering wheels on either the left or the right side could remain but were to drive on the left. Eight years later, the Prime Minister reversed the ban on importing left-hand-drive vehicles. He said that the change was due to rules of the World Trade Organization of which Samoa had become a member and because people wanted to bring in American vehicles. This 2017 article sums it up well:

> https://www.talanei.com/2017/03/06/
> samoa-will-accept-right-hand-drive-cars-again/
> The PM said while left hand drive vehicles from American Samoa and the US will be allowed, Samoa will strictly enforce the policy of only vehicles manufactured in 2009 up to now will be accepted.
>
> He said no begging on bended knee to get the minister or CEO of the Land Transport Authority to give exceptions to this rule will work.
>
> "And don't think of coming to me...I'll just send you back to the minister," said Tuilaepa.
>
> The Samoa Observer quotes the Land Transport Authority

saying that up to 100 left hand drive vehicles will be allowed in per month.

Since the switch to right hand drive vehicles, traffic jams in urban Āpia at peak hours in the morning and after work have been exacerbated.

*At the fale 'i tai . . . the water is beautifully blue and so clear that I can see dozens of fish swimming about. Someone took the clothesline I'd put up here. Truthfully, I'm surprised it took that long; it had been up about a month.*

## The People Will Come

About the same time as the protest march, New Zealand's Minister for Pacific Affairs visited Samoa. Through Tuatagaloa Joe's connections, his delegation came to Poutasi and were greeted with an 'ava ceremony at our *fale tele*. A fale tele (round house) or a *fale āfolau* (long house) were the main buildings on a family compound and the pride of the extended family. It was a meeting house, a space for funerals or parties, or to welcome guests. And it was a good place for kids to play on rainy days or for women to weave mats. It's size, floor height, number of beams, décor, and carvings all reflected the owner's social standing within the village. Ours was the only fale tele in the village; all others were long houses.

Our family fale tele from my front door. Meleisea Seti and Mataomanu's family
compound is behind the fale tele.

That morning I photographed the preparations—young men
climbing the breadfruit tree for leaves to wrap around the soon-to-be
baking palusami, starting the umu fire, scraping coconuts for coconut
cream, and cutting and braiding palm leaves to bedeck the posts at the
fale tele. Very early I'd heard a pig squeal, so I assumed he was part of
the entree. But I puzzled over whether I should have been there.

*This afternoon I walked to the store and Mataomanu called to
me. She said they missed me at the ceremony. I said I didn't know
I was invited. She said I should come to everything in the village. This is a cultural quandary. I just finished reading* To A
God Unknown *by John Steinbeck. In the book, an Anglo man
in frontier California decides to have a fiesta and wonders aloud
to a Mexican man, "Who should I invite?" The old man responds,
"Invite? You do not 'invite,' señor . . . I will tell that you make a fiesta on the New Year, and the people will come." Maybe it's like that*

*in Samoa. Maybe I shouldn't wait to be "invited," but (assuming I know about it), just go.*

The following weekend I visited Manunu bearing gifts for Donna La'itiiti. It was the end of April and she was turning one already!

*When one of the family says, "Donna," sometimes I respond, though they're not talking to me but to Donna La'itiiti. I thought it'd be an honorary name, so I'm always a little surprised and I cherish the accolade.*

It was always a treat to be there for a couple of days. Like Sinalei, it felt farther away than it was. As the crow flies it was only ten miles directly across the central mountain range from Poutasi, but it took two bus rides with an overnight stop in Āpia to get there. Inland at an elevation of five hundred feet, surrounded by flourishing greenery on low mountains, Manunu was a substantial change from my usual life on the beach.

And then I heard the unsettling news of another Group 78 departure.

### Mark's Village Drives Him Away

One afternoon Mark called to tell me he'd resigned. His village had been approved for a sizeable grant upon his request. However, the village was supposed to match ten percent in cash and the matai said he should pay it. He'd paid to have the family dog neutered and it later died, so they blamed him. And he was concerned about what he saw as child abuse when the children were disciplined. In two months, we'd lost four people from Group 78.

It was interesting for me to observe myself and others as we came to Samoa for various reasons, adapting or not, and putting in our time.

I'd thought that the young people would have a harder time because they were just starting out in life, while those of us who were older had years of experience. However, the first to leave voluntarily were Renee and Paul and they "should" have fit into the life experience category. Then again, us "older" folks are set in our ways or may have particular expectations, whereas young people are more flexible and adventurous.

*As for me, my pride and desire to achieve and prove myself will keep me here for at least some period. In fairness, I've been dealt a good hand—village-wise and family-wise. Of course, people sometimes win even without the best hand, so it's not always clear cut. I don't know what I would've done in Mark's situation.*

When I went to Samoa I had intended to stay for the entire two years of service (plus the three months of training), and after that travel to Australia and New Zealand for fun. By now, Group 78 had been in the country for eleven months and our scheduled departure date was a year and four months away. After Mark left, I deliberated with myself for several days. I'd originally planned to fly to the States in June of the following year, three months before the official end of our service, to celebrate my son Geoffrey's wedding. I was going to make the trip and then return to finish my service in Samoa. However after my ponderings, I concluded that I'd go home the following summer and cut my service short by three months.

Maybe it was my fellow volunteers' departures, the emotional ups and downs, or my inherent practicality that wanted to save money on airfare, but I persuaded myself that by that time I'd have been in the country for two years, and that was enough. And perhaps having a sooner date for my ultimate departure made the present a bit easier to bear. My decision would mean traveling to New Zealand and Australia earlier than I'd planned. So I contacted my friend Rona in New Zealand about a visit in October and made plans with my Colorado friend Rosi to meet in Australia in August.

*Things are generally going well, but I'll be glad to be home to the comforts and familiarities of life in the USA. I'll miss the people and living next to the ocean, but I'll be ready to leave. At this point it's mostly a job I've got to finish.*

*There's such a love/hate connection for Peace Corps volunteers. Frustration, anger, hurt feelings, misunderstandings, loneliness, boredom, inertia—friendship, exhilaration, gratitude, kindness, satisfaction, appreciation, amusement. Sweat, lice, diarrhea, centipedes, pisupo, scary dogs, cold showers—sea breezes, beaches, mangoes, sunsets, snorkeling, no shoes, the laughter of children.*

*It's like being on a small boat at sea. Sometimes the ocean swells are coming from afar, and although the weather's fine in Samoa, I can feel the effect of a storm thousands of miles away. Sometimes the sea is rough, and my fragile boat rises with a huge wave and then plunges into the trough, over and over again. Occasionally a storm threatens and I'm caught unaware, holding on for dear life, hoping I'll live to tell the tale. And sometimes it's blessedly peaceful, as I glide over the crystal-clear water with ease, a few white fluffy clouds in the brilliantly blue sky, the warmth of the sun on my back, looking to the horizon with anticipation.*

*Only seven days left in April! Next month I can say that "next month" it'll be only one year until I go home. We each do what we can, and that's enough.*

### Bumbye: Adapting to Life on Samoan Time

Even though I was counting the months, the actual dates didn't mean much. I rarely had a specific personal or work-related agenda to focus on, so the time just slipped gently by.

One may think that Samoa was in a time zone like all those distributed around the world, but you'd be wrong. Yes, technically, if you're measuring such temporal necessities, our time zone name was "Western Samoa Time," and our clocks were set one hour earlier than Hawai'i. We were a short distance from the International Date Line and the last sunset on the planet each evening.[7] But the reality was that Samoa was in its own time zone called "Whenever."

The constant delays were maddening as I tried to figure out how to manage my projects. The carpenter would promise to be there in the afternoon and not show up. And then the next day, maybe he'd come and maybe he wouldn't. I called the electrician to set up a time for an estimate and he didn't return my calls. And then when we finally connected, it was the same as the carpenter; maybe he'd show up and maybe he wouldn't.

*I don't want to be too pushy, but if this was a project in the States it'd be a piece of cake. I'd just organize, assign, and get it done.*

Our PC Committee meetings never started on time. Fortunately, the meetings were at our family's house, so I could patiently read or write while I waited.

*We held our PC Komiti meeting today, even though we started two hours after the "scheduled" time. Surprise, surprise. Fa'aSāmoa. Meleisea Seti wasn't there, and Valasi is in Pago Pago because her niece died of dengue fever. A teenager, so sad.*

---

7 Samoa switched time zones on December 29, 2011. This change resulted in Samoa being west of the International Date Line (IDL) sharing the same day of the week with Australia and New Zealand, two of its major trading partners. The IDL now passes between Samoa and American Samoa, which remains on the east side of the line.

I could go on and on with examples. When one vacations in other countries where the concept of time is like that in Samoa, it's charmingly refreshing. Of course, with my penchant for efficiency inherited from my German forefathers, and my American ways of doing things, neither "charming" nor "refreshing" were words that came to mind. I did become much more patient and understanding though. I began to never expect things to actually happen when they said they would, and so occasionally I was pleasantly surprised.

I thought that living in Hawai'i would prepare me for living in Wheneverland since life moves at a slower pace there too. But I'll never again complain about living on "Hawaiian Time." It seems positively punctual by comparison. A word from Hawaiian pidgin comes to mind—"bumbye." When the missionaries came to Hawai'i, they taught the Hawaiians many traditional hymns. One of the hymns was "In the Sweet By and By," suggesting we'll be together in heaven someday—maybe not today, maybe not tomorrow, but someday—by and by. It became "bumbye" in pidgin and means I'll get around to it. So to be on "Samoan time" was to rarely be hurried, to get to it when you get to it, and understand that sometimes it's just not that important.

### Crystal Evaporates and I'm Feeling Blue

My boat was rocked again when I got a text message telling me that Crystal was leaving. She was fed up with trying to work with a difficult counterpart in her village. I knew she'd had some challenges, but I thought she was coping okay.

*I'm surprised but not shocked. At this point, I wouldn't be shocked if any of us left. I've decided that earlier I was too inwardly critical of the decisions of some Group 78 volunteers to leave. If you want to go home, so be it. Sometimes we criticize what we don't like or fear about ourselves.*

*At this point I'd feel like a quitter, like I'd disappoint my family and friends who said all those wonderful things about being so proud of me. I'd let down the village—but they'd get over it. Hmmm, this is the most serious thought I've given to it or given voice to. Maybe it's because others are leaving. Maybe it's just this point in PC service.*

But my malaise continued into May.

*I can't break out of feeling sorry for myself. There's nothing big, just small shit. I know little things here can get me down more than in "real life" but I'm not sure how to get past it. Niu, Saina, and friends are talking loudly and break out in riotous laughter in the kitchen; I've lost count of the number of children shouting and racing through the house; three old ladies are prattling outside my window; the church bell is ringing; and a rooster has decided to crow outside the other window in the middle of the afternoon. And, I don't feel well. I'm achy, have a stuffy nose, and an upset stomach. I don't have any meds to take, and there's no Walmart down the street with a plethora of drugs to cure anything that ails you.*

I began to have lingering thoughts of going home sooner than June of the following year. The Homework Center would be established with the long-term goal to leave it for the village to operate. The Marine Project would still be in progress, but Tuatagaloa Joe could continue to manage it. I was worried about Mom's health and Uncle Bob and I missed the kids and their families. Even though they were spread all over the country, at home I could talk, text, or Skype with them often—practically for free compared to international rates, with no time limit. And I could be with them from time to time.

*I struggle with both sides of the question. On one hand I'd feel like I wimped out and disappointed the village, Group 78, and myself.*

*On the other hand, if I stay until the end of the year, I'll have been in Samoa for a year and a half and I'll have started some good projects. In any case I'm not leaving until after my trip to New Zealand in October. But maybe I'll be home by Christmas, or maybe everything will be going so great that I'll stay for the duration.*

*I skipped going to church this afternoon, ostensibly because I have a cold. I'm just weary of church. I read an entire book today, City of Light by Lauren Belfer. Now I'm out of books and Radio Australia is off the air, maybe for a few hours or (hopefully not) for a few days. So, I'll resort to crosswords and computer games. I'll stay in Poutasi tomorrow, which I like to do on Mondays if I can, so that I can spend time with Saina. New solitaire record: 11,778; 63 seconds.*

Mother's Day in Samoa was the same date in May as in the States (although Father's Day was in August not June) and it was another occasion for lots of church. At the three-hour morning service, all the mothers wore a new puletasi and hats with ribbons, flowers, and feathers, all in white. Uncharacteristically, the women took center stage and led the prayer, read the Bible selection, and gave a short sermon. That was followed by songs and dances, and an entertaining skit in costume portraying great mothers in history—Eve, Ruth, Mary, and ending with Winnie Mandela. I loved the music and dance in Samoa, which was everywhere and always. From wee childhood, Samoan youth were taught, and expected, to perform at church, school, village, and family events. It was second nature, and no one felt too shy or less talented.

Early that Sunday morning, Niu, Saina, Tamamasui, and the kids drove to town to attend church and celebrate the day with Saina's mother and family. I ate Sunday dinner with Tuatagaloa Joe, Tui, their son, daughter, and their families on the deck overlooking the bay at their new fale. I reveled in the food from Sinalei—delicious beef Wellington, scalloped potatoes, an eggplant and tomato dish, boysenberry ice cream with bread pudding, and a glass of white wine. Stuffed, I took a nap, then sat at the fale ʻi tai and "traveled to" Atlanta, Denver, and San Diego as my sons called me, and I called Mom. I always tried to illustrate the view before me with words—the small cove with the vast ocean beyond, the white coral beach on Nuʻusafeʻe Island glistening in the midday sun—knowing full well that I could never really describe what it was like. Mostly I wanted to hear news from home even though the conversations were too short. Geoffrey talked about wedding plans; Jay laughed as he told me about Jayden's first steps; Thomas said it was still below freezing at night in Colorado; and Mom loved the two dozen multi-colored roses I'd sent.

*It's been blessedly quiet with everyone gone. I'm a bit beyond my wanting to go home phase. I wasn't* seriously *contemplating it at the moment, but when I feel that way it's hard to take on new challenges, or put up with the usual ones. I'm by the sea reading* North Toward Home *by Willie Morris. Tuatagaloa Joe said next Wednesday is okay for our next village meeting with MNRE about the Marine Project. I'll set that up then we can announce it at both church services on Sunday, so that people will know.*

# Chapter 9

# Projects Come to Fruition

*Ua tofo i tino matagi lelei*
*"A favorable wind is felt on the body"*
*One feels the joy of expectation.*

Despite my sporadic discontent I had been busily coordinating the finishing touches on the Homework Center: tear out the concrete wall between the storeroom and shower to make it longer, disconnect plumbing, construct a new concrete block wall and a louvered window, do electrical work, build the countertop along the wall for three computers and printer/copier, add bookshelves (eventually filled with donated books, puzzles, and school/craft supplies), install equipment, and voila: a Homework Center. That straight forward rendition of tasks makes it sound simpler than it was. It took seven months to get the funding, do the construction, and figure out how to teach computer classes and help kids with homework.

*I'm watching the ocean from the fale 'i tai in the afternoon breeze. It's too hot inside the house. The electrician is working at the Homework Center. The carpenter is supposed to come tomorrow.*

Of course, the carpenter didn't come the next day, but eventually he did, and then it was finally done! We'd scheduled a Ribbon Cutting for May 25th, and that was only a few days away. Niu suggested that we have a sign painted for the "Poutasi Homework Center" and requested it from a guy he knew who'd recently made signs for the national park.

*Yay! The computers all work! I need a USB connection to the print-er which I'll buy in Āpia next week, but the copier function works. The room is ready and looks great!*

It was a beautiful sunny day for the Ribbon Cutting, with a light breeze rippling the edge of the small white tent that faced the berib-boned red wooden door of the center. Under the welcome shade, vil-lage leaders and invited dignitaries took their places on folding chairs, women in their finest colorful puletasi and men in their business attire of aloha shirts and lāvalava.

Niu at the Ribbon Cutting.

Niu was well versed in chiefly language and spoke eloquently as he recounted the short story of how we'd come to this day. After the proper introductions, there were speeches by representatives from the NZ High Commission, the Country Director of Peace Corps, and the Division of Internal Affairs. Then, dressed in pastor's-wife-white, wear-ing a bright red hat, Logo cut the ribbon across the door. It was finally official after an 'ava ceremony with the matai at our family fale tele with more elaborate and lengthy speechifying. Back at the hall, the village then presented fine mats and roast suckling pigs in baskets woven from coconut fronds to the honored guests, followed by music, dancing, and lots of food, while I gave tours of our tiny Homework Center.

That part was exhilarating, but after three hours of these festivities the real fun began when the village's sixty primary school children sat cross-legged in the hall and boisterously sang the Samoan national anthem. They'd all heard about "The Homework Center" but at that moment they were more enthused about what was about to happen—a kids craft fair! Three Group 78 volunteers, Erin, Justin, and Hannah (and her Samoan boyfriend Leleiga) painted hearts, flowers, Samoan flags or Superman logos on smiling young faces and helped the kids make paper plate masks and paper bag puppets. I manned the coloring station with photocopied coloring book pages, popular with all ages and sexes, which gave me freedom to wander about taking photos, always with the "requirement" that I show the pictures to the kids on the viewing screen immediately after.

Then I walked home and took a nap—Samoan style.

Poutasi children ready to sing in the church hall on Ribbon Cutting Day.

Hemara and her friend Lemapu with their paper bag puppets.

Paper plate mask fun.

I loved seeing their beautiful smiles.

Homework center before; shower at end removed and blocked off.

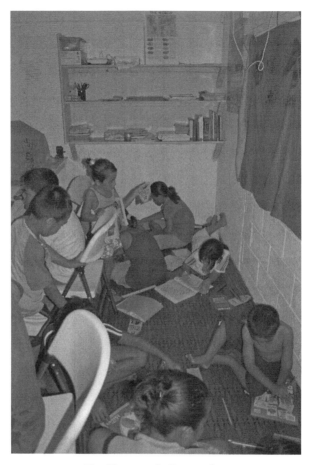

The Homework Center after.

It had been a slog to get to this point—the delays, the no-shows, the confusion, the expectations, and the pressure I put on myself. But it all came together that day, unquestionably one of the best days I spent in Samoa. So many emotions flowed through me—apprehension, joy, pride, elation, enthusiasm, relief, hope. When those eager young voices reverberated in the hall, excited faces looking toward me, I knew that although I was still inwardly anxious at the prospect of teaching them how to use a computer, I could do it.

## One Year in Samoa

*It's early morning by the beautiful sea. The drums are calling for some event. The center won't be officially "open" to the public until after school starts on June 9th. I'm trying to devise a schedule and lessons. I don't want to be tied to it every day, yet it needs to be often to make it useful. It'll help the boredom and keep me be occupied enough to feel productive.*

The supervision of the remodel of the Homework Center, preparations for opening day, and the simultaneous beginning of the Marine Project had kept me busy. By this time, I'd settled in with the family and into a routine of sorts, although no day was ever the same. On a typical morning, I'd walk the half mile to the edge of Sāleilua and back, enjoy breakfast at the fale 'i tai, and work on "PC paperwork." Sometimes I'd attend a village event, but many days were spent reading, writing, and watching the clouds, the ocean, and the sunset. After dinner I'd pop a DVD into my laptop or read, then listen to Radio Australia until I fell asleep.

On weekends and school breaks I spent time with the kids (and usually their friends) and became their pālagi aunty. Although I often wrote about my frustration and need for quiet time, in hindsight I have no doubt that this chattering trio of Samoan children kept me from loneliness and brought me many more smiles than frowns.

*Fetū and Tia are sitting on the floor coloring and Hemara is laying on my bed reading. I know they have nothing else to do other than watch TV, so I'm being patient. Only one more week before school starts again.*

During the school break, Niu took a Monday off so we could go play and picnic on my first trip to Nu'usafe'e. We clambered into a small fishing boat loaded with food baskets and towels and sped over the small bay to the island. Once ashore, the kids ran in and out of the waves, shrieking happily when one caught them unaware. I snorkeled, but the water was too choppy to see well. Mostly I relaxed in the sun with Niu and Saina, using a fallen tree weathered smooth by the wind and sea as our makeshift table. I gazed back at the village—the exact opposite view from the one I had looking toward the island. Poutasi looked small and insignificant from even that short distance, but our family's turquoise roof was easy to identify across from the fale 'i tai.

Looking out to sea toward the reef from the white sand beach.

*Since I plan to stay through October at a minimum, I wrote the number of weeks left until then on my calendar—twenty-three weeks. It's not very long when I look at it that way. From the* Incredible Lightness of Being *by Milan Kundera: "Being in a foreign country means walking a tightrope high above the ground without the net afforded a person by the country where he has his family, colleagues, and friends, and where he can easily say what he has to say in a language he has known from childhood."*

### *Mary's Illness Separates Her From Nick*

One week before Group 78 had been in Samoa for a year, Mary called to say she was reluctantly resigning. Over the months she'd contracted several staph and strep infections from relatively small cuts, and was even hospitalized in Āpia twice. The local doctor recommended that she go home. Nick decided to stay in their village while she went to live with their daughter in the States.

> *I'm glad for her health's sake, but I'll miss her. I'll be the only woman left from our group not living in Āpia. I'll get through the next few months and see how things are going.*

To celebrate our one-year anniversary, the four remaining Group 78 women, Kaitlen, Erin, Hannah, and I, nibbled cucumber sandwiches and squishy cream puff bites at high afternoon tea at the Plantation House in Āpia. The dining area was under a fale tele open to tropical green, fishponds, and trailing bougainvillea in many colorful shades. Surrounded by potted palms, we perched on wicker chairs and toasted our future with delicate teacups. I hesitantly told them how I felt about going home by the end of the year, feeling like one more dropout but also with a sense of relief that I'd said it out loud. It wasn't just a conversation I was having with myself in my head anymore. It was real.

There was serious doubt about whether the four of us would be in Samoa for one more year. Kaitlen seemed iffy. She'd moved from her village on Savai'i to an office at the Ministry of Agriculture, but she also felt the pull of home. Hannah was trying to change from her non-profit job to teach biology at a secondary school in Āpia but didn't know yet if that would happen. She and Leleiga, my "brother" in Manunu, were making plans to marry and working on paperwork for him to emigrate. Erin had been frustrated with her job at Fisheries from the beginning but was on a plateau for the moment.

*As for me, I'm in a good mood again. Maybe it's just part of the cycle. Maybe it's because I've decided (at this point) to go home at the end of the year. And yet, it feels like more effort than I want to expend right now. That sums up a lot of how it is here in Samoa. Everything is such an effort. It just wears you out after a while. And it's not like things are*  *going badly. Quite the contrary. One never knows how it'll be until they try something. For me, one year is enough, a year and a half will be a real test, and if I make it to two years, I'll be surprised.*

*I know I only see Niu, Saina, the family, the village, PC staff, and everyone in the country, from my own perspective—from the window through which I see the world, tinted with the events of my lifetime. And they see me through their windows, which are similarly colored with their own prism of experiences. No matter how we try to empathize and understand, to put ourselves in the shoes of others, that's never entirely possible. I'm sure that from their point of view, I often seem foolish and hard to understand.*

*On a totally different subject, I heard that the American economy is in a slump and gas is nearly $4.00 USD /gallon. Clinton conceded the nomination to Obama last weekend. I wish I could follow the election more closely, but I'm relieved not to have to put up with the spin and excesses of the process. Sometimes it's nice to hear only the big news from the States, and not to have to deal with the day-to-day stuff, or the bad news.*

*The evening bell is ringing—it's 6:00. I'm losing the light at the fale 'i tai.*

I whined a lot to myself in May and early June when I hit a new low in my ability to cope. Was it because fellow volunteers seemed to go home every time I turned around? Or because I was jittery about teaching computer classes? The perceived weight of the expectations of the village on my shoulders? Our group's one-year anniversary on my grandson's first birthday? Missing Jackson? Add to that the intimacy of life in a Samoan household and village. It was probably all the above.

*I've been studying computer lessons from the PC office and trying to get my courage up to teach at the Homework Center. Tomorrow will be our official opening. I've just finished a light dinner and I'm sitting at the fale 'i tai. Despite how hard it's been up till now, I dread it becoming just a job.*

## I Get Tattooed

I was also trying to muster up my courage to do what almost every PCV in Samoa did—get a tattoo. Not many Polynesian words have entered the English language, but perhaps the most widely used is tattoo. Exactly where and when the word originated is open to debate but it's certain that it was a corruption of the Polynesian word *tatau*, picked up by early European sailors exploring the Southern Ocean.

Since more than half of volunteers got inked, there was even a specific tattooist that our Peace Corps Medical Officer recommended. Most PCVs chose traditional designs applied with traditional implements—pointed metal combs (made of bone in the old days) dipped in black dye and tapped into the skin with a wooden mallet. I watched several times as the master tattooist was assisted by up to six helpers who often wished to become masters themselves. One mixed the dyes, another wiped away the blood, another dipped the instruments into the dye and received used ones, another cleaned and sharpened the teeth of the metal combs, and one or two held the skin tight. Young women sat by the person being tattooed, held them down to limit movement, massaged the head, and cooled the sweat with a laufala fan.

In my case, I had the tattoo artist use his electric instruments because I wanted color that wasn't applied with the traditional tools. I sketched an idea of what I wanted, and together we created the finished pattern—a pink and yellow frangipani flower with a black border design. It took only about a half hour to ink it on the back of my right shoulder. It hurt, but it helped to take my mind off getting punctured with needles by closing my eyes and thinking of something pleasant, like sitting by the pool at Sinalei, which I planned to do that afternoon.

Nearly all Samoan men and women were tattooed. The most prized tattoos for men covered their bodies from their bellies to above the knees and took forty or fifty hours over multiple sessions to complete. The ink coverage was so extensive and the design so intricate, that on first glance it looked like they wore tight, short pants, like bike shorts. The ships' logs of many early explorers recorded the presence of "britches" on Samoan males. Women's traditional tattoos were smaller and more delicate tribal designs that wrapped around both thighs.

### Banishment Hits Close to Home

One morning over breakfast with Tui and Tuatagaloa Joe, he told me that the weekly matai council meeting had lasted for ten hours! The topic that kept the chiefs all day was banishment of two people from the village. The matai made the decision after Tuatagaloa Joe left at 3:00 PM to go to a meeting in Āpia, but he planned to meet separately with the other high chiefs to discuss it further.

Over the next few days, I heard various details. One of those banished was a married man having an affair with a single woman in the village. In an unrelated tryst, a woman was banished as well. She'd left her husband in another village some time before and moved back to Poutasi. At that time, a delegation had gone from Poutasi and made a formal apology to her husband's family and his village. She'd then had an affair with a man in Poutasi, who'd since left the village. The matai discussed her case first and decided on lifetime banishment. Then the other case came up, and since they'd set a precedent, so to speak, he received the same punishment.

> *I knew about banishment, but I thought it only applied to serious crimes. I don't know if there'll be punishment for the other parties in the adultery. I'll await further developments.*

It had been four decades since Dad abandoned our family for an affair. I was sixteen when he left, and he missed my first serious boy-friend, my senior prom, and wasn't there for high school graduation. When he and Mom reconciled three years later, I was in college in another state. With their whole hearts, they began a new phase of their marriage and they were deeply in love the rest of their lives. The affair was never spoken of again. Ever. I truly forgave Dad, and as the years went by I rarely thought of it. Yet, I've wondered how it affected my relationships and my ambivalence about commitment.

Dad died at eighty-one, eighteen months before I left for Samoa. His name was Donald and I was his namesake. We loved one another in that special way of daughters and dads, and he was always my biggest fan. Traveling was one of his favorite pursuits. I know he'd have loved to hear my stories from Samoa and would've bragged to everyone he knew about his adventurous daughter in the Peace Corps.

### The Poutasi Homework Center

*"Āoga komepiuta i lenei aso?"* ("Is there computer school today?") asked twelve-year-old Milana as he deferentially approached me. I was sitting in my usual chair at the fale 'i tai, facing the ocean, working on my PC quarterly report with my laptop on a tray.

My office by the sea.

*"Leai. Auā, e mafai ona 'ou alu i le center i tasi itula."* ("No. But I can go to the center in one hour.")

*"Fa'afetai!"* ("Thanks!") he said with a smile and scampered away down the dusty road.

Computer school, as he called it, would be good for me. I'd been feeling bored and kind of lonesome. Going to the Homework Center always lifted my spirits.

I'd been so nervous about "teaching computers." But as it turned out, tutoring someone who'd never seen one was easier than I thought—how to turn it on and off and use a mouse, how to create and save a file, open a file, work on a project, and save it again. I also taught key-boarding basics and beginning word processing.

In the days before school resumed, I'd made sure all the connections and programs worked and installed educational games. One of my favorites was Sobran word and math games in many languages, including Samoan. I also installed Snood, a puzzle game excellent for learning mouse skills. I eventually had to limit the amount of time they played it because it was such good fun that even I nearly became addicted after adding it to my laptop! Another favorite was Typer Shark.[8] It was great for learning the keyboard and had different levels. My rules were that they had to take basic keyboarding lessons before they could play it, and stay in home position, not hunt-and-peck.

While I was attending to these last-minute details, I was delighted that about ten boys and girls dropped by at various times through word of mouth. They practiced, while I practiced on them. I discovered that MS Paint was not only good for mouse skills, but could be turned into a geography lesson when they picked a flag from the back of a donated atlas, drew it with Paint, read about the country, and found it on the world map taped to the wall.

The week before the official opening, I'd given a Homework Center schedule to Letone and the priest to announce on Sunday. The following Tuesday I was positively overwhelmed! I was there for seven straight hours!

I'd scheduled lesson time for adults from 2:00 to 4:00 PM. At first no one came, and then Fuifui, who used a computer at her Āpia job, came to write a church announcement, and then Logo came. She knew how to type but had never used a computer. While Fuifui typed, I showed Logo some basics. So, it started off nice and slow.

---

8 "Typer Shark® Sink your teeth into an action-packed educational adventure. Hungry sharks and piranhas are on the hunt for food as you SCUBA dive into the deep blue unknown. But if you can type words fast enough, they'll be zapped before they can turn you into lunch."

Logo practices at her computer lesson.

The time for kids to start was at 4:00 PM. They began showing up a little after 3:00 and an hour later there were thirty excited boys and girls waiting outside! This presented quite a challenge for a room that was only the size of a large closet. Logo came to my rescue and acted as doorkeeper and monitor. We rotated in groups with one at a computer and two watching, then switched. When it became obvious that not everyone would get a chance, I told the girls that their turn would be later that week since we'd started with the boys.

I'd planned to take a short break and then help with homework from 6:00 to 7:00. There was no time for a break, and then fifteen kids showed up for homework help. With Valasi's assistance, we did homework until after 8:00. I ate a quick dinner that Logo kindly fixed for me since she knew I'd been there all afternoon, printed documents, and got back to my house at 9:00, where I flopped onto the bed with a huge sigh.

*What was I thinking? Obviously there needs to be a Plan B! While I'm thrilled at the response, I haven't yet figured out how to accommodate this surprising level of interest. I was grateful when Logo stepped in to keep some semblance of order and control. No one can do that with kids in a Samoan village like a pastor or his wife! It's supposed to be good to get out of your comfort zone and challenge yourself, but right now that feels like a lot of BS. Maybe whatever I do in "real life" after this will seem easy.*

Since on that first day we'd unexpectedly sorted the kids into "Boys' Day" and "Girls' Day," that's what it became. Tuesday was Boys' Day after school, then homework help for all in the evening and Girls' Day was on Thursday, with evening homework help. During the week I taught computer/keyboarding lessons for adults, and for adults and youth on Saturday mornings.

In the beginning, all the kids who came learned the basics, and of course I always made time for individual instruction for new arrivals. After that, the afternoon sessions became "free time" when they could do whatever they wanted—games, word processing, or Paint—rotating and taking turns. Teaching opportunities abounded with the kids waiting their turn as they sat cross-legged reading, making puzzles, doing crosswords, drawing, or coloring. When they were finished, they'd excitedly bring their artwork to me to tape on the painted block wall by the door, until it was covered to the ceiling in layers.

The Homework Center was tiny in terms of dollars and scope compared to the Marine Project, but it's the one that I always mention first when people ask what I did in Peace Corps. My work on the Marine Project was intermittent and often behind the scenes, but I was at the Homework Center at my regularly scheduled time three days a week.

On a typical afternoon, I'd walk toward the hall just before 4:00 and spy a few kids waiting outside the door. Depending on the day, the girls would whisper secrets and giggle in a circle, or the boys would elbow each other to be first in line when they spotted me walking down the road. I'd unlock the red wooden door, turn on the lights and fan, and let in the first nine for the computers and the rest to sit on the floor. From that moment on I bounced from one to the next, giving instructions, answering questions, watching the time so that everyone would get a turn. Then I'd go home for an hour and go back for homework help for another hour or so, with assistance from one of the village teachers.

I didn't know enough about truly "teaching computers" to have gone far beyond the basics, but for whatever benefit they derived from it, I gained more than I could ever enumerate—another insight into Samoan culture, fun and rejoicing, something to fill my time, the satisfaction of those "Aha!" moments that every teacher lives for, and the memory of smiles and laughter.

*The kids are delightfully eager to learn, and like kids everywhere, they pick it up quickly. They're totally fearless, even though for most of them it's the first time they've ever used a computer. I must admit that I'm moved when I think about how exciting this is for them!*

I sent an email to family and friends and told them that the best way to describe my work at the Homework Center was to tell them about the people:

*Ten-year-old Poiva always has an impish grin on his coppery-brown face with his dark, mischievous eyes. Not long ago, he tried to teach me how to fish with a spool of line, a hook, and some bait. Of course I didn't catch a thing, but I watched him pull in three pan-size fish. This week I taught him how to use a computer.*

*High school senior Penelope is learning how to type. She's a shy, beautiful young girl with long black braids. Last night, she finished a research paper (with some typing help from me) on running a small business for which she interviewed the owner of a local general store.*

*Siliafai is fifty, pleasantly plump, with a ready smile and a twinkle in her eye. She learned on a typewriter when she was young but had never used a computer until last Saturday. Now she can turn it on, go to Word, and type a letter to print and mail to her family in New Zealand.*

*I'm happy to report that I walk to my house after an afternoon at the Homework Center with a big smile on my face.*

I asked those friends and family for donations of puzzles, a pencil sharpener, children's books, dictionaries, coloring books, crayons, and colored pencils.

*Puzzles with frames would be appreciated, and some a bit harder. Most boxed jigsaw puzzles are too difficult, even though kids the same age in the States would be able to do them. I think most haven't ever done a puzzle. I took it for granted that they'd know how since I grew up with puzzles. Initially, they don't understand the concept of looking for the pieces with the matching pattern or that the smooth edges go on the sides. They just pick up pieces at random and try to force them together.*

I received eight big boxes stuffed with goodies for the kids—everything I'd asked for and more, including lettered wooden blocks that turned out to be a real hit! And here and there were handwritten notes of encouragement, a pair of earrings, or a box of my favorite tea.

## The United Nations Marine Project

Although the Homework Center won my heart, the Marine Project fed my mind. It was a fascinating, auspicious, and enlightening learning experience. I loved sitting by the sea at the fale 'i tai; however, that was a beautiful, but superficial view. The Marine Project gave me the opportunity to discover the deeper connections between the sea life and the shore life of this amazing ecosystem.

The stated purpose of the project was to rehabilitate, protect, and conserve Poutasi's marine environment. Coral and other marine life were decreasing, and the banks of the river were being denuded of natural flora, including mangroves,[9] due to poor management and muddy run-off from higher ground. The drainage pipe between the spring-fed brackish lagoon and the ocean was poorly constructed, contributing to a build-up of silt and debris that impeded the normal migration of spawning fish, and the beach was eroding.

The village matai had wanted a request for a seawall included in the proposal. That component was turned down by the United Nations as I'd anticipated. Many seawalls are effective, saving homes that otherwise would be destroyed. However, we were taught in PC training that they have two specific weaknesses: wave reflection from the wall lowers the sand level on the fronting beach and accelerates erosion of adjacent, unprotected coastline.

*Tuatagaloa Joe will talk to the matai Monday about establishing a Marine Project committee. I'm not kidding myself into believing that there's a lot of support for the project, yet. If I come back to*

---

9 Mangroves only grow in areas with low-oxygen soil, where slow-moving waters allow fine sediments to accumulate at tropical/subtropical latitudes near the equator. Their dense tangle of prop roots make the trees appear to be standing on stilts above the water. Mangrove forests stabilize the coastline, reducing erosion from storm surges, currents, waves, and tides and their intricate root system makes them attractive to fish and other organisms seeking food and shelter from predators.

*Samoa in ten years I won't be surprised if not much remains. But there will be a short-term impact. I'll do my best to get it started and maybe I'll be pleasantly surprised. Like most of us in PC, our best chance for "success" is to impact individuals in small ways that may make a difference.*

About the same time as the opening of the Homework Center, Tuatagaloa Joe presided over our first Marine Project Committee meeting at a long table on the ocean-facing deck of his and Tui's house. A late afternoon breeze kept the temperature manageable. Everyone sat expectantly while Leiloa, their house girl, served tea and coffee. Seven of the eleven committee members were there—a respectable turnout by Samoan standards. Tuatagaloa Joe detailed the project and asked for their commitment and support. Because some villagers had expressed concern about the proposed Marine Protected Area, thinking that it would reduce their ability to catch fish and other seafood, Tuatagaloa Joe asked the committee to be ambassadors for the project.

After the meeting, Tui, Tuatagaloa Joe, and I relaxed on the deck with a glass of wine and watched another magnificent sunset behind 'Ili'ili Point. I reviewed my notes with them to make sure I got everything right and they asked me to stay for dinner, which I gladly accepted.

The first steps would be getting technical assessments from government departments such as the Divisions of Fisheries, Environment, Conservation and Forestry, and the Ministry of Works. In the following months, the villagers completed a shoreline and village-wide cleanup that resulted in several dump truck loads of rubbish, and the natural spring was cleaned and restored with new retaining walls. Niu capably organized the young men to plant saplings along the edge of the lagoon and the riverfront, and steps were underway to protect the mangroves and cultivate giant clams. The next phase would be the actual physical creation of the Marine Protected Area and submission of an MPA management plan that I'd begun to draft.

Nuʻusafeʻe Island and the fringing reef at the top. The mangroves grow where the freshwater flows from the river on the left. The oval in the center represents the MPA.

Although Poutasi's marine resources were under threat like those of many other villages, the establishment of MPAs and protection of waterways was becoming more common. A couple of weeks later, the United Nations invited us to a two-day seminar at another southside village that had a Marine Protected Area. When I called Tuatagaloa Joe to remind him of it, he told me he'd forgotten to put it on his calendar and could only stay for the morning of the first day. We arrived about 8:00 AM and after all the welcoming speeches, ʻava ceremony, and a tea break, it was nearly 11:00 before we started, and Tuatagaloa Joe left shortly thereafter.

*It was good that his presence was noted, but now I'm here for the day to try to understand everything in Samoan. We're seated on fala mats in an open fale. I had to stretch my legs out and cover my feet with a mat a long time ago. At least I have a pole to lean on! I'll keep looking like I'm taking notes and try to stay awake until lunch time. Last night Tuatagaloa Joe asked Pauga to come [a matai supportive of the project], but when we went to his house to pick him up this morning, he'd gone fishing.*

At the end of the day I got a ride to Sinalei, then waited for Tuatagaloa Joe to pick me up on his way back from Āpia. He told me he couldn't attend the second day, but I should drive his pickup to the seminar with Pauga and Matatamali'i (another matai on the Marine Project Committee). But driving would require Peace Corps approval.

*I'm trying to decide if I should just do it and take the slight risk, or call the PC office in the morning and ask for a vacation day so I can officially drive. I hate to "waste" the vacation day. This argues for a beg for forgiveness rather than ask for permission approach.*

So that's what I did. I decided if there was an incident on the way, I'd tell PC that I was going to call at 8:00 AM and ask for a vacation day, since we had to leave before the office opened. I saw the two chiefs look uneasily at one another when I put the truck into gear as we headed out of the village. But once we were cruising along on the government road, they relaxed and told me about the villages along the way. Since it'd been easy to drive there, I decided to drive back without calling the Peace Corps office. I figured that it'd be an inglorious ending, but the worst that could happen was that they'd send me home.

To determine if our future marine reserve would make a difference in the fish and coral population, we needed to do a baseline survey. On a sunny morning in late June, Malama and her team from the Ministry of Natural Resources and Environment drove to Poutasi in their government pickup loaded with snorkel gear, waterproof measuring tapes, and skinny white PVC pipes marked in meters. The bay was calm and brightly reflecting the midday light as we waded out at low tide.

With Matatamali'i and Pauga at the UN seminar.

Malama asked me to take photos with her underwater camera, which I did with delight. I snorkeled in the warm, crystal-clear water for two hours as they measured and wrote observations. I was once again amazed at the circle of life under the surface. I floated above the multicolored stalks, antlers, and shelves, boulders that looked like giant brains, and blossom-like lettuce and leaf corals. I watched tiny fish faces quickly poke out of the maze of hiding places that provided them food and shelter, then dart away to go about their fishy business. Malama said that the presence of many small fish meant that an MPA was promising. Although there was a lot of dead coral, it was great to see young polyps growing, and even dead coral provides habitat to light-avoiding species that are part of the food chain.

Malama measuring coral in Poutasi Bay.

We stashed the snorkeling gear in the bed of the pickup, gathered more measuring tools and cameras, and tramped though the mangrove marshes to places I'd never been. There were numerous spring-fed channels between the coastal road and the government road above it, with clumps of head-high ferns and stilted mangroves. Walking in water up to mid-thigh, I once stepped onto the bank out of the main channel into knee-deep, sucking black mud. I had to stick my hand in and muck around to find my flip flop. After that I carried them.

# Chapter 10

# Yearning for Home

*'E 'o'o le vao*
*"The grass is thin"*
*Nothing can be hidden.*

*Today's the first day in a couple of weeks that I've had an entire day all to myself. Adapting to the change of pace is almost as taxing as trying to manage the time when there was nothing to do. I finally feel like I'm justifying my existence here in the village and recently it's seemed as if I could stay until June next year. I'll see how it's going but it does help to be busy. I enjoy feeling productive, and it certainly makes the days go faster, but I also miss time to read and relax.*

*Yesterday I heard that after more discussion by the Matai Council, it was decided that only the men involved in the two affairs are to be banished. The families of the women must pay a fine of $1,000 tala, plus a cow (worth about $1,000 tala), which is a lot! Not only are there no secrets in a Samoan village, can you imagine your affairs (pun intended) being discussed publicly?*

I visited my family in Manunu again, stayed Sunday night and returned Monday; it was harder to stay the whole weekend now since I taught computer classes on Saturday mornings. I'd been back a half dozen times and knew I was always welcome, so I didn't tell them I was coming this time. I didn't want them to go to a lot of trouble, buying special food and serving meals at pālagi times when they wouldn't otherwise. Niu always went to pick up Saina and the kids on Saturday, so I rode with him to Āpia, stayed the night at Saina's mother's house, and splurged on a taxi for the hour-long ride along the north shore, then inland up the winding road. I surprised them when I showed up shortly before morning church. Wilma, in a bright white puletasi, saw me first when she opened the door, curious to see who'd arrived by taxi. She rushed out to hug me and I told her I'd meet her at the church next door. As I walked in and placed my offering in the basket, I was greeted with smiles, hugs, and kisses, and ushered to the front pew to wait for Wilma. In his preamble, Roma welcomed me warmly as I sat smiling and fanning myself.

Along with the deacons and their wives, we were served Sunday dinner in the open fale between the church and the house by the church young people, who then ate our leftovers.

From right to left: pork on bone, chicken leg, spaghetti mix, pisupo, chicken soup with watercress, another piece of pork, and umu baked breadfruit, taro, and palusami at top.

Afterwards, I laughed and played with Donna La'itiiti, who at fourteen months was doing the toddler dance of taking a few unsteady steps, wobble, fall on her padded butt, spider upright, and do it again. This time I'd brought her a sturdy, tiny book about learning numbers with colorful pictures of animals. With the usual Sunday mālōlō and afternoon church, the day went fast, and I took the early bus back to Āpia Monday morning.

When I got back to Poutasi, I heard that two young men were lost at sea near Nu'usafe'e when their twin-hulled fishing boat capsized. It had been dark, and the fishermen drove the boat onto the reef. Each had a piece of debris to hold on to, floated together for a while, and then got separated. One man swam to shore in Poutasi, but the others didn't make it. The two who were lost were from Sāleilua. Only one body was found at the southwestern tip of the island.

Early Polynesian navigators could stand firmly planted on the decks of their double-hulled sailing canoes and sense the direction and movement of the waves from their feet right up through their bodies. They understood the complex patterns produced by ocean swells that are refracted and reflected among the islands. This knowledge was especially important when canoes neared an island on a dark, moonless night, allowing the navigator to stay clear of the surrounding reefs until daylight. In our modern era, absent that traditional knowledge, accidents happen.

### I'm Sick though Things are Going Well

*I've reached another language level. I'm beginning to understand without going through the translation process in my head. Except for common phrases, I've been hearing the words and then mentally translating into English. As my familiarity and vocabulary increased that process got faster, but lately there's been a leap to the next level. I'm far from being fluent, but it feels good. It's a process of letting go and just letting the words flow over you.*

Early in July, Tuatagaloa Joe invited a musical group from New Zealand to perform at several venues—at the university, on Savai'i Island, and at the secondary school in Poutasi. And through his connection with that group, the Poutasi Congregational choir would record a CD to sell as a fundraiser.

Everyone in the choir was excited! For two weeks we had daily evening practices, and I was thrilled that I'd have the CD to take with me when I left. The Sunday before our recording sessions were scheduled, I'd promised to take photos of the choir for the CD cover following the afternoon service. If it hadn't been for the photo shoot, I wouldn't have gone to church for the second time that day. A couple of days before, I'd begun to feel crummy. By Sunday I had a nasty sore throat and was fairly sure that I had a fever, although I didn't have a thermometer.

The following week I toughed it out. I certainly didn't want to miss the recording sessions, so I rode to Sinalei in the back of a pickup with a dozen others for two back-to-back afternoons as we recorded eight hymns. I drug myself to the Homework Center for Girls' Day and Boys' Day. I kept thinking I'd start to feel better, but on Friday I called Teuila, our Peace Corps Medical Officer, who telephoned the village medical clinic so I could walk there and pick up some antibiotics.

Poutasi Congregational choir after recording session at Sinalei.
My blond head is on the left, back row.

By Sunday I felt wretched. There was some improvement after the antibiotics, and the sore throat was finally gone, but my head was congested, and my eyes were itchy and watery. However, the worst part was the cough and asthma. My life-long asthma was well managed with an inhaler, but now I was using it two or three times a day, and the wheezing and coughing never went away.

The next morning, I rode to Āpia with the family in Niu's pickup. Saina sat in front with Fetū on her lap, Tia, Hemara, and Feonu'u and Uiti's two girls sat in the back beside me with the two younger girls on their sisters' laps. When I got to the Peace Corps office, Teuila sent me to the doctor, who told me I had pneumonia! He doubled the antibiotic dosage, prescribed some Prednisone, and told me not to work for a week. On the midmorning green bus back to Poutasi, I had the seat to myself, and for two hours I was cheered as I read *Me Talk Pretty One Day* by David Sedaris.

It had been raining all day, so even with my umbrella I was soaked from the waist down by the time I walked to the house from the government road. I changed my wet clothes, made myself a cup of instant hot chocolate (thanks Mom!), and laid in bed with my laptop playing the new Bookworm word puzzle game I'd recently found for Hemara.

*I have a perverse satisfaction in being diagnosed with something other than a common cold. I've got to get well—it just occurred to me that I leave for Australia in three weeks. I've been so busy that I haven't thought about how close it is!*

The next morning, I thought, "I feel good." Then, I began moving around and started coughing. I took my medicine and a spoon of cough syrup, used my inhaler, and rubbed Vicks on my chest. After a half hour of morning stuff and minor tidying up I was exhausted, but I finally felt like eating. I pulled some bread out of my shoebox-sized freezer to thaw to see if it was toastable. Those few slices of bread and some hot dogs had thawed and refrozen the day before, and probably the previous week too when we'd had no power. I'd planned to make an egg sandwich, but the bread was a total loss. So I tossed it to the chickens and scrambled a couple of eggs.

That afternoon I was concerned that I wouldn't be at the Homework Center for the kids. I wished I could put a note on the door, but it was pouring rain. Then the power went off, so I knew they wouldn't expect me, and I relaxed and read in the dull afternoon light until I fell asleep. By the fourth day on the medications, I was able to sit at the fale 'i tai with some tea and masi popo.

*Still coughing, but grateful to be outdoors. There are heavy clouds over the mountains, but for now I'm enjoying the sunshine. It's delightful here—I've missed it so! I'm looking forward to the Homework Center this afternoon. Penelope came by the house yesterday. She's writing a paper on tourism. I answered a couple of questions and told her to do her best and I'd read it today to help her improve it.*

*Niu asked me to look over some paperwork for a project that he and three other cattle farmers want to do. I wrote a support letter and jotted down some ideas, but he and the others did the actual proposal. He told me that because of me he's learning how to write proposals. That's what it's all about!*

*Later . . . I had a good time this afternoon with the girls at the Homework Center. Penelope worked on her research paper and Avasa wrote a speech about visiting New Zealand. Girls of all ages were sitting on the floor, making puzzles, coloring, drawing, and doing crosswords. This is what I hoped this small space could be.*

Penelope reading in the Homework Center.

*I just glanced at earlier entries in this journal. I've been so cheerful lately that I haven't looked at the "weeks left" that I noted on my calendar to help me get through it when I was feeling low. I'll see how things are going at the end of the year. I'm sure there'll be more ups and downs, but I'm glad that passed.*

I was sick for two weeks and the cough lingered for a couple more. If I'd fallen seriously ill, I would've wanted to be back in America. Although Peace Corps provided medical and dental care for volunteers, local medicine left something to be desired. I had persistent shoulder pain while I was there that later required arthroscopic rotator cuff surgery less than a year after I returned to America. My Samoan experience with my shoulder was both good and bad. Teuila first sent me to "physical therapy," which was merely a massage with coconut oil. When that didn't help, she sent me to a bearded pālagi doctor in an aloha shirt and shorts at his bungalow on the beach near Āpia. He gave me an epidural steroid injection that worked great, got me through the rest of my service, and cost (PC) only $35 USD!

The worst illnesses I had were the pneumonia and a couple of bouts of food poisoning. The first time was when several of us PCVs went to the Miss Samoa pageant a few months after we arrived. An hour into the program it hit me with terrible cramps and nausea. While beautiful women sang and danced, I violently expelled whatever it was out of my system in the Ladies Room, alternately sitting on the toilet, flushing, sitting on the floor to puke into said toilet, all the while sweating profusely. Wearing my nice puletasi. In a dirty public bathroom stall. Gradually I recovered, splashed cold water on my face, and rejoined my friends just as they announced the winner.

Others in Group 78 had dysentery, dengue fever, mumps (despite being vaccinated), dog bites, and centipede bites. And we all had diarrhea, which was a rather constant companion. Peace Corps volunteers called it the "little d" (diarrhea) versus the "big D" (dengue fever).

About this time, I had a blister on my foot, a healing wound where

I'd dug out a splinter the day we trekked through the bush to the man-groves, and a rash on my backside. That heat rash was from the two-hour bus rides, especially the sweltering, sweaty trip home, sitting be-side someone just as hot as I was. I got "Butt Aid" for the rash from Teuila. It was zinc oxide powder, essentially for diaper rash, although it did have a section labeled "For use on adults: Apply liberally and smooth on the irritated or chafed skin."

*Further down on the label: "For total butt maintenance, also try our Baby's Butt Aid Ointment. It's an effective, doctor recommend-ed, treatment for babies . . . and the baby in all of us." I won't be experiencing total butt maintenance, but hopefully, this will help.*

### And Then Kaitlen was Gone

In mid-July, I heard that Kaitlen was going home. She'd moved from her village to a ministry job in Āpia, but decided to go home early to start her Master's degree. Now it was me, Hannah, and Erin left of the eight women who came together.

*We're only volunteering, and if one isn't happy here, it should be perfectly acceptable to go home. Then there's a middle ground. You're not miserable, you could stay if you had to, but you'd rather be home. There are those PCVs who aren't suited to service in a for-eign country, can't cope with the culture, or are lazy, immature, or not willing to give it their best effort. And that's not even mention-ing those sent home for illness or misconduct. And the commitment that you made for two years always reminds you that even if it's hard, you should stay the course. It's certainly not black and white.*

*I'm not blue today, but I looked at my calendar for the first time in quite a while—fifteen weeks from now is my decision point to stay or go, after I get back from New Zealand. Today I'd say it's 50-50.*

As I got my strength back, I was looking forward to flying to American Samoa for the Festival of Pacific Arts at the end of July. This was the tenth festival, hosted every four years by one of the Pacific island nations. Representatives attended the cultural gathering from twenty-two island groups including Wallis and Futuna, Nauru, Palau, and the more well-known Hawai'i, Australia, New Zealand (Aotearoa), and Easter Island (Rapa Nui).

Our next village meeting for the Marine Project would be to present the results of the fish and coral baseline survey. When Malama at the Ministry of Natural Resources and Environment recommended a date during the time I'd be gone to American Samoa, I told her, "I don't need to be there. If I'm not, it'll reinforce the fact that this is the village's project, not *my* project."

*I've spent hours by the ocean this week, and it's been good for my body and for my spirit. I've had no obligations other than the Homework Center. I remember those days almost a year ago when I first came to Poutasi and how sitting here at the fale 'i tai was a similar respite. It was a time of great stress and uncertainty as I sat here and let the beauty soothe me. It still does. I take photo after photo trying to capture its essence. It's hard to put into words how much I absolutely adore this one little place in Samoa.*

*These are the days I will remember—this gloriously blue sea, the slight breeze, the muffled roar of the breakers on the reef, the rustling of the palms, roosters crowing, birds singing, waves sloshing lightly as they break on the sandy beach.*

*From* Brideshead Revisited *by Evelyn Waugh: "These memories which are my life—for we possess nothing certainly except the past . . ."*

### *In America for the Weekend, then off to Brisbane*

Two days before I flew to American Samoa, U. S. Secretary of State Condoleezza Rice stopped in Āpia to meet with her counterparts from Pacific Island Forum states to strengthen cooperation within the region. All the volunteers in the country were invited to meet with her at Aggie Grey's Hotel. She posed for photos and spoke to us briefly, telling us how she always met with PCVs in each country she visited. She praised our work and said we were carrying on a proud tradition. I didn't agree with her conservative political views, but I respected her accomplishments and was thrilled with the opportunity. She was much smaller and thinner than I expected.

When I arrived in Pago Pago for the festival, my first impression was that it was both very American and very Samoan. It reminded me of rural areas of Hawai'i, yet despite the American influence and official status as a U.S. territory, it was still Samoa. The villages were organized under the matai system and fa'aSāmoa was the way of life. Everyone spoke English, but Samoan was the everyday language. I thought that this statement made by one of the speakers at the festival was very enlightening: "One family, one culture, one country—two different forms of government."

In a large grassy field, each visiting nation set up a fale where they sold handicrafts, and canoe makers, tattoo artists, bark cloth artists, and other artisans demonstrated their skills. I met a woman who told me that the land where the festival village was built was given to the United States by her family for the naval hospital during World War II. I love to watch dance and I was spellbound for two days, enthralled with dancers on the main stage from Tahiti, Fiji, Hawai'i, New Caledonia, Guam, Papua New Guinea, Samoa, American Samoa, the Cook Islands, the Solomon Islands, and more.

For weeks before there'd been a controversial public discussion, which was thoroughly covered by the Samoan media, about whether women who traditionally danced topless in their own countries would be allowed to do so. Since both Samoa and American Samoa were religiously conservative, it was quite an issue. Some years before, when the festival was held in Samoa, a woman dancer from Papua New Guinea was slapped by a Samoan man because of her "nakedness." The current discussions were one-sided, as is often the case on issues of gender. No one seemed to care that the handsome young men from Rapa Nui danced with the male version of a G-string. In the end, everyone did their traditional dances in whatever manner they wished, and women from the Solomon Islands and Papua New Guinea were indeed topless. All the dancing was impressively athletic, told moving stories, and entertained with gusto. I couldn't get enough of it!

I opted to be there for the last two days of the ten-day event, which included the closing ceremony. After the parade of nations, I watched in awe as the lights went down and one hundred Samoan fire knife dancers performed in long lines.[10] The dancers held the knife blade, spinning circles of fire, tossing it high into the air and catching it to the sound of pulsating drums.

Before I went, I'd asked Tuatagaloa Joe to recommend a place to stay. He replied, "Oh, you can stay with my cousin!" So I stayed with extended family, exceedingly kind and generous hosts who fed me and drove me around Tutuila Island sightseeing. On the way to the airport, I asked them to stop at Kentucky Fried Chicken so that I could fulfill a special request from Tuatagaloa Joe and Tui, and I bought them two large crispy buckets. I couldn't resist the enticing aroma and ate two pieces on the plane on the way home.

American Samoa was great fun and expanded my knowledge about the Samoan archipelago. Before the trip, I'd been busy starting up the Homework Center, moving the Marine Project forward, and relished

---

10 The fire knife dance has been traced to the days when Samoan warriors twirled war clubs to display their strength, celebrate victory in battle, and on other ceremonial occasions. After the introduction of metal, the club evolved into a machete. Starting in the 1940s, both ends were wrapped in towels soaked in white gas and lit aflame.

the progress we'd made. I'd been feeling upbeat, despite the pneumonia, and then at the beginning of August:

*I don't feel as low as I was in May, but I have that "been there, done that" feeling. I can't figure out why I'm melancholy. Maybe staying in a modern American-style house, eating American food, and speaking English in American Samoa made me yearn for home. Whatever the reason, it's challenging me right now. It's Sunday morning and I'm ditching church. I hear the familiar hymns wafting from next door and I smell the umu fires cooking Sunday dinner. The kids are in Āpia, and Niu and Saina have gone to Savai'i, so I can stay home without explanation. If not for my flight to New Zealand in October I don't know what I'd do. But the NZ trip will keep me here and then I'll decide how long I'll stay.*

Four days after I got back from American Samoa, I flew to meet my friend Rosi in Brisbane. We'd met when I was campaign manager for a candidate for the Colorado state legislature and she was on our executive team. She was a city planner and had spent the previous two months in Australia exploring the possibility of relocating Down Under.

The first evening, I took a hot shower and it felt so good that I immediately filled the bathtub and took a long, hot bath. Our "holiday apartment" (Australian for condo) on Sunshine Beach faced the ocean, with five-star restaurants within walking distance, and vivid red, green, blue, and orange rainbow lorikeets landed in the morning on the tree beside our balcony. Exploring Queensland together for eight days, we hiked to the summit of Mount Beerburrum, rewarded by a breathtaking 360° view of the Glass House Mountains, and watched kangaroos and koalas in the wild, at Steve Irwin's iconic Australia Zoo, and at the Lone Pine Koala Sanctuary. We listened to amazing bird songs on forest walks, cruised the Brisbane River, strolled through a Picasso exhibition, and shopped until we dropped.

The highlight for me was a short flight from Bundaberg to Lady Elliot Island, the southern-most coral cay of the Great Barrier Reef. It appeared like a jewel in the indigo ocean surrounded by the azure water of the shallow fringing reef. The small plane dropped onto the grassy landing strip slicing through the middle of the island, as hundreds of squawking seabirds grudgingly made way. We explored and relaxed in the morning, and that afternoon I was finally able to snorkel the Great Barrier Reef—one of the dreams on my "Bucket List." Colorful fish were everywhere—yellow, orange, blue, striped, spotted, and combinations of all the above! Floating, suspended motionless in the Coral Sea, on the Tropic of Capricorn, blue sky above, crystal clear water below, I could clearly see to the sunlit sand sixty feet beneath me.

*I'm at the hotel in Brisbane with my bags packed for my return flight to Samoa. I'm not ready to go back. Partly because I wish I could see more of Australia, but also because being here has solidified my desire to go home. Australia is more like the U.S. than Samoa, and I was able to talk to Rosi and think about this out loud. Unless I change my mind, I'll go home by Christmas. So, with my return to Samoa I'll begin my phase-out period (at least in my own mind). I won't tell PC or the village until after I return from New Zealand. I could force myself to stay six months longer, but I don't think it'd be worth it, for me or for them.*

When I landed in Samoa, the familiarity of the place came rushing back. I did email and computer stuff at the PC office and waited for 'Afakasi's bus in the full sun for nearly an hour. Either I missed it, or he didn't make a noontime run to Poutasi. So I waited for the Sinalei shuttle at Aggie Grey's.

*There wasn't room for me in the shuttle, but I sent my suitcase and shopping bags. Now I'm on the yellow Laumoso'oi bus. I'll get there eventually. Welcome back to Samoa!*

Village life resumed its normal pace. Tuatagaloa Joe was pleased with the village meeting that had convened while I was gone where they'd reviewed the baseline survey and planned for the next steps of the Marine Project. I sorted through paperwork, caught up on village news with Saina, and worked my shifts at the Homework Center. One afternoon, Mataomanu stopped by to make copies for her students as I taught a new boy how to use the computer. While other boys played games and drew flags, she smiled and said, "I can see why they want to come here!"

Even so, thoughts of wrapping up still preoccupied me:

*I've spent nearly the entire day at the fale 'i tai. The girls did puzzles in my room last night until we got into a giggling pillow fight. It's nearly time for afternoon church. It's easier to go since I've had a break from it. I'll miss two Sundays while in New Zealand, so I only have to do this about a dozen more times. I feel like the countdown has started!*

### Justin Fades Away

Then another Group 78 volunteer went home. Justin came to Samoa only a few days after college graduation. I didn't hear the circumstances of his departure but knew that he'd been frustrated since he had expertise in water systems which wasn't being utilized.

*That means exactly half of our group of sixteen will have gone home. I wouldn't have predicted that one year ago when we were sworn in.*

*Peace Corps is by its very nature a hiatus time in our lives, younger or older, when we altruistically think we'll help someone in need. We're all in transition. No matter why we joined, altruism, boredom, fear of the future, looking for something, seeking adventure, while we're here we're always on the cusp of the next thing. Perhaps we create a "job," but it's temporary, amorphous. So we wake each morning with the day spread before us, with feelings as varied as the weather—sometimes with anticipation, often with longing for home and familiar patterns of life as we've known them. Even occasionally with a grudging attitude, which our hosts don't deserve.*

*Whatever the mood of the day, it comes, and you deal with it, and then the next, and the next, until you can leave, go on to the next thing, reinvent yourself, go back to some similarity of the way it was (never just the same), try something totally different, or keep searching. Being in a place and time such as this makes you focus on the search and be aware of it in ways you otherwise wouldn't. I have time to think, to be in the moment. It's all part of the transition to what lies ahead, the unknown future, which will reveal itself to me, as will the little things that I'll find to fill this day.*

So what did I do to fill my day? I read most of *The Serpentine Cave* by Jill Paton Walsh. Three girls came to the fale 'i tai and asked, "Ā'oga computer?" I told them I'd be there at 4:00, even though it wasn't a scheduled day. About mid-afternoon, I realized it was my one-year anniversary of arriving in the village. I took it as a good sign that it didn't occur to me until late in the day.

*I'm going to miss this place so much! The water is various shades of aquamarine and deep blue with the dark patches of coral clearly visible. It's choppy today. There's a strong breeze from some unsettled weather. It looks like there may be rain showers on the horizon.*

## *A Birthday Gift for Hemara*

In September, for Hemara's twelfth birthday I took her to the Miss Samoa pageant. I rode to town with Niu early in the morning, got out at the PC office, and walked with fellow Group 78 volunteers Christian and Benj to Beach Road to watch the annual Teuila Festival parade. We found a good spot along the water and waited, and waited. It finally started an hour late, led by the Royal Samoa Police Band. Each of the nine contestants sat regally on floats intricately decorated with vegetation—dark green palm branches, yellow-green ti leaves, pink and red teuila flowers, orange birds of paradise, multi-colored croton leaves, and many more. Miss Samoa Australia's float even included a life-size kangaroo made of small tan seeds. Each contender was sponsored by a local business or organization, such as Miss Samoa Realty, Miss Susana o Samoa (an Āpia clothing designer and shop owner), or was sent by expat Samoan communities in Australia, New Zealand, and the United States.

After the parade, I did my usual Āpia errands, then met Hemara at Saina's mother's house to get dressed up for our big night on the town. We took a taxi, picked up some food on the way, and got there early to get a good seat. Hemara was tickled pink to meet and take a photo with the reigning Miss Samoa who mingled with the crowd before starting time.

After formalities, the pageant started with drums, music, and haka and fire knife dancers, followed by the typical competition with unique Samoan variations. There were contests in sarongs (instead of bathing suits), in traditional native Samoan attire, and in evening wear (floor-length puletasi instead of gowns, though more revealing than those worn in church or business, with spaghetti straps or cutouts). Local designers such as Susana o Samoa and Miss Cece's House of Fashion were recognized for the custom-made puletasi styles. The talent competition was amusing. One singer and one pianist were good, but not great. Another girl did a massage to music. One contestant arranged flowers with a narration. Others gave speeches or performed interpretive dance. The interviews were in English and some of the local girls clearly were not fluent. The winner was Miss Samoa USA from Utah—the first time a contestant from America had won.

We ate, talked, laughed, and I don't think Hemara stopped smiling all evening. Me neither!

From *To The Wedding* by John Berger: "*. . . they wait for the moments during which life counts. When they arrive, these moments, they come and they pass quickly. Afterwards, nothing is quite the same and they wait once more.*"

# Chapter 11

## The Beginning of the End

*'E lele se'ae lama te ti'otala*
*"The grasshopper flies about but the kingfisher is watching"*
**An incautious person will be surprised by his enemy.**

*To make it sound dramatic—I got beat up by a large, crazed Samoan woman today.*

One morning later in September, Hemara came to my room and told me that someone was in the back of the house and wanted to see me. I later learned that Ala (not her real name) was the cousin of a village family and was visiting from Australia. She was tall with her dark hair in a bun, probably in her forties, with a pretty smile.

She asked me loudly, "Where is the American boy who was here?" Apparently she was referring to Christian, the pisikoa who'd visited me a few days prior because he was studying mangroves.

"He's not here anymore," I replied.

She said to tell him that she loved him and wanted to marry him, going on and on about it, mostly in English but some Samoan. As odd as this may sound, Peace Corps volunteers heard variations of this all the time. Even Saina would smile and say to me—"you should marry him"— pointing to someone in the village or in Āpia. Yet I could tell that something wasn't quite right, as if she was drunk, but I thought that unlikely so early in the morning.

"I have to leave, thank you," I said, and went to my room.

Then she stood outside my curtained window shouting at me to let her in. I ignored her, but when she continued, I went to the kitchen where Niu was, and he said, "Don't open the door because she isn't right in the head." Soon after, she left.

After lunch, when I walked to the Homework Center, a bunch of kids and the Sunday School teachers were playing volleyball next door. Ala was playing with them and shouted at me as I walked by. Not wanting to reengage, I just waved to everyone.

A half hour later, she burst into the Homework Center shouting, "Why are these kids touching the computers? They shouldn't be touching the computers!"

*"Ua lelei. O a'u o le faiā'oga computer,"* ("It's okay, I'm the computer teacher.") I replied. Oddly, I spoke in Samoan, although she was speaking English.

Then she rushed over to Milana seated at a computer and pushed him to the floor. Ala sat in his chair and started slamming the mouse on the counter and pounding the keyboard with her fists.

*"Aua! Alu i fafo!"* ("Don't! Go outside!")

She jumped up and hurled the keyboard to the floor, its letters popping off everywhere.

"Alu i fafo!" I shouted again.

Suddenly, she whirled around and punched me with her fist, hard, like a boxer. Then she hit me again, over and over on my upper right arm and shoulder.

I shouted to Milana, "Go get someone!" (You revert to your native language quickly in a true emergency.)

From the window I saw Logo outside rushing toward the door. Then Niu, Uiti, and Samu burst in, the three big guys filling the small space, and in the confusion Ala left. I told them what had happened and burst into tears. My body hurt, but I was also shocked and afraid. I quickly wiped away the tears and started picking up keyboard keys.

"Leave everything and lock the door," Niu said.

I told him I wanted to pick up the pieces so that no one stepped on them. Then, as I crouched on the floor, I noticed two little kids who'd cowered in the corner under the counter. I calmly asked them to help me pick up, including the puzzles that they'd been putting together before she came in. Even though Ala had fled, I didn't know where she was, so we hastily put everything on the counter and locked up. The adrenaline rush from being attacked masked the pain, and I was so stunned that I didn't know what to do. So I watched the young people playing volleyball for a while, and then walked back to the house.

Meanwhile, Niu had gone to get Saina in Āpia and they weren't back yet. 'Ofisa was the only one home and she said I should tell Tuatagaloa Joe, but I was sure everyone in the village already knew by then. When Niu and Saina returned, they told me Ala's family had brought her from Australia because of her "problems." I debated whether to call Fono, our Peace Corps Security Officer, to report the incident, and with Niu and Saina's encouragement, I decided that I would, in case anything came of it.

*I have red welts and five ugly bruises, each the size of a fist, on my right upper arm and shoulder. Milana said Ala hit me in the face but I don't remember that and there's no mark. My neck is stiff, it hurts to turn it to the left, and my teeth are sore on the right side, so maybe she did. My right hand and wrist are bruised. Did I put my hand up defensively and she hit it? I know I didn't hit her back, but maybe I tried to. It's funny how you remember part of something like that, but not everything. I do remember Milana cringing when Ala approached him—the instinctive flinching of a child who's been hit, which applies to all children in Samoa. For the first time in Poutasi I'll double-check the locks on the doors tonight. I've never been afraid here, but I'm afraid of Ala.*

The attack happened on Saturday, and over the next couple of days the bruises spread and got uglier. Fono called me on Monday and asked me to come to the Peace Corps office. The next day in town, I recounted the story to him and the Country Director. Teuila examined me then sent me to a doctor to check me out, and to document and photograph my injuries. At Fono's request, I also filed a police report. I told them I didn't want to press charges but just file a report for the record. Even so, later that week the police and Fono came to Poutasi and talked to Ala's family.

*Maybe I'm making a big deal out of an unfortunate incident, but then again, it <u>was</u> a big deal. I've never been attacked like that and I was frightened. In the States someone could be charged with assault and battery and a restraining order obtained. Here it's usually best to let the village handle it, and I'm content to do that for now.*

Tuatagaloa Joe told me that the day that I went to the PC office to make my report, Ala's family came to him and asked for help. They told him that Ala was bipolar, came to Samoa with no medication, and she hadn't slept for forty-eight hours. The family tried to control her by beating her. I'd heard her shouting in the night since their family compound was nearby. After my incident, her young niece had told me that they hit Ala with a "board," but I wasn't sure if I understood correctly. Apparently, I did. Tuatagaloa Joe said she was black and blue all over. He called a doctor he knew to make arrangements, then he and family members forced her into Tuatagaloa Joe's pickup and drove her to the hospital in Āpia. There she received a shot to calm her until she could get on the correct medication.

That afternoon, I walked to the Homework Center with a sense of relief that she wasn't in the village. But she was back the next morning. While Tuatagaloa Joe and I talked at his house about the upcoming Marine Project committee meeting, she came to the open door, loudly calling my name. "Donna forgive me. Forgive me please Donna." I had no desire to talk to her. Tuatagaloa Joe talked to her quietly, then Leiloa took her home.

*Fono told me to always make sure someone is with me when I go out. A little while ago, 'Ofisa walked with me to the Homework Center to make copies for tomorrow's meeting. I forgot something the first time and we had to go home and back. Both times Ala shouted at me from their house. I can't even sit at the fale 'i tai today, or maybe as long as she's in the village, since it's within sight of their family compound. I helped Hemara with a report about keeping the environment healthy and read Craig Danner's* Himalayan Dhaba *about a fellow American seeking direction in her life. A good day, except for feeling like I'm under house arrest.*

It quickly became clear that I couldn't ask someone to accompany me every time I left the house, so instead I just kept a watchful eye out for Ala. On Thursday afternoon at the Homework Center I was tired and frustrated, and it didn't energize me as it usually did. As I walked along the beach road afterward, I came upon Ala's cousin picking up strips of laufala laid to dry on the sand, later to be woven into fine mats. She apologized for Ala's attack and told me that earlier that day they'd taken her to a Samoan healer. She gave me a quick hug, and then said in a hurried voice, "You should go before she sees us talking."

*I went to photograph the sunset from the fale 'i tai and Ala shouted to me to come to talk to her. I said I was busy and went back to the house. She may not be a physical threat at this point but she keeps calling me from outside as I write this. I just don't want to have anything to do with her.*

Four days later, at 3:45 AM, I got up to go to the bathroom and was back in bed half asleep when Rocky started barking. I heard footsteps, and then Ala called my name in front of my bedroom window several times. I ignored her, so she went to the back of the house muttering, calling my name, and calling Saina's name for ten or fifteen minutes. Fortunately, she wasn't shouting. I thought about waking Niu

(Saina was in Āpia) but decided to wait and see what happened. When Ala finally left, it sounded like she headed toward Tuatagaloa Joe and Tui's house.

After that I was wide awake, with my alarm set for 5:15 to catch the bus. I couldn't go back to sleep, so I gave up, packed my things for a day trip to town, and read until time to go. From my room I heard 'Afakasi start the bus several times and I could hear him messing with the engine. Then he drove off without turning down the beach road past our house like he always did. Usually, I would've walked the short distance to be the first passenger aboard, but I'd quit doing that because I didn't want to run into Ala. I had some Marine Project work to do in Āpia, but mostly I wanted to get away from the village. Fortunately, I later caught a ride with Niu instead, who said that he'd heard Ala early that morning too, but like me didn't want her to know we'd awakened, or we'd have a hard time getting rid of her.

*My interlude of being in a better mood, that continued even with the anxiety of Ala's presence, has ended and I have that "I want to go home" feeling again. She seems calmer, though certainly not normal. However, walking around the village in the middle of the night is not a good sign.*

Day after day, she was a constant presence in my mind. Fono said he'd talk again to Ala's family after I'd told him about her night wanderings, but I asked him to be sure to tell them that I didn't want to cause trouble. He said he'd make it clear that he and the police were only there because it was Peace Corps policy. I never knew when or where she'd pop up. When the Marine Project Committee gathered in front of Tuatagaloa Joe's fale for a field trip to see an MPA in a nearby village, she said she wanted to go with us. I firmly told her that only the committee was going and that we were working, and eventually satisfied, she walked away.

The next morning, I went to the Homework Center to install a new educational game. When I started to leave, I opened the door just an inch, and heard her voice next door asking Logo, "Where's Donna?" I didn't hear the response but hoped no one knew I was still there. I quickly pulled the door almost shut and peeked out to watch her walk toward her family compound. When she was out of sight, I slipped away, dashed around the far side of the hall, and ran down the beach to our house.

*I hate this feeling of wondering where she is, what she'll do next, and trying to avoid her. I'm so bored and lonely today, and I can't even go to the fale 'i tai for respite.*

On Sunday morning, she decided to sit with the choir. I almost sat in another row to avoid being in the pew directly in front of her, then I talked myself into sitting where I always did. Ala leaned forward and said, "Hello darling. How are you, darling? I love you Donna."

Then, just before afternoon church, when I was in my room, she walked in the front door of the house. I heard her talking to Fetū, asking among other things, "Where is Donna?" I worried that he'd bring her to my door, so I quickly locked it. I heard her walk through to the kitchen where the rest of the family was, and they were shocked to see her in the house. Saina talked with her and led her out. Thankfully, at the second service she was two rows back and didn't speak to me.

*Now it occurs to me that she might walk into the house anytime during the week, when I'm here alone. I have a stalker. And it's weird and disconcerting as hell.*

On Monday, I was irritable and I snapped at the kids, which I never did. That night I slept for nearly ten hours and woke with a migraine headache.

The next day, I went to town to get away from the constant menace. I was briefly cheered by an email from Jackson sending his love and kisses, with photos of roses, since he couldn't send me the real thing for my birthday. But that mood didn't last:

*I sent a positive email update to everyone. I keep trying to talk myself out of this blue mood. It's not working. Usually just being in town breaks the spell, but I felt vulnerable all day. A couple of times I thought I'd burst into tears at the slightest provocation.*

That afternoon I rode home on the green bus packed with people. I sat on the aisle with one bun on the seat, next to a large woman holding her daughter on her lap, with my bags on the narrow bit of floor in front of me. It ranked among the most uncomfortable bus rides ever. When I finally got home, I dumped my stuff in my room, grabbed my camera, and walked toward the fale 'i tai to check on the sunset. Just offshore, Leiloa's son Poiva and two of his friends floated in one of Tuatagaloa Joe's canoes. They waved at me and in chorus shouted, *"Sau Donna! E fia ti 'eti 'e i le paopao?"* ("Come Donna! Do you want to ride in the canoe?") Their cheery voices and the inviting scene before me were too enticing to refuse, so I waded into the waist-deep water in my t-shirt and lāvalava, circling them with my camera taking photos. Then I clumsily climbed into the canoe and rode with them as the sun set behind 'Ili'ili Point. They had no idea how much that small reprieve from my trials with Ala meant to me!

Poiva and friends in Tuatagaloa Joe's canoe.

## *I Just Want to Go Home*

For the next few days I didn't see much of Ala. Whenever I wasn't in Āpia, I hardly left the house except for church or the Homework Center.

*I hear occasional cheering from the direction of the grassy malae in front of the school. Perhaps there's some sporting event today. I've come to believe that I don't know about happenings in the village not because of any thoughtlessness or insensitivity. Everyone knows everything because they interact with one another so much—women weaving at the Committee House, young men fishing during the day and hanging out in the evening, kids in school, not to mention the ever-present church activities. It just never occurs to them that I don't know.*

*I've been hearing news from the U.S. about the financial crisis and a bill pending in Congress. It's a $700 billion bailout bill to keep major U.S. companies (financial companies?) afloat. It's controversial (of course I don't have many details) but they say if they don't do something, we'll have a depression, with credit card companies pulling credit lines and a general lack of credit.*

Then I got more disconcerting news. Tuatagaloa Joe and Tui had recently told me that a German doctor was coming to Poutasi in November to volunteer for three months at the clinic. That was great for the village of course, but at the beginning of October, Niu offered to have him stay in the empty bedroom next to mine when he arrived.

*I've lived with a family when I wanted to live alone (and come to love them). I've appreciated the little bit of privacy I have when Niu, Saina and the kids are in Āpia during the day. Now I'll have to share my bathroom (well, I already share it with the kids, but not someone else too!) and what little space I have to myself will feel invaded. He'll arrive when I'm in New Zealand. Perhaps Herr Doktor will turn out to be an interesting conversationalist, a pleasant distraction from the mind-numbing boredom that my life has become. If he turns out to be a boorish Germanic prig, I don't know what I'll do other than hunker down in my tiny space, biding my time until the flight to freedom. It's time to go home.*

*Last night I had odd dreams of living in a huge room with no furniture other than a bed; falling asleep with my Sunday clothes on, including my hat; Tia, Fetū, and Hemara with ear infections; and, I was trying to rewind yards and yards of spilt red dental floss.*

Even my rewarding tasks, like teaching the children at the center, felt burdensome.

*I was exhausted after a couple of hours today in the Homework Center! The small kids were practicing their White Sunday program in the fale next door, so I let them in. I had nineteen preschool-aged kids sitting butt to butt, coloring, playing with puzzles and blocks. With two kids at each computer, there were twenty-five kids in that expanded closet at one time!*

Preschool children with Samu in the background.

Soon it was only a few days until I'd go to Namu'a Island for Group 78's next in-service conference, followed by two days in Āpia, and then off to New Zealand for nine days.

*I'm deeply and profoundly homesick. For some reason I've avoided that word. Maybe because somehow it signifies an inability to adapt, to survive this, to stick it out. So, I've used other words like lonely or feeling blue. But you can't define homesickness more clearly than by saying, "I just want to go home." If the poetic definition stands— "home is where the heart is"—then my home is where I can be with family and friends.*

*I can survive one more week. I'll go to Āpia tomorrow and again on Friday, and to Manunu for White Sunday. So I only have to spend a few more days in the village where homesickness and isolation overwhelm me. As the time approaches to leave, it becomes both easier and more difficult. I tell myself, "You only have to do this thing—go to church, take the bus to Āpia, borrow another book from the PC library—a few more times." But visions of home and resuming a life there become more frequent. Thoughts that had been pushed aside before are now allowed to linger and become plans.*

The next morning when I was with the kids at the Homework Center, Ala came to the door and asked if she could go to *people.com*. I stood in the doorway and was glad that there were villagers outside as I told her there was no internet. Later when I wasn't looking, she came inside and said she wanted to use the computer where Romani was sitting. I backed against the bookcase on the far wall and told her that today was the day for boys only. She was strident and belligerent. I urgently called to Uiti, *"Sau mai!"* ("Come!"), and she left.

Before I went back to the center for the afternoon session, I read *Water for Elephants* by Sara Gruen and wrote a quarterly report to the United Nations for the Marine Project. We'd made good progress, but I was anxious to see our next major milestone met when the Marine Protected Area was established in the bay. The buoys to mark the MPA still hadn't been delivered. I'd thought of sitting at the fale 'i tai but stayed in the house since Ala was still wandering about. I didn't want to deal with her again.

I ended up working three hours at the Homework Center and was worn out, on my feet, constantly vigilant, with no break. Just as I was ready to quit, Uiti and Samu curiously came in after their White

Sunday practice with the Sunday School kids next door. I wanted to demonstrate what the kids had learned, so I showed them Paint flags that they'd made and some of the other programs, including Snood, which sucked them in, so I stayed longer.

By the time I got back to my room, I was weak from thirst and hunger. I immediately drank two glasses of water, then warmed some leftover pasta and scarfed it down. Just as I finished eating, I heard Ala yelling and slapping someone in front of our house. I turned on our outside lights and cautiously stepped onto the front porch. Others had heard too and came running—Leiloa from Tuatagaloa Joe's house, 'Ofisa from our house, and Ala's family. They struggled to subdue her but finally got her back to her fale.

*'Ofisa told me she was hitting one of her cousins. Perhaps she's not taking her medication. Apparently, my continued caution is justified, and it pays to stay away from her, although I clearly can't manage to do so all the time. This morning I saw her from my window walking about outside our house and quickly pulled the curtain shut. I'd planned to walk to the Homework Center on the beach if it was low tide. It wasn't, so I ran down the road, and*

*knocked next door to make sure Letone or Logo were home before*
*I went inside the center. This is no way to live.*


## So Much Hitting

*A couple of new kids have come to the Homework Center . . . I was*
*showing one of the boys how to type today. An older teenage girl*
*sat next to him watching and slapped him on the arm whenever*
*he made a mistake. Hannah says half of her school kids do "the*
*cringe" when she puts her hand on their shoulder. And they hit*
*each other—hard. Mostly teasing, but still, hard punches or slaps.*

In training, we'd learned about the fact of corporal punishment in
Samoa and I thought I could deal with it as long as it wasn't out and
out child abuse. Part of the culture of hitting children was Biblical:
"Spare the rod, spoil the child." However, it was also important to recognize that this practice had been the custom for generations. Early
twentieth century anthropologists studying cultures throughout the
South Pacific noted the physical punishment of children.

The younger volunteers found it especially challenging. Because it's
now met with disapproval and legal protections in the United States,
it's difficult for Americans to realize that nearly the world over, corporal punishment is still socially and legally accepted in childrearing.
Despite being illegal in Samoan schools, it was still prevalent there as
well. I was told that prosecutions happened only when someone was
beaten badly enough to need medical care.

Gradually, things were changing. To spontaneous applause, the
winner of the Miss Samoa 2007 pageant said that her platform would
be to combat child abuse and corporal punishment in Samoa. But I
had seen how pervasive and harsh it was. Soon after I got to Poutasi, I
wrote in my journal:

*As much as we try to fit in and understand Samoan culture and be fa'aSāmoa, it'll never totally happen. There's a young boy crying with heart-wrenching sobs, sitting under the breadfruit tree alongside the road in front of my house. Two of his friends are nearby, watching, listening. I ask them why he's crying, and they say something about "tupe," which means "money," and "sāsā," which means "hit." Maybe he took money from someone and got a beating for it. Maybe he lost some money and got a beating for it. I don't dare get involved, even though my instinct wants to find out what's wrong and to comfort, make it right somehow. I can't because I don't understand the language or the culture. I come into the house and tell 'Ofisa, who is folding laundry in the front room, and can't help but hear. She looks at me and goes back to folding laundry. Samoan children get beaten all the time. No big deal. That's the way it is.*

Soon after the Homework Center had opened, Tui and I stood talking in front of the church after the morning service as we often did, and she asked if I'd had a problem with two of the boys at the center. I couldn't think of anything, and then she told me two boys were punished at Sunday School that morning for something relating to the Homework Center. Later, I remembered the day I was overwhelmed with the number of kids who showed up and Logo stepped in to help. She gave the kids a good behavior lecture and when she said it would be boys only that day, two stepped forward to come in. When I said that those two had already been at the computers, she scolded them, and made sure that boys who hadn't yet had a turn were next. I wondered if those were the boys who were punished. Tui said they were made to puff out their cheeks, and then one of the Sunday School teachers hit them on the face, hard. And then not long after I heard of another incident.

*Saina told me that two boys got their hands slapped at Sunday School for taking pencils from the Homework Center. I bought a couple dozen pencils for them to use. They're on the shelf and I would've gladly given one to any of the children, as I already have. One of the boys apologized to me later in the week for taking pencils. I can rationalize that they should've asked, and I certainly don't want them to think that they can take anything on the shelves, but I didn't approve of them being hit for it.*

When Niu or Saina broke off a small branch and gave the kids a good switching, I didn't like it, but essentially it was none of my business. However, when it came to the two occasions involving the Homework Center, I bore some responsibility and I felt badly about it. There was nothing I could do, especially after the fact, but I kept the possibility in the back of my mind, so I wouldn't contribute to it happening again.

The second Sunday in October was nearly here so the children were all excitedly anticipating the White Sunday holiday. Some of the older Sunday School kids had been festively practicing in the front room of our house, but the story of their play was unsettling:

*The skit's about a mother and father who punish their children for doing bad things by beating them. One of the boys dies in the end, which shows what happens when he doesn't listen to his parents. I told Hemara that in America we don't hit our children. She smiled and said, "Yes, I know. They don't in New Zealand either."*

I watched for a bit, but then came back to my room because I was uncomfortable with the hitting, which they thought was very funny. I'd also seen Samoans laugh raucously at violent scenes in movies that made me cringe and close my eyes. Not being a psychologist, I don't pretend to understand this behavior. Perhaps it was a coping mechanism or catharsis of sorts, or maybe just the jubilant physicality of a not-so-long-ago warrior culture.

About this time, I'd been reading *Where We Once Belonged* by Sia Figiel, the first Samoan woman novelist to be published in the United States. In her moving story about a thirteen-year-old navigating the mores and restrictions of her Samoan village, Figiel illustrates the extraordinary burdens on Samoan children. I adapted one of her moving passages on this subject to reflect what I observed:

*No one listens to the children.*

*Washing dishes. Wiping babies. Carrying sisters, brothers, cousins, nieces, nephews on their hips. Sweeping the fale. Picking up bread-fruit leaves, cigarette butts, beer bottles.*

*No one listens to the children.*

*Slapped by the teacher for being cheeky. Rapped on the head with a long stick for not being attentive during the prayer. Hands smacked by the pastor for being late to Bible study after school. Switched with a branch for using the wrong bucket to fetch the water.*

*No one listens to the children.*

### White Sunday Brings Joy Amidst my Disquiet

Under a clear, blue-sky on the Saturday afternoon before White Sunday, I walked past the Congregational church and Feonuʻu's store, on to the Catholic church. I sat in the open fale next to the priest's house on the edge of the sea and watched the younger Catholic kids laugh and practice for the next day's program while the older ones boisterously played volleyball. There was a definite holiday air in the village, preceded by weeks of shopping and practicing.

*I'm at the fale 'i tai at sunset. I haven't seen Ala all day. Maybe she's calm today, or out of the village. For whatever reason, it's good for me and I'm hoping she doesn't show up.*

With PC permission, the next morning I made the hour-and-a-half drive over the mountains in Tuatagaloa Joe's pickup to Manunu for the holiday. I arrived just before the children started the White Sunday March in their new finery, circling the church twice, their knees lifted high. I heard the exuberant shout-singing of the littlest ones as they walked past, followed by the more harmonious voices of the older young people. As usual, the children conducted the service with Bible readings, skits, songs, and dances. It wasn't exceptionally long like Poutasi's four-hour service the year before—only a little over two hours—and there was no afternoon service. After Sunday dinner, I took a long nap and slept so soundly in my old room at Roma and Wilma's that I had a hard time waking up. I drove back in the evening as the sun set.

*What a lovely day! The kind of day that reminds me that there'll be people and places that I'll miss in Samoa.*

Back in the village, the next day Tuatagaloa Joe told me that there'd been a lengthy discussion by the Matai Council about how I operated the Homework Center. Some of the matai said that the Catholic kids were being discriminated against and at times kids couldn't use the computers because adults were. He said he grew weary of the discussion which was going nowhere and suggested that the mayor be appointed to look into the matter.

*All of that is bullshit. I don't even know which kids are Catholic and which aren't except for a select few, and the second part isn't true at all. I've known that things in my village have gone very smoothly compared to stories I've heard from other PCVs, but I've also been sheltered by Tuatagaloa Joe being the spokesperson for PC projects at the Matai Council meetings. I've just worked toward what I thought I could accomplish, kept a relatively low profile, and tried not to worry about village politics. I'm not surprised that something has come up, but I'll deal with it and know that I'll soon be gone. Yet, I do hope that the kids will be able in some way to continue what I started!*

I made a poster-size display for the mayor to take to the next Matai Council with photos of the kids in the center, including Catholic kids. It was also a chance to show the matai, most of whom hadn't seen inside, what it looked like and see the kids engaged and learning. I still constantly looked over my shoulder for Ala whenever I was in the village. I rarely sat at the fale 'i tai because if she saw me, she'd make a beeline in my direction and I'd scurry back inside the house. I'd recently asked Fono what was said when he and the police talked to the family. He told me that they said she was too much for them to handle and they were thinking of sending her to back to Australia where her siblings could care for her.

*Soon we'll have our three-day Group 78 conference. Then I'm off
to New Zealand, and it's over whenever I want to go home. That
seems hard to believe! I'm ready, but it doesn't seem real.*

*Later . . . ah, right on cue, as if I needed some reinforcement, I
went to the kitchen to visit with Saina, and there was Ala. She said,
"Hello, Donna." I waved and went back to my room. She'll be one
of the reasons that I go.*

It may seem odd that I didn't make a bigger deal about Ala's stalking
and threatening behavior. I could've made my feelings of fear and in-
timidation more clearly known, but most of the time I believed that
if I tried to avoid her I'd be okay. I wanted to abide by the cultural
norms of letting the family and village manage the situation. If it had
happened at the beginning of my Peace Corps experience, I might have
handled it differently. I liked her family and I felt badly about their situation. It emphasized the sad lack of mental health assistance in Samoa.
I didn't tell anyone back home about Ala until after I returned. I knew
that from afar I couldn't convey the circumstances in a way that would
make them not worry.

In addition to all of this, Mom told me that she was going to have
back surgery in December. She already knew I was thinking of coming
home early, so she asked if I'd stay with her during her recovery.

*Maybe that's what I'll tell the village—that my mother needs me.
This is true but leaves out the parts I don't necessarily want to share.
December is only seven weeks from today! That's amazing! After
all the tears and struggles, it's so close. Predictably, I'm having, not
second thoughts, but pangs of guilt, and preliminary sadness.*

## We Don't Want to Stay in this Paradise

Group 78's mid-service conference was held later than it normally would've been, with just ten months left for those who'd stay the whole course. It was delayed due to significant changes that had happened since we'd arrived. Our Country Director had left when her term was up, replaced by a temporary, and then a new Country Director. In addition, the Associate Director who oversaw our Village-Based Development Program had also left, and that position was vacant for ten months.

In the middle of October, our conference was held on Namuʻa, one of the four tiny Aleipata Islands east of ʻUpolu. It was uninhabited like Nuʻusafeʻe, but slightly larger. By now, we didn't need a bus to shuttle us from Āpia—the PC van was big enough for all of us. Benj, Jacob, and Nick were doing well in their villages on Savaiʻi Island; the Intercoastal Management volunteers, Hannah, Erin, and Christian worked in Āpia; and Shane (who got a grant for his village to build a preschool) was on the far southeastern tip of ʻUpolu.

With our island destination in sight offshore, we pulled our bags out of the van and waited under the coconut palms for the boat to Namuʻa, drinking sodas from the small shop nearby. Soon a motorized aluminum rowboat putted to shore to take us in small groups across the shallow water on a ten-minute bouncy ride. Our accommodations were small beach huts (the only ones on the island) rented by a local family. They were thatched on the sides, with a metal roof and a tarp to pull down inside at night or in rainy weather. There was also a large open fale for meetings and eating. You could walk the island perimeter along the white sand beach and through the tropical forest in about an hour, and it was the typical vision of an untouched island paradise.

*We're all disappointed, as we'd hoped for a different type of location. There's no electricity, no store, and—would it be too much to ask?— no hot water. Past groups have gone to one of the small resorts for conferences but the new Country Director has been instructed to cut back on costs. Nick didn't come; said he's too busy. So, there are only seven of our original sixteen plus three PC staff, including the new Associate Director, Kellye. We've been here about an hour and we're bored already. It's beautiful, but I can do beautiful every day in Poutasi. I'll think positive. I'm out of the village and prepared to go to New Zealand on Saturday. Many people would pay a lot of money to come to a place like this. At least it's not lonely.*

That night, I had one of the creepiest experiences of my life. I woke about 1:00 AM and brushed the side of my head because I felt a bug fluttering near my ear—I thought. But it was *inside* my ear! It was the strangest sensation. Every now and then I heard and felt it flitter, so I assumed it had wings. I woke Kevin, a PC trainer, trying not to awaken anyone else. He peered into my ear with a flashlight but didn't see anything. I hated to wake Teuila in the middle of the night but decided this was a matter for the PC Medical Officer. When I called, she asked if we had baby oil or coconut oil. Kevin had a natural insect repellent made of coconut oil with citronella. Teuila told us to heat the oil, pour it into my ear, and let it run out. So there we were in the middle of the night, sitting cross-legged in his beach fale, heating the oil in a spoon with his lighter. Three times he poured the warm liquid in my ear and I let it run out. We didn't see a bug come out, but it stopped moving.

*It's still disconcerting to think that there may be a dead insect in my ear for the next twenty-four hours until I see Teuila at the PC office. After finally going to sleep again last night (which wasn't easy), I dreamed that I blew my nose and bugs came out. I've been very aware of it all day.*

To my relief, Teuila found no evidence of the insect when we returned to town the next day, so it must have washed out.

On the morning of the conference's second day, Benj left to go back to Savaiʻi to meet up with a United Nations team filming a documentary. They'd been discussing it for weeks, but luckily the UN finally called several days before his village completed their water tanks project. After that, the six of us left told the trainers that we'd rather to go back to Āpia after we finished that day's language and training sessions, instead of the next morning as scheduled.

In the late afternoon before our return motorboat, Hannah, Erin, and I snorkeled over coral communities that provided habitat for countless creatures. Tiny orange and white parrotfish nibbled the coral and its polyps, to be pooped out later creating new white sand. Yellow and blue striped wrasse darted in and out, and giant clams lazed on the seafloor with wide bluish-purple mouths. The night before, by a roaring bonfire on the beach, with our faces glowing in the light, we'd all shared stories of PC and before, and talked about what we'd do after.

*It feels, as Hannah said today, as if the sun has set on Group 78 before we had a chance to shine. There were many reasons, but some of our group might still be here if there hadn't been the turnover in upper-level PC staff and they'd received the PC support they needed. Hannah also reminded me of something that I know is true but is good to hear from someone else. With the sort of people in my village—Niu and Saina, Tuatagaloa Joe and Tui, others—I can have confidence that the projects I started won't come to a halt. Some things may move more slowly, but I believe that they will continue.*

# Chapter 12

# Homeward Bound

*'Ua toe o se aga*
*"Only a handbreadth away"*
*We're almost there.*

After the conference, I slept two nights in Āpia at Saina's mother's house, then I was off to New Zealand. Like Australia, it was a place I'd always wanted to go. I stayed two hotel nights in Auckland—city of one hundred nationalities and the largest Polynesian population of any city in the world. From there I drove to Hamilton to meet my friend Rona. We'd met in Veracruz, Mexico, on a Jimmy Carter Work Project for Habitat for Humanity, where we had the honor of meeting this great man and his wife Rosalynn who worked alongside us. Two thousand volunteers from thirty-two countries built seventy-five small concrete block homes in five days! Rona, part Scottish and part Maori, was my assigned roommate and we hit it off immediately. In her work and personal life, she was a passionate advocate for abused and neglected children.

Together we toured the North Island for four days. There was so much beauty, natural history, and culture to take in! The precise date of first settlement is a matter of debate, but it's currently believed that the first voyagers came from East Polynesia five to six hundred years ago. I lived in the Hawaiian Islands at the northern tip of the Polynesian triangle, and now I was at the southwest corner, excited to learn about the Maori *tangata* (people). Rona added much-welcomed, thought-provoking, and educational commentary. And as always, I was fascinated with the language and the similarities to Hawaiian and Samoan since they are sister languages.[11]

Some of the highlights included the breathtaking (and terrifying) view atop Auckland's thousand-foot-high Sky Tower, the tallest building in the Southern Hemisphere; silently gliding on the underground river in Waitomo Caves, craning our necks upward to the ceiling lit with glow worms like a starry night; and breakfast at the beach followed by lunch at a snowy ski resort . . . I didn't want to go back to Samoa.

After the plane landed on 'Upolu, I could've taken an earlier bus to Poutasi, but instead I hung out at the PC office until it was time to catch 'Afakasi's 4:30 bus. Back in the village, the homesickness was overwhelming, and although I hadn't seen Ala yet, her presence still loomed. To get away I went to Āpia the next day, and the day after.

I checked out the Homework Center when I returned. It had obviously been used while I was gone, which pleased me. I fretted momentarily about the gum stuck to the floor, the fan that wasn't turned off, and the windows left open. But I told myself that it was time to let go and let it be their Homework Center, not mine. I'd decided to leave Samoa the first of December, and here it was nearly November and I hadn't told anyone in Samoa except Hannah and Erin. I knew I needed to talk soon to Tuatagaloa Joe and Tui, Niu and Saina, and the kids, but I didn't yet have the nerve and courage to tell them.

*It seems as if I should be able to cope better than this since I'll be leaving in less than five weeks. I thought about talking to Teuila when I was in town because I was so miserable, but I knew I'd tell her I wanted to go home, and I didn't want to do that today. Instead, I sucked it in and did the things I needed to do. I found a book at the library entitled* Haiku of Hawai'i *by Annette Morrow. Here's a particularly poignant one for today:*

---

11 The connection is shown in the word for "people": tangata (Maori), tagata (Samoan), and kanaka (Hawaiian).

*Loneliness sits on*
*My shoulder, like a black crow,*
*Ah—come home, come home!*

However, despite my inner resolve, the next day was more of the same.

*The electricity was off most of the day, but I don't think I'd have done much anyway. I'm depressed. I dozed and read all morning—* One Red Paperclip *by Kyle MacDonald. Even this quirky story of one man achieving his dream can't rouse me. I don't think I can stay until December.*

I called Teuila on her mobile and learned that she'd taken the day off—I heard her kids laughing in the background. She asked if it was urgent, and I said no. She said she'd be in the PC office the next day and I told her I'd see her then. I called Hannah after she'd finished teaching for the day, but only briefly because I didn't have much phone credit. Talking helped, but not enough.

*Tomorrow I'll talk to Teuila about going home. Kellye is supposed to come for a site visit soon. I'd feel hypocritical telling her what I plan to do in the village, knowing full well that I'm leaving. It feels like I should be able to get up and do something, but I can't. It's dragging me down day by day, little by little. I want to go home, and I don't want to be here anymore.*

A couple of hours later, Kellye called me. She said she'd read my blog and wanted to recommend it to Peace Corps in Washington, D.C. as an example of Peace Corps' third goal—to help promote a better understanding of other people and cultures by Americans. It cheered me to hear something heartening, but I still felt despondent. When she asked how things were going, I replied, "So-so. It's hard to come back after vacation."

The next day, my crisis had passed, so I didn't talk to Teuila or Kellye. Instead, I met Hannah in town for lunch. Belying her consistently sunny personality, she was wise and understanding beyond her years. Using her as a sounding board, I made a plan for the following week to announce my resignation. Now I'd have to think about how and when to tell everyone else, which I found more difficult to face than I'd thought.


### After New Zealand it All Comes Together

Three days later I heard the welcome news—after six weeks in Poutasi, Ala went back to live with family in Australia! Just as we sometimes don't realize how sick we were until we're well again, I didn't fully comprehend the weight of Ala's constant presence in the village and on my mind until she was gone. My relief was immeasurable.

> *I feel like I've been freed! I'm at the fale ʻi tai in the early evening—setting sun time again. Someone's blowing a conch shell. Tonight, standing at the edge of the sea with waves lapping at my bare feet, the water was pink and blue, and the sky an astonishing display of color.*

The roller coaster continued until the end, but I could relax and have fun again as things started coming together. Tuatagaloa Joe's cousin in American Samoa (the family I stayed with) collected donated buoys to mark the boundary of our Marine Protected Area. The same day that I heard about Ala's departure, the floats arrived on the ferry from Pago Pago in a horse trailer crammed back to front and top to bottom. Some were battered and beaten, but after several young village men painted them bright red and white, they were beautiful, hung to dry like shiny Christmas ornaments in the fale 'i tai. The Marine Project Committee had adopted a management plan for the MPA which set out fines for villagers who fished within the restricted area and steps were underway to protect the mangroves, cultivate giant clams, and bring ecotourists to the village. While I was disappointed that the Marine Project wouldn't be completed before I left, I had every confidence in Tuatagaloa Joe, Niu, and the others to keep it moving forward. It was always intended to be an ongoing endeavor.

We'd had hot temperatures and not enough rain, and I'd read in the *Samoan Observer* that the lake with the dam that produced most of the electricity for the country was nearly dry. There'd also been a problem with the island's backup generator, so we began to have periodic outages for a few hours every day. Since Poutasi's household water came from a spring in Sāleilua and depended on an electric pump, we intermittently had no water in the village. Even in town there was sometimes no water at the PC office.

*Since there's no power, and thankfully no Ala, I'm sitting at the fale 'i tai in the sea breeze. With these daily outages I don't know what I would've done if she was still here. I'm drenched with sweat if I stay indoors, with no air moving, 90+ ° in that concrete block box. I found lettuce at the market yesterday, but when I wanted to make a salad, there was no electricity, therefore no water to wash it. I only have enough boiled water for drinking because the power was on this morning only long enough for me to boil that much and shower.*

*Assuming there's electricity later today, I'll go to the Homework Center and until then read* One for the Road *by Tony Horwitz. Can't use my laptop because I've used up most of the battery.*

## *I'm Going Home!*

Early the next morning, I rode to town with Niu listening to the Samoan morning news on his pickup's radio. My decision to move my departure date earlier than December 1st meant that I suddenly had only two weeks left instead of the month that I'd planned.

I need to tell you something," I said reluctantly. "I'm going to Colorado to help my mother after her surgery, and I'm not coming back." I told him that I loved living in Poutasi and was incredibly grateful for all his family had done for me, but I missed home and needed to leave before the end of my service. Typical of Niu, he didn't say much then, just a brief acknowledgment, although he expressed his love and appreciation many times before I went home.

When he dropped me off at the Peace Corps office, I tapped on Kellye's slightly open door and peered around the corner at her invitation. "Can I talk to you?" I asked, dreading the conversation. I'd thought carefully about what I'd say, anticipating a discussion and that perhaps she'd try to talk me out of it. After I explained my reasons, adding that Monday, November 17th would be my preferred date to leave on the once-a-week flight, to my surprise she said, "I understand. Peace Corps and Poutasi will miss you." We talked for a while about the village's projects and my plans, then she told me to check with Teuila about a final physical and that staff would arrange for my ticket.

Evidenced by my procrastination and reluctance to talk to my Samoan families and Peace Corps, notwithstanding the inner knowledge that it was the right thing to do, I hated the idea of leaving early. I wanted to see things through. But there'd never be an "end." Our goal was to create sustaining projects, which by definition meant we'd walk away. And it would always be hard. Whether you left after six months or extended for an additional year, one day it would end. The hard part for me was saying it out loud and making it official.

Of course, Niu called Saina and she called me soon thereafter. I was at McDonalds and asked her to take a taxi there and told her that

I'd buy her lunch. I can't remember what we said, but I do recall the complexity of emotions I felt, desperately needing to go back to the States, and also knowing how much I'd miss her laughter, cheeky jokes, and her strength and support.

It was Election Day in America, and even though there had been intermittent power outages throughout the day, apparently the American Embassy was prepared for such things, so we came together for a party that afternoon. Embassy staff, most of the PCVs in the country, and a few American students watched the CNN results trickle in with palpable anticipation. I'd mailed my official ballot, but we also held a mock election for "'Upolu County" which went overwhelmingly for Obama (90%). With his Hawai'i connection, he was also the favorite of the Samoans.

McCain made a worthy concession speech, but Obama energized and enthralled everyone, as he did so well. The satellite reception went off briefly before he spoke, and we were afraid we wouldn't get to hear him. But it came back, although the picture was occasionally jerky and pixilated. We clapped at various junctures as if we were in the huge crowd in Chicago. When Obama said, "And to those of you across the globe huddled by radios listening . . , " a huge cheer went up. It felt like he was talking to us and there were tears in the eyes of many of the young people. In the spirit of the event, we had popcorn and potato chips, hot dogs, baked beans, cole slaw, and potato salad, followed by chocolate cake and homemade cookies. The potato salad was the Samoan version—mayonnaise, potatoes, and salt—and the hot dog buns were large rolls, but other than that, it was close to 100% real American food.

After the party, most of us went to celebrate at Cocktails On The Rocks. The popular club on Beach Road faced the ocean and was a favorite PC hangout, filled with sea breezes, the beat of live music, expats, tourists, and locals. Abruptly, I was full-on sick—throwing up with diarrhea. I took a taxi the few blocks to the Peace Corps office where I could be ill in private. It seemed like food poisoning, but I'd eaten what everyone else did at the Embassy. However, I'd ordered four McDonald's chicken wings earlier that day and later learned that several people who'd eaten there recently had been sick. Fortunately, Saina didn't eat the chicken!

That night Hemara and I cried together when I told her I was leaving. She held me tight with her head on my shoulder and said, "Oh Aunty! I'll miss you so much! I love you."

I kissed the top of her head, inhaled the coconut oil fragrance of her hair, and replied, "I'll miss you too! I love you! I'll write to you."

I think at that moment, holding that dear little girl whom I'd miss so much, was when it really hit me that I was leaving.

Later, I photographed another perfect sunset from the fale 'i tai, then reluctantly walked to Tuatagaloa Joe and Tui's house to tell them I was going home. Leiloa opened the door at my knock and Tui called for me to come in.

"Tālofa! Is Tuatagaloa Joe here? Is this a good time to talk to both of you?"

As Leiloa brought us steaming cups of tea, we faced Poutasi Bay from their deck, looking at the MPA marked by the red and white buoys. I told them my plans and said I was sorry to leave things unfinished. They both quickly disabused me of any regret and told me how profoundly thankful they were for all I'd done for the village, especially the Homework Center. I was exceptionally grateful to have met these two Poutasi leaders, and family who'd become friends.

*7:30 PM. No power, no water, and I'm dying for a shower. Although like others in the village, I've been washing and cooling off in the brackish spring water where it runs into the ocean. I didn't sleep well last night and lay awake for hours. There's a lot to think about right now.*

I was grateful that I was able to spend these last weeks without Ala in the village. I'd already resolved to leave because of my homesickness, plus I was worried about Mom's upcoming surgery. But Ala's intimidating actions certainly pushed me the last bit toward home. Now, there was no water and no power, which meant I couldn't do one of the things that gave me the most joy—teaching the kids at the Homework Center.

And, I was thinking about Jackson. I liked having him back in my life. We were talking dreamily of a future together, perhaps splitting time between Colorado and Hawai'i. The distance between us had forced us to communicate by email, conducive to sharing inner thoughts. We wrote lists of the top ten things we loved about each other and sent romantic poems. But it was complicated since I had no plan for my own future, with Jackson or without him. I knew I needed to be back in Hawai'i one day, but I intended to stay in Colorado to help Mom recover until I figured out what was next.

The following morning, I was able to shower, wash my hair, and boil enough water for the day before the power went off. I called Roma and Wilma to tell them of my plan to leave and began sorting and packing. I'd go home with the two suitcases I came with and a new carry-on bag bought in Āpia. I still had the small bag that was run over by the bus, so I put some odds and ends inside it for Saina, and I'd give her the electric skillet, toaster, and tea pot. The rest I'd leave at the PC office for other volunteers.

*It's too hot in the house. I'll go read* Floating *by Nancy Corbett at the fale 'i tai. We've only been able to have one session at the Homework Center since I returned from New Zealand, and that only lasted an hour before the power went off. I heard that Herr Doktor arrived while I was gone, but he's staying at Sinalei for a few days before beginning his volunteer work in the village.*

## *A Picture-Postcard Mini Vacation*

Earlier in the year, I'd requested prints of the kids at the computers in the Homework Center for a follow-up report to the NZ High Commission, along with some of my other favorite island photos. As I spread them on the counter in the shop, Hilda had admired some of my shots and said, "I'm looking for photos for new postcards. You should bring some in."

I'd dropped off some of what I thought were my best postcard-variety photos and she called and invited me to lunch. While we munched salads at Sydney Side Cafe, she reiterated that she'd like to buy some. I told her that because I couldn't drive, there were many places that I hadn't been to, so she offered to provide a car and driver to take me on a photo shoot to additional scenic places on 'Upolu. Consequently, I'd been chauffeured by Hilda's son on a scenic tour of 'Upolu Island a few weeks prior. And now, she and I would tour Savai'i Island together taking photos for three days before I left Samoa the following week

I rode 'Afakasi's bus to meet Hilda in Āpia for the hour-long drive to the wharf to board the blue and white "Lady Samoa" ferry. That day Savai'i was visible on the horizon fifty miles away. After an hour in the queue, we drove into the dark hold. Upstairs on the deck, I sat by the window musing and making small talk for the one-hour-and-fifteen-minute trip over the open ocean—the beautiful weather and moderate waves made it a fine crossing.

We initially stayed at a small resort owned by Herman's father. When we'd first talked of going, Hilda said, "We can stay at my father-in-law's," and I envisioned a Samoan fale, but it turned out to be more like an American interstate motel, with hot water, TV, and air conditioning! We had a sumptuous breakfast the next morning—American style pancakes, poached eggs, bacon, whole wheat toast, mango, papaya and orange slices, and cornflakes. I ate some of everything!

To write in detail about the places we went would add at least another chapter. The guaranteed-to-make-you-say-Wow! Alofa'aga

Blowholes, swimming with turtles rescued from fishermen's nets at Satoalepai Turtle Sanctuary, climbing up into the canopy of huge banyan trees to walk the swinging bridge in the Falealupo Rainforest Preserve, and so many lovely beaches kept me and my camera busy as we circled the island.

*We're at Lauiula Beach where we'll spend the night and return to reality tomorrow. At lunch I ate all the boiled shrimp I could eat. Then I slept in the fale on the beach like I'd been drugged, woke, and went for a swim. Now I'm writing by the sea. This is truly what people envision as paradise. I've seen behind the scenes and know that a fantastic view, perfect weather, and wonderful beach don't make paradise, but nonetheless it's been a fabulous experience. This part of Samoa I'll miss immensely.*

I'd told Hilda from the beginning that I didn't want any compensation—just some free postcards. The next morning, we rode the Lady Samoa back to life on 'Upolu.

*It was a lovely trip. I'm on the bus waiting to leave for Poutasi. I'm dripping sweat and I need to pee. I'll go at Pacific Express. I hope the "facilities" aren't too horrid. I'll have no other option. No electricity here again this afternoon.*

By the sea with my camera in hand. (Photo courtesy of Hilda Kruse.)

## *One Last Computer Class*

Before I left Samoa, I had another happy and unexpected bonus. The primary school in Sāleilua had been given a couple dozen used computers when it had opened three years earlier. All this time they'd sat in dust and disarray in an unused room. I'd always wanted to help them set up a computer lab, but it never seemed to work out. A combination of scheduling and logistics problems, missed communications, and village turf wars had kept getting in the way of this tiny project.

But finally, even that came together. Before my trip with Hilda, I'd walked the mile to the school and at long last connected with the principal. I suggested that Meghan and I finish setting up the lab and teach a couple of classes for the Level 8 students the following week and he readily agreed. Meghan checked out the computers and taped notes on each indicating which ones worked and which didn't, and I made plans to install the Typer Shark typing practice program. Then we'd teach a couple of introductory classes. But new obstacles emerged.

*I walked to the school this morning and tried to put Typer Shark on the computers. They're very dirty and so old they don't have USB ports. I brought only my flash drive, so I'll go back with a disk. Before I could check them all the power went off.*

After I'd walked to the school a couple more times, we were finally ready. But the power outages continued.

*It's an overcast morning with small breaks in the clouds where the sun shines through now and then, and there's a warm breeze here at the fale 'i tai. The power is already off again. I don't know if Meghan and I will be able to teach the first class tomorrow or not.*

The next morning dawned sunny and hot, but there was electricity! 'Upolu's backup generator had been fixed. Meghan and I met at the school and taught a class to excited girls and boys. I knew some of them from the Homework Center and they proudly showed off their knowledge to their peers.

Meghan teaching the girls at the primary school in Sāleilua.

I didn't have half of the computer and software expertise that Meghan did, but I'd been able to interact with village kids at the Poutasi Homework Center in a more informal, definitely cozy, setting. The computer classes Meghan taught at the secondary school in Si'umu were more technical and in English, as required, whereas I'd been teaching all ages in my inept Samoan, often making it up as I went along. So we made a good team, and we had a blast showing them what they could do when given the chance.

The next morning, my last Friday in Samoa, we taught another class. Afterwards, in the Samoan way, the principal made a speech of thanks and the kids sang for us and gave us each a lei and a lāvalava. I felt like we'd done so little for the gratitude that was expressed to us. In the end, after all the procrastination, miscommunication, and delay, we spent two fabulous days with the kids. Meghan's PC group went home soon thereafter, but a volunteer from the next group was assigned to pick up where Meghan and I left off in that first ever computer lab at Sāleilua Primary School.

## My Homeward Journey has One More Unexpected Turn

In addition to the primary school classes, the week before I left was filled with last-minute details—PC paperwork, turning over the Homework Center to the village, working with Tuatagaloa Joe on the Marine Project, and spending time with Niu, Saina, and the kids.

I sent an email to friends and family back home:

*Life has often been compared to a journey, and like a journey, we never know what we'll find around the next bend in the road. My assignment with Peace Corps in Samoa was scheduled to conclude in the summer of 2009, but I'll be leaving a few months early to be with my mother in Colorado as she undergoes back surgery. To be honest, lately my thoughts have been turning more and more toward home.*

*Perhaps this will come as a surprise to some because I've tried to keep an optimistic outlook and upbeat attitude, but damn, it's hard sometimes! Peace Corps life is supposed to be a challenge and it is. But not in the ways that I thought it would be. Of course, there are language and culture issues, which one expects. However, my biggest source of distress has been the loneliness. I miss laughing with loved ones, talking about the events of the day, and sharing life.*

My Hawaiian friend Laura, whom I'd met when I worked for the Volcano Art Center, sent a reply that touched me deeply:

Laura R
11/12/2008

Aloha Donna,

First, I want to say that I am sorry about your Mom's health, and I will say a prayer for a successful surgery and a quick recovery. It is strange how God works... Like you said, lately, your thoughts have been turning to home, and friends and family. God opened a door for you to leave in a timely fashion. Otherwise, it may have dragged the leaving out for too long.

I have to confess and be a little selfish . . . I feel that MY time in Poutasi is coming to an end also. I have enjoyed hearing about Samoa and your life experiences, very much. I have never been out of the State of Hawai'i, and I thank you for taking me to Samoa this year and a half.

You did great and wonderful things there, you have so

much to be proud of. Having an adventure that most people would never be brave enough for, that alone is amazing!

Good luck in all that you will do, and I look forward to hearing from you!

Aloha and a hui hou,
Laura

During my last days in Poutasi, I finally met Herr Doktor—my age, graying, wire rimmed glasses, no wedding ring—that could've been interesting if I'd stayed. But I was looking forward to seeing Jackson, and I was more enthusiastic about our relationship than I'd ever been despite my ambivalence.

*Conrad the German doctor is staying at Sinalei for a few more days. He seems nice and said he was looking forward to talking with me about what he should know about life in the village. Hmmm . . .*

I began to say my goodbyes. After our first computer class at the primary school, I took the bus to Āpia, and that evening I shared a jovial and mouthwatering meal with Hilda and Herman at their home—sashimi appetizer followed by freshly caught swordfish, green beans, boiled potatoes, and pineapple pie for dessert. Hilda gave me a calendar that she'd printed with some of my photos, and an envelope with $500 tala. I protested vigorously and said once again that I didn't want any compensation. But she insisted that it was a gift and said, "Use it to buy yourself something at the duty-free shop at the airport." It would've been very rude to refuse a thank you gift from a Samoan, so I accepted and expressed my gratitude profusely.

I'd planned to take a taxi back to Poutasi, but Hilda offered her little blue Toyota to me for a couple of days. So, I drove off—without PC approval! Friday morning, I picked Meghan up in Si'umu for our second computer class and took her home after. We hugged a quick goodbye with promises to keep in touch. I hurried back to Poutasi to meet with a representative from the Ministry of Natural Resources and Environment about the marine reserve management plan. By the time I got to the village I was late for the meeting, but of course he wasn't there yet. He came about an hour later and we sat and talked at the fale 'i tai with Tuatagaloa Joe.

I decided to use my gift from Hilda to treat myself to a sumptuous send off at Sinalei with Hannah and Erin. I checked to see if they could do it and then I called Tui to make the arrangements.

*Massages by the sea, Asian buffet for dinner, and a beautiful room with hot water. What a wonderful way to end my Samoan adventure!*

That afternoon, on a picture-perfect day with deep blue sky, fluffy white clouds, and a light breeze, I made the fifteen-minute drive to Sinalei to meet Erin and Hannah. Hannah and Leleiga planned to leave in April and marry back in the States, so Erin would be the only woman from Group 78 at the close of service conference a few months later.

Each in our own tiny beach fale, open to the ocean on one side, facing the immaculately landscaped grounds on the other, we luxuriated with an hour-long, full-body, coconut oil massage, followed by a facial. In the photos I took of us afterwards, we look muzzy with the endorphins rushing through our bloodstreams. We enjoyed drinks and dinner, toasting our unknown futures as the sun set in a blaze of glory. Later we swam and talked in the warm pool while the nearly full moon rose above us.

Early Saturday morning, as I leisurely drove Hilda's car back to Āpia, it felt like I was beginning my transition back to life in America. I *drove through* McDonalds for a Coke float and apple pie and dropped the car off at Hilda's shop. After hugs and many thanks, I took a taxi back to Sinalei and found Hannah and Erin reading on the beach. We ate lunch at the restaurant on the pier, and soon after I left for Poutasi.

I encouraged the girls to stay through the afternoon and paid for the taxis to take them to and from Āpia. Tui gave me a massive discount of course—the total for everything was just over the $500 tala that Hilda gave me.

## I Bid Farewell to My Village

That night, tables and chairs lined the walls of the church hall at my going away party, and everyone briskly waved their laufala fans in the hot muggy air. On a long table in the center were plates of deviled eggs, egg salad and tuna sandwiches, thick white bread with butter, biscuits, and cakes, with hot tea and coffee. I piled my plate full and sat at the front of the room in the place of honor.

One by one, the women of each family presented me with Samoan gifts—a stunning siapo with a plumeria flower design like my tattoo; lāvalava after lāvalava—red, black, yellow, green, and more; intricately woven laufala baskets, handbags, and fans; and a fierce, intricately carved, black war club with the hooked beak of a sea eagle.

As I humbly accepted their gifts and their gratitude, I wished I'd written a long eloquent speech sprinkled with proverbs and honorific phrases. Instead, I spoke from my heart. I thanked them for the joy I'd received from the kids at the Homework Center, for the opportunity to live by the sea and learn about its wonders and treasures, and for the many kindnesses I'd been given. I ended with these few words before the tears might come.

*"Faʻafetai tele lava mo le avanoa e sau i Poutasi e galue mo le nuʻu i le pisikoa. ʻOu te alofa le nuʻu ma le tagata o Poutasi. O le a ʻou misi ʻoutou."* ("Thank you very, very much for the opportunity to come to Poutasi to work for the village in the Peace Corps. I love the village and the people of Poutasi. I will miss you.")

Then we gathered for a smaller party at the house—Niu, Saina, and the three kids, Tuatagaloa Joe and Tui, Samu and Lupe, Feonuʻu and Uiti, 'Ofisa and her husband Tavita, and Conrad, the German doctor. We merrily drank Vailima beer and rosé wine as we stuffed ourselves on leftover sandwiches, cake, and coconut buns. I expressed my meager words of thanks and gave Niu and Saina a plaque I bought at Hilda's shop that said: "Bless this house o Lord we pray, Make it safe by night and day."

The next morning, I attended Sunday church services for the last time. After all the days when I didn't want to go or was bored with it, I suddenly knew I'd miss this too. The warm glow of the sun shining through the red cross at the front of the sanctuary, Letone's slightly raspy voice as he read from the Bible, the way the songs of the choir bounced off the vaulted wooden ceiling, and all that had been a fundamental part of my routine—from now on, it would different.

After the service, I stood up front and thanked everyone, especially Pastor Letone and his wife Logo, for welcoming me to the congregation and the choir, for the use of the church hall for the Homework Center, and for the opportunity to teach their children. As usual, Tamamasui had risen at dawn to start the Sunday umu fire, and at dinner with the family I ate my fill of smoky baked taro with palusami, breadfruit, and fried lamb chops accompanied by chicken soup.

In the late afternoon, I walked to the Catholic service and said farewell and thank you to those villagers as well. Afterwards, by the statue of Mary in her tiny alcove in front of the church, I hugged goodbye to Tumema. I'd always be indebted to her for inviting me to trek beside her on the household monthly inspections in my early days in Poutasi. My friend Soloao, who'd been a key part of the Marine Project, gave me a lovely laufala fan as I hugged her and said goodbye.

I'd spent the afternoon between church services drafting an interim United Nations grant report for the Marine Project. That evening, I sat in the cool breeze with Tuatagaloa Joe and Tui on their deck facing the bay as we reviewed the report and talked about next steps for the project.

I'd always felt uniquely at ease with Tuatagaloa Joe and Tui and we'd become good friends. Somehow, I knew I'd see them again. They'd traveled the world, including Hawai'i, and it was likely they'd be there again one day. We made sure that we had one another's email addresses and I stood to go. I embraced Tui, "Goodbye dear friend, I love you."

Tui hugged me tightly as she replied, "We love you and we'll miss you."

Joe hugged me too and added, "Yes, we'll miss you very much. Come back for a visit soon. You always have a home in Poutasi."

Then I walked to the fale 'i tai next door.

*The sun's sinking lower and lower over 'Ili'ili Point. The color of the sea changes all day depending on the light. Tonight, the water to the east is deep blue, while the water to the west reflects so brightly that I can't even look at it, as if shining on a mirror. It'll gradually turn golden and then pink, as a few bright clouds reflect the last rays of the sun. Soon, only silhouettes on the horizon.*

It's difficult to convey in mere words the depth and complexity of how much the fale 'i tai meant to me. The structure itself was at the core of my sojourn in Poutasi from the beginning when the mayor pointed it out on my first drive through the village. It's easy to see how I'd be enchanted by its location at the edge of the sea with the ever-changing, breathtaking view. But it became so much more than that. It was *my* space. I read, photographed sunset after sunset, worked on project paperwork, played with the kids, and learned about the village and the people in it.

"*'Ou te alu i le fale 'i tai*" ("I'm going to the house by the sea") was such a common refrain, that if I appeared with my journal, book, and camera, looking as if I was about to set off somewhere, the family would ask, "*E alu i le fale 'i tai?*" ("Are you going to the house by the sea?").

It was the center of my world, and the village revolved around me with a 360° view. Villagers passed by on the way to church or walked to the government road for school, to catch a bus, go to the store, or visit friends. Offshore, fishing boats came and went to deeper waters and there was constant canoe traffic. The paddlers would shout "Tālofa!" and wave if they passed close to shore on their way to a destination in Poutasi or a neighboring village.

*One of the more spectacular sunsets. I swam at high tide in the twilight. As I lay floating, one perfect star appeared in the darkening sky right above me.*

Later as I finished packing, the kids bounced in and out of my room. Sprawled on the floor, Tia, Fetū, and Hemara drew hearts sprinkled with glitter on construction paper and made cards expressing how much they'd miss me. I still have them.

On Monday morning I woke up at 4:30, tossed and turned, then I gave up on going back to sleep and got up an hour later. At dawn, the village was quiet and the air was cool as my flip flops crunched on the tiny pebbles between our house and Meleisea Seti and Mataomanu's compound. I walked along the edge of the ocean inhaling the fragrance of the light sea breeze and moso'oi flowers. I passed the church hall with the Homework Center in the back, then on to Soloao's house at the fork leading to the government road. Smoke from morning cooking fires was beginning to drift in the warming air. I walked on to the edge of Sāleilua, accompanied by the morning chorus of chirping birds and crowing roosters, with occasional crying babies, and the sounds of the village stirring.

As I turned around, I faced Poutasi. I stopped to take it all in, and as I gazed at lovely Nu'usafe'e Island, I took a deep breath and thought, "This is it!" Tomorrow I'd be on to the next thing in my life, even though I didn't know exactly what that was yet. I was reluctant to say goodbye but looked forward to the unknown future. Then I briskly walked back.

Usually the kids would've left with Niu to be dropped off at school, but all three had colds so they stayed home that morning. As Niu and

I hugged our goodbye, I told him once more how grateful I was for all he and the family had done for me and we promised to keep in touch. Notwithstanding the occasional fa'aSāmoa procrastination and lateness, Niu had always been there for me and our projects.

I piled my baggage in front of the house, including the refrigerator to return to Roma and Wilma on the way to Āpia. With my cup of tea, and Saina with her coffee and cigarette, we sat on the shady side of the house as Fetū, Tia, and Hemara ran in and out, belying their runny-nosed condition. Papu, the PC driver, drove up in front of the house at 9:30, although he was supposed to come at 10:00. Go figure—the one time in Samoa when someone comes early!

"I love you Donna!" Saina said with tear-filled eyes. "You're my pālagi sister."

"I love you, too, my Samoan sister!" I replied, my eyes also gleaming with tears.

Donna and Saina relaxing outside the church hall.

We held each other in a tight circle with the kids, and then, unwillingly, I pulled away and climbed into the PC pickup. I waved, shouted

*"Fā! Fā! Fā!"* ("Bye! Bye! Bye!") and threw kisses out the open window until they were out of sight.

I was lost in thought along the route I'd taken so many times in 'Afakasi's bus, passing waterfalls, down to the Falefa River valley, and through bustling villages along the way. As we turned off the highway toward Manunu, I was prepared to tell Papu we'd have to wait for Roma and Wilma if they weren't yet back from their planned trip to Āpia. But they were home, having canceled the trip so they wouldn't miss seeing me. While Papu listened to the radio and patiently smoked a few cigarettes in the cab with the doors open, I gratefully returned the little refrigerator. With our steaming cups of tea, Roma, Wilma, and I nibbled biscuits at the kitchen table and said our farewells as Donna La'itiiti, now nearly eighteen months old, toddled around. As I got up to leave, I scooped her up for one last snuggle. I didn't know when I'd see them again, but I knew we'd keep in touch.

When we arrived in Āpia, I finished up paperwork at the PC office, said goodbye to everyone there, then dropped off the United Nations progress report, and I was done! All I had to do was relax until the nighttime flight to LAX. At Mari's cafe, I met Hannah and Erin for a late and leisurely lunch at a front table with an ocean view. As their surrogate mom and friend, I was proud of these two young Group 78 women, and I looked forward to hearing of their future adventures and successes.

Twenty-four hours later, the plane touched down at DIA on the plains at the edge of Denver. The landscape was cold, harsh, and barren, with the snowcapped Rockies standing in stark contrast to the low green mountains of Samoa. But it was America, and I was home.

### Everything Changed and Nothing had Changed

Jackson pulled me into his arms for a kiss at the airport curbside pick-up and I relaxed into his embrace. Once we were in the city, we excitedly talked over a lunch of cheap Mexican food and I savored every spicy bite. I was exhausted from traveling with little sleep and jet lag, so we made plans to see each other that evening. With my house still rented and Mom's surgery in less than two weeks, I planned to stay with her.

*First thoughts on being back in America:*

*We take so much for granted in this wonderful country. We have so much. We buy so much. We want so much. I spent little money for eighteen months but ironically (thus far), I'm not interested in buying or shopping. Because of the approaching holidays, constant commercials on TV advertise gluttonous stuff nobody needs. It's obnoxious.*

The hot showers felt luxurious. Not having hot water may be the thing I missed most besides friends and family. The size of the supermarkets and their abundance nearly overwhelmed my vision. I'd so missed having a variety of affordable fresh vegetables! I'll never take them for granted again.

*Time goes so much faster when you don't have to search for something to fill every moment of every day. So many things to do and places to go! And I can get in my car and drive there! I can pick up my phone and call anyone or chat online while watching interesting TV. Amazing!*

In *I'm a Stranger Here Myself: Notes on Returning to America After 20 Years Away*—one of more than one hundred books that I read while in Samoa—Bill Bryson said that coming back to one's native land after an absence is "a surprisingly unsettling business." He wrote:

Happily, there is a flipside to this. The many good things about America also took on a bewitching air of novelty. I was as dazzled as any newcomer by the famous ease and convenience of daily life, the giddying abundance of absolutely everything . . . and that rooms can have more than one electrical socket.

*I feel like I'm on vacation, that I'll be going back, and yet simultaneously Samoa seems far away and long ago. I worked up to the last minute, tying up loose ends, talking to people, and now, it's just over. I'll keep in touch, but it's really over.*

When Peace Corps volunteers return home one of the toughest parts may still be ahead—what PC calls "readjustment"—the period of disorientation after returning to one's native culture after living abroad. It may last for a few weeks or a few months, and it may be recognizable, or so subtle that it may almost be missed. Returning home is a process, just like getting used to one's host country. Once I got back home, I automatically spoke Samoan to all little kids and dogs as I always did in Samoa, because there they were certain not to know English. I'd even say to my own toddling grandson "*Aua!*" ("Don't!") or "*Sau mai*" ("Come to me"), a habit it took a few weeks to break.

But more significantly, at the time it was hard to have any real perspective on what the PC experience had meant to me or how the world back home had changed, or not, while I was gone. There had been small changes, but basically everyone else's lives seemed pretty much the same. They continued the circle of their daily life and I couldn't describe how I was different, how my life would be *forever* different.

And then there was the readjustment to Jackson.

*Since I've been back it isn't what I thought it would be. I don't feel the love from either of us. Maybe my expectations were unrealistic. Perhaps having him waiting back home was simply a good way for me to get through a difficult experience in Samoa and nothing more.*

Because I was different, I needed someone different. After I'd been back for a couple of weeks, my friend Dana asked me how it was going for me and Jackson, and she said that my body language spoke volumes before I opened my mouth. Then I got an email from Harmut, the German engineer. It wasn't remotely romantic, but perhaps the memory of a perfect afternoon by the sea at Sinalei with a handsome, blue-eyed man helped me to see myself more honestly. That day, three weeks after I returned from Samoa, I broke up with Jackson by email. After that exchange, we saw each other only once.

*So, that's over. Not one tear and a huge sense of relief. I read the* Samoan Observer *online and I'm listening to Radio Australia. Of course, ironically Radio Australia makes me think of Samoa, not Australia. Connecting with Samoa feels good. I'd enjoy going back someday. I have Christmas cookies in the oven and the house smells of ginger, chocolate, and evergreen.*

One characteristic of the return to America is almost non-stop enthusiasm and telling about the experience. I was guilty on all counts. In the beginning, it was expected and welcomed, but I couldn't stop talking about life in Samoa. They never said it, but my friends and family sometimes probably wanted me to "shut up about it already!"

And then there's the feeling that you've lost the purpose in your life that existed in Peace Corps. Yes, it was temporary and frustrating, and I'd wanted so much to go home, but it was rewarding beyond comprehension. And I knew that the village of Poutasi appreciated the work that I'd done there. How would I now find something in my life that I'd feel that passionate about?

Despite all the ups and downs and my relief at being back home, I immediately missed Samoa and my Samoan families. I also missed the excitement and stimulation that came with the PC experience and the adventure of living in a foreign country. Indeed, in the weeks that followed, I applied for and was accepted by WorldTeach, to teach English as a second language for one year in American Samoa. I was "on the rebound" from my relationship with Samoa. I worried that I'd lose my ability to speak the language, I didn't want to lose touch with the people there whom I'd grown to love, and I missed living by the sea with the fale 'i tai a stone's throw away. I thought that going to American Samoa would keep me in touch with those things. Although I ultimately didn't accept that offer, my application precisely illustrates this syndrome of post-PC disorientation.

### One Last Goodbye

I went to Samoa with two suitcases, a small carry-on, and a red journal, and came home with so much more. That journal and the fale 'i tai made all the difference. The house by the sea was my physical haven and my journal was my psychological refuge. I resumed avid journaling when I got back to the States and have never stopped.

> *I started a new journal entitled "Life After Peace Corps." Time to move on . . . Goodbye dear friend. Our journey together was amazing!*

# Chapter 13

## Crisis Brings Closure

*A logo tai 'ua logo uta*
*"When it is felt toward the sea, it is felt toward the land"*
*When something happens in our family, no matter how far away*
*they might be, we all feel the effect.*

I sent periodic gift packages to Manunu and Poutasi, mailed letters to Hemara, and sent emails to Tuatagaloa Joe and Tui, and to Niu and Saina via his office. Then, ten months after I came home to the States, on September 30, 2009, I wrote:

*It's the day after the earthquake and tsunami in Samoa. I can't write much. I'm numb, exhausted, emotionally drained. My heart is broken.*

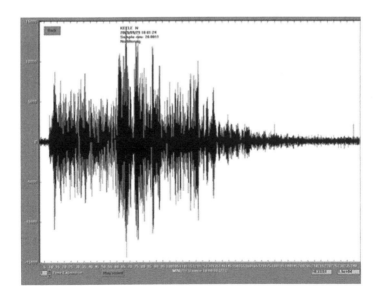

With a massive moment magnitude of 8.1, the earthquake struck at 6:48 AM. Locals said it lasted up to three minutes.[12] Only a few minutes passed between the quake and the tsunami, not enough time to sound a warning. Eyewitnesses described between one and four giant walls of water reaching up to forty-five feet high as they hit 'Upolu's south side head-on.

It was mid-morning by the time that I heard a radio announcer briefly describe the event, and I literally stopped in my tracks in disbelief. Although Group 78 had finished their service and gone home one month before, I had contacts at the PC office and friends still there in subsequent groups. The phones didn't work, so I frantically sent them emails and began to search online for news while I waited to hear. Then late that afternoon, I got a reply from the PC Country Director who told me that Poutasi was one of the hardest hit villages, with initial reports saying it was devastated, flattened, with many killed. But the most shattering news was that Tui was among the dead. I didn't yet know if the rest of my family was safe.

*Today will be another hard day. I slept very little last night. Every time I closed my eyes, I could only see my beautiful village as it was and imagine what must have happened. And I see the children and know that their lives are changed forever.*

Those first days of not knowing were terrifying—a physical dread deep inside me that wouldn't go away. I spent hours and hours online day and night, combing through news reports from all over the South Pacific. What I found alarmed me—photos of places I knew intimately that were demolished. I kept thinking, "If Tui had been killed, how could the rest have survived?"

I got answers forty-eight hours later in an email from a PCV in Āpia.

---

12 There were actually two separate earthquakes of magnitude 8.1 and 8.0 eighty seconds apart, an extremely rare event known as a "doublet." The quakes originated near the Tonga Trench, one of the most seismically active areas in the world.

At my behest, he'd contacted Niu's office at the Ministry of Natural Resources and Environment and learned that Niu, Saina, Tamamasui, and the kids were safe. They'd been in Āpia the morning of the disaster. However, I learned nothing more about Tuatagaloa Joe at that point, other than that he was alive. I was so drained by living with the terror of not knowing for hour after hour that I immediately fell into a deep, dream-filled sleep in the middle of the afternoon.

*I still can't come to grips with the fact that Tui is dead. It's even hard to write the words.*

All my family connections and friendships in Samoa are precious to me. I look back and see how each fit uniquely into my Peace Corps life, and beyond. Tui's death, two days before her sixty-fourth birthday, was made all the worse by its suddenness and the surrounding tragedy. When I think of Tui, her kindness and caring always come first to mind. She automatically reached out to others in need, including a lonesome pisikoa.

She and I had spent many hours together chatting by the sea at her house next to the fale 'i tai or at Sinalei. We'd gone together to Āpia for Peace Corps projects, and to fun events that I wouldn't have attended without her kind invitation. Our friendship was easy, and we were part of the same Samoan family. When we were together, I forgot about my troubles and relaxed in a way that I rarely did in Poutasi—just two friends chatting over a glass of rosé wine. I was confident that Niu and Saina would have gone to Poutasi by this time, without access to phones or email, so the first details I learned were from a *tvnz.co.nz* article online. Reading the story in print made it seem real, and I let the tears flow for the first time since I'd heard the news.

Tui Annandale wasn't one of the lucky ones. Annandale and her husband Joe were having morning prayers at home in the village of Poutasi when the earthquake struck. Annandale tried to flee the wave by car, but she was sucked out and drowned.

Tui's friend Leiloa was on foot behind the car and miraculously lived. "The wave picked me up and threw me into the church. I held onto the pillar until the water passed," she says.

Tui at Sinalei. (Photo courtesy of Tuatagaloa Joe Annandale.)

### *My Peace Corps Family Supports Each Other*

Meghan, like all of us former Samoa PCVs, had been searching online. When she found the news of Tui's death, she sent me a heartfelt email with the simple subject line: "I am so sorry." I was relieved to hear that her Samoan family was safe since they lived far enough inland that the waves didn't reach them.

I began an email conversation with Shane, the other member of Group 78 whose south-facing village was hard hit. He told me sorrowfully that he lost five family members, some of his students, and a friend who was schoolteacher. I grieved with him when he told me about the makeshift funeral in his village that he watched on YouTube. He wrote:

> *There is literally nothing left. I recognize everyone in the video. I've never felt this bad. It's hard to drag myself away from the computer, but I have to. Call me if you want to talk.*

And I replied:

> *Tonight, I don't want to think about "it" anymore. The deaths of our friends and Samoan families are hard enough, but our villages have a special place in our hearts unlike anywhere else we've ever lived, or probably ever will. If miraculously no one in Poutasi had been killed, I would still be heartbroken. The village I knew is gone forever.*

### *Contact with Samoa Brings Sadness and Relief*

Finally, several days later, Niu and Saina were able to telephone me. I slumped with relief to hear their voices! They told me that they'd all slept at Saina's mother's house (two miles inland from the sea) the night before. After they felt the earthquake, they tried to calm down and turned on the radio. When they heard the news of the tsunami and the mention of Poutasi, they immediately left for the village.

Even on that side of the island people living close to the ocean fled inland after the earthquake damaged many buildings. Boats of all sizes were immediately underway every direction in Āpia Harbor, trying to avoid being bashed ashore by the four-foot waves that hit the north side.

Niu kept a stiff upper lip, but Saina began to cry as they told me that the reports I'd heard about Poutasi were true. Everything along the bayfront was demolished, except the two churches, now gutted and windowless. Our house and Tuatagaloa Joe and Tui's were partially standing, but uninhabitable. Saina laughed a little when she told me, "Hemara is angry at the tsunami because she wrote a letter to you and it washed away." I told her to tell Hemara and the others that I'd mailed their White Sunday gifts just before the wave, so there would be a box of goodies arriving soon.

I learned more sorrowful details. A few days after the ordeal, Tui's mother, Anna Ruland Schaafhausen, succumbed to her injuries.

My friend Logo Letone Uili, the pastor's wife, died. Letone had taken the children to school in Āpia and she was home alone. I remember how her eyes smiled, and the day I breathed in the delightful aroma of a juicy pear she gave me as we sat and talked next to the Homework Center. It was the only one I ate in Samoa.

'Ofisa's mother, Vaimoana Fui Fa'asavalu, was swept away along with 'Ofisa's baby boy, Filisi Tavita Fa'atau. On my first abrupt visit to the village when I didn't know what to do, I'd gone fale to fale and introduced myself. Moana's home was the first place in Poutasi that I'd sat cross-legged, talking in my halting Samoan as she wove a fala mat.

'Afakasi's two children, Nonumaifele Tofilau, who slept on my lap on the bus with the clinking bottles, and his baby sister, Maupenei Tofilau drowned along with Siliva Fa'pulou, another of Mataomanu and Meleisea Seti's grandchildren.

Eleven-year-old Amataga Tiotio died. He came often to the Homework Center. I remember his smiling face filled with excitement and delight.

The tsunami killed 149 people in Samoa, and nearly fifty percent of them were children under the age of ten. Other lives were lost in American Samoa and Tonga.

With phone service restored, I was also able to talk to Roma and Wilma. Since they lived on high ground far from the sea on the north side of the island, I hadn't been as franticly concerned about their safety. But I recognized that I'd been more worried than I thought as my anxiety diminished when I heard their happy greeting.

Wilma and Roma had just arisen for the day. Wilma said she was sleepily standing in the center room folding the sheets they'd covered with the night before when the earthquake hit, and Roma had been walking toward the kitchen. They said it felt like it would never stop. Wilma grabbed Donna La'itiiti, called to the other children, and they all ran outside. They were relieved to see that there was no damage. And then they heard the news of the tsunami on the radio and like me, they stood still listening intently in shock and disbelief.

The beach in Poutasi looking across the bay toward the reef.

The beach after the tsunami. It took weeks to remove debris from the bay.

The church hall with the Homework Center in the rear.

The church hall after the tsunami.

In Poutasi, the first days after the disaster were filled with grief, trauma, and the challenges presented by the loss of necessities like roads, transportation, and water. Since the natural spring behind the Catholic church had been restored as part of our Marine Project, it became the only source of fresh water for the village immediately following the earthquake and tsunami. Within days, the washed-out bridge at the fork was replaced by the Samoan government and work begun on an additional village access road behind the Catholic church. Relief aid and donations flowed in from around the world, with Australia and New Zealand leading the efforts.

In the coming weeks, Niu emailed to tell me that with government assistance and a bank loan, he and Saina planned to build a new house on Tuatagaloa family land on the government road, slightly higher and further from the sea.

### My Return to Samoa

Immediately after the catastrophe I wanted to go back and help somehow, but it didn't seem as if there was much I could do. So I waited until recovery had begun, and in 2010, eight months after the tsunami, I went back with trepidation for a two-week visit. I was anxiously looking forward to seeing my Samoan families, but I harbored a different kind of anxiety about what I'd find when I returned to Poutasi. As ʻUpolu appeared out of my plane window, I wrote:

*I'm unsettled and nervous. I don't feel like I'm mentally ready for this trip. Maybe there isn't a way to be ready. I have tenuous arrangements to show up and that's about it. Fa'aSāmoa. I have no plan!*

As we approached for landing, everything on that part of the island looked the same—the densely forested mountains, coconut groves, villages dotting the shoreline, and the cerulean sea. I stepped out of the plane, walked across the tarmac to customs, and instantly realized that I'd forgotten the intensity of Samoa's heat and humidity! I surprised the taxi driver when this pālagi in jeans greeted him in Samoan and gave him directions to Mari's Cafe and Bakeshop, where I immediately saw familiar faces.

Saina's mother, Paugata, was seated as always at her small table with ledger and pencil. I said, *"Tālofa Tinā!"* ("Greetings Mother!"), leaning over and kissing her on the cheek as the aroma of baking bread enveloped me. She called to one of the shop girls to bring me an ice-cold bottle of orange Fanta and an egg sandwich. I sat down beside her, and in between customers, vendors, and employee interruptions, we caught up on family news and talked of the tsunami with great sadness. A half hour later one of the numerous cousins gave me a ride to Paugata's family compound in Āpia. As we drove up, I spotted Saina seated in the shade with a cup of coffee and a cigarette.

I leaped out of the car and dashed to her. We embraced, as she said with a grin, "My sister!"

"My sister!" I replied, holding her tightly.

Niu had been promoted to Principal Terrestrial Biodiversity Officer for the Ministry of Natural Resources and Environment. He was at an environmental conference in Kenya, due to return the following week. I looked forward to seeing him too, but I was happy to have Saina all to myself for a few days. On the front porch I sank into the overstuffed tropical print cushions and began to relax from travel fatigue and ease into the fa'aSāmoa ambiance. She and I planned to go together to Poutasi that afternoon after the kids came home from school.

The people of Poutasi hadn't had many photos when I'd lived there, and knowing many families lost everything, I took with me over six hundred photographs to give them. In addition, I'd made an album for Niu and Saina with pictures of the family, house, and village—before the devastation. Seated side by side, Saina and I looked at the photos, crying over some as she tried to tell me what village life was like now.

"Oh Donna, you won't believe it!" she said, eyes closed, shaking her head. She told me that Tuatagaloa Joe was getting his strength back and had restored the house he and Tui had built by the sea.

When a cab brought the kids from school, all three swarmed out and ran squealing to me. I scooped them up en masse as far as my arms would reach.

As we taxied into Poutasi that afternoon, I saw that every fale along the seashore was swept away or left in ruin. At the fork where I'd walked straight toward Sāleilua or turned toward the government road, Soloao's house was gone. The wave surged to the edge of the medical clinic, roared through the church hall leaving a mangled mess, and swept away Logo and their house. Meleisea Seti and Mataomanu's family compound was gone, save for the stone and concrete foundations. The big mango tree behind their main house and a few breadfruit had survived, but the bayfront was mostly denuded of vegetation with lonely snags here and there.

Next door, one entire side of our house had been torn off, metal roof twisted, and all the doors and windows blown out. Across the road, the fale 'i tai was a pile of rubble.

My room was on the right, behind the Red Cross emergency water tanks.

Niu, Saina, and the kids had been staying in town at Paugata's, coming to the village whenever they could while their new home was being built. At the old house, the former kitchen in the rear still had a roof on it, so they'd set up housekeeping there. Nailed boards replaced windows and ripped-off walls. Fortunately, one of the bathrooms was still usable after water had been reconnected. Tuatagaloa Joe intended to reconstruct the house for guests and family gatherings.

Saina told me that I'd be more comfortable at Sinalei in the room Tuatagaloa Joe had offered, but I told her I wanted to stay in Poutasi. I didn't want her to go to a lot of trouble for my sake, but she insisted on borrowing a single bed for me. So we all slept together in the kitchen, me in my small bed, and Saina and the kids nearby on mats on the floor.

*How odd to wake up in the morning in Samoa with no roosters crowing at our house, or next door, or next door. Despite my protestations, I'm grateful for the bed and mosquito net. I'm also glad that I stayed here with the family. Even if parts of the house aren't here, it feels like home.*

The next morning, Hemara, Tia, Fetū, and I walked about the village. In the old days, Rocky would've run along panting beside us, but of course he was washed away. Of sixteen family compounds on the bay front, only four had been partially rebuilt. Damaged structures still stood, green shoots of vegetation sprouting inside, with lots of open space where houses, the church hall and the Homework Center, and the district school had once been. Both churches remained, repaired and painted inside, pock-marked outside, with a new alcove for Mary—facing the ocean—at the Catholic church.

As we walked, village kids joined us, shyly ducking their heads as they said, *"Tālofa, Donna, ke alu i fea?"* ("Greetings, Donna, where are you going?") and then they strutted along with our little parade. More than once, they playfully pushed each other from behind, and shouted "Tsunami!" and then sprinted ahead laughing.

I carried my huge packet of photos, organized by families, and bequeathed them to their new owners wherever someone was at home. Every time, I sat quietly as each short stack was eagerly devoured with a quick look through, then slowly savored with exclamations of joy and sadness, sometimes tears, and always a hug and *"Fa'afetai! Ia fa'amanuia mai le Atua "* ("Thank you! God bless you").

Aunese looks at a photo of her former home by the ocean.

That afternoon, I walked the familiar yet alien path of my usual morning route along the ocean. At the crossroad where my friend Soloao once lived, there was nothing but a flat cement pad. In her new house, slightly inland, one of the few rebuilt near the sea, she told me her tsunami story. At the time, her husband was in New Zealand having surgery for a toe amputation as the result of diabetes. After the earthquake, she began to check around the house to see if everything was okay. Then her son called out when he saw the wave coming. Her daughter sped up the road clutching her baby, and Soloao ran with her son holding her hand. She said she could see that she wouldn't be able to keep up and shouted at him to go ahead. They lost touch of each other's hands as the first wave hit, and the wall of water washed her up to the clinic. She lay there gasping, bruised and battered, and saw the second wave take out Logo and Letone's house, and probably our house. She was hospitalized for nine days. She told me she didn't know what to do in her new house because none of her things were there, but she was glad to be back teaching her fourth-grade class.

Me with Tui on the left and Soloao on the right in happier times.

It was a lot to take in.

*It seems like I should be writing more about how it feels coming back. Maybe I need time to process it. It does make it real to see the village as it is now, and how much has changed.*

The next day was Sunday, a beautiful sunny day. I was welcomed genuinely and profusely at the Congregational church. It felt odd to sit in the back with Saina and not up front with the choir. Instead of the usual $20 tala that I'd offered every Sunday during Peace Corps, I gave $100 tala which put me at the top of the tithes for the day. I understood a bit more then why it was read aloud after a hint of pride snuck into my thoughts. After Sunday dinner and a nap, Tumema came by the house and we reminisced as I shared more photos. Living on the government road next to the store, her home wasn't affected, though her life in the shattered village certainly was.

As usual, Monday was Saina's day off, so we walked through the village in the early morning coolness on new pathways. She showed me young trees the villagers had planted along the edge of the inland lagoon where it emptied into the ocean under the new bridge. We walked past the new church hall and pastor's house under construction on the government road and down the newly constructed road behind the Catholic church, sharing photos along the way.

Each family's traditional land went from the ocean toward the mountain, so once again, next to Niu and Saina's new home on the government road, was Mataomanu and Meleisea Seti's new family compound. Saina walked on and I stopped and sat on the floor with Mataomanu. As she wove a laufala mat, we talked about family and the tsunami. She was found unconscious near Tui. Meleisea Seti had gone to feed the pigs, so he was further back from the sea, although still caught in the waves. Mataomanu pulled up the hem of her lāvalava and showed me the scars of a terrible wound on her calf. She said she was fortunate that volunteer doctors had come from New Zealand and Australia and with four operations were able to save her leg.

She told me that in the hospital she'd dreamt of walking to a beautiful white house. Everything was brilliant white, the flowers, even the leaves on the plants. She said she kept walking, and walking, and she was so happy, and looked forward to arriving at the white house at the end of the road. Then the plants started to turn green, the flowers were brightly colored, and she heard Meleisea Seti's voice. Still dreaming, she turned and saw him seated at a table with three black envelopes laid before him (she did not yet know that three of her grandchildren had been killed in the tsunami). Then she felt someone touching her feet and heard Meleisea Seti thanking the doctors for saving her life.

'Afakasi and his family were also living at the new family compound. I said hello to him as he sat staring at the ocean. He was a shell of his former self and there was no light in his eyes.

So that Saina could work her evening shifts at the store, we went back to Āpia and I slept with her and the kids at her mother's house. Despite the constant reminders of tragedy, I was enjoying my time with her immensely. During my PC days, she'd stayed in town much of the time, and when she'd been in Poutasi I'd always felt I was imposing on her limited time at home. Sharing our still-fresh grief, and this opportunity to spend so much time with her, brought us even closer.

I slipped out in the cool morning to write on the front porch as Saina slept on the floor nearby. As the family began to arouse, Paugata's house girl brought me a cup of tea and a hot dog in a bun with catsup. That held me until noon when Saina and I enjoyed an unhurried lunch at Mari's Cafe, which was the same except for the new big-screen TV. Reruns of the Vancouver Winter Olympics were playing, and it was especially incongruous watching Japanese women curling while I sipped coconut water with a straw directly from the source. Then Saina and I shopped ourselves silly from store to store—me trying to buy stuff for her, her trying to buy stuff for me, both of us protesting, laughing together, buying nonetheless.

The next day, June 1st, was Samoan Independence Day. Hemara and I sleepily got up to a damp dawn and took a taxi to the parade grounds. Her school class marched smartly in their blue and white uniforms in the huge parade, passing by the review stand where the Head of State of Samoa, the Prime Minister, the King of Tonga, and other dignitaries sat with their wives, all splendidly dressed. It went on seemingly forever, and as it began to rain, I was grateful for my "elderly" status which had accorded me a chair under a tent. Hemara was soaked to the skin when we reunited, and she asked, excitedly "Did you see me? Did you see me?" I assured her that I did indeed and after we were dry and fed back at Paugata's, I took a taxi to Sinalei.

## Tui's Story

I looked forward to seeing Tuatagaloa Joe. He'd been relentlessly working toward healing and restoring the village and getting Sinalei open again. As I sat reading by the pool, despite the familiarity of the place, it seemed like a world away, as it always did when I lived a few miles down the road.

*This is what I needed today—to get away from reality, although Tui's presence is everywhere. I see her in the water-filled pottery basins with tiny flowers arranged in intricate floating geometric designs, in the sign she hung on the kitchen door with pictures of fish species that Sinalei won't buy under a certain size, and in the delicate attention to detail in every corner.*

I stayed at the resort that night and the next. It had been considerably damaged by the tsunami, but fortunately no one was killed. The waves reached the edge of the swimming pool. The fale where I first stayed, and others nearby, were washed away along with the seaside restaurant and the pier. Most had been rebuilt, re-opened five months prior to my visit. The new massage fale was named *Tui i Lagi Spa*—Tui in Heaven Spa.

*Tuatagaloa Joe told me his tsunami story yesterday. Leiloa was cooking in the kitchen while he and Tui were in the midst of their morning devotions in their bedroom when the earthquake struck. While it was still shaking, he ran to Tui's ninety-five year old mother's room. Anna was in bed and he held her hand and told her that it would be okay. Within minutes Tui shouted when she saw the water receding. He looked out the window and could see the coral exposed. He gathered Anna in his arms and put her beside him in the pickup cab. Leiloa sped off on foot, while Tui and Anna's nurse/caregiver jumped into the truck bed. He said the wall of water was "immense." He realized that they wouldn't be able to make it to the government road, so he sped straight inland toward the big mango tree behind Mataomanu and Meleisea Seti's house. Then the massive wave hit, and Tuatagaloa Joe's pickup rolled over and over. With all his strength he held on to the steering wheel and Anna. When the truck came to a stop it was on its side in standing water in the fao trees at the edge of the inland lagoon. Water was waist-deep everywhere—he said it looked like a huge lake. He pulled Anna out of the truck and called to some boys on a little rise. They came running, padded a wheelbarrow with grass, and carted her to safety. Then he began calling for Tui. He said it was absolute bedlam. From all directions people were screaming, calling for their families, crying out in pain. He first made his way back to their house, thinking that perhaps Tui would do the same. When she wasn't there, he followed the path they'd taken behind Meleisea Seti's house, and beyond. Shortly, some boys came and said that they'd found Tui. He said he could tell immediately by their voices and body language that the news wasn't good. She was in a fao tree and it was likely from her position that she had a broken neck. They brought her to the store and cleaned her. He saw Mataomanu there with the huge gash on her leg, bleeding badly. Tuatagaloa Joe got into the back of another villager's pickup, cradling Tui in his arms, and they headed for Sinalei. By some quirk of fate, they met their daughter's car at the crossroad at Si'umu as she rushed toward Poutasi from Āpia. Devastated, they made their way together toward Sinalei.*

Tui had always told him she wanted to be buried in the traditional Samoan way—within twenty-four hours with no coffin. At sunrise the next morning, she was buried wrapped in siapo, high up on the mountain at the family homestead, a place she loved. Some family members wanted to wait so that extended family could come, but loyal to his partner of forty years, he put his foot down and insisted. Soon thereafter, he developed aspiration pneumonia known as "tsunami lung" from inhaling saltwater contaminated with mud and bacteria.

*Tuatagaloa Joe is just beginning to recover mentally and physically. He still has a chronic cough. He told me he's been in a deep, dark hole and how much he misses her. How he almost gave up and wanted to leave Poutasi. But he decided to come back, rebuild the house, and face his fears.*

*It'll take more time, but Saina tells me he's smiling more, and she can tell he's healing. When I try to imagine his loss, I feel my deep sadness at the tragic passing of my dear friend, but I know that can't compare to what he feels. A crack in his heart is the best I can do to describe it. Even when it's filled, there's a nugget of grief that'll be there always, along with the happy memories.*

### Connecting with Family

Tuatagaloa Joe loaned me Sinalei's small, white pickup for the rest of my visit, so now I had wheels to go wherever and whenever I wanted. Niu had returned from Kenya and I met him at their new house under construction in Poutasi. He drove up in his same blue Toyota pickup and the kids jumped out eagerly. Built on a slight rise, not far from F&K store, a slice of ocean was visible over the trees from the wide front veranda.

Niu looked happy and healthy as he told me about his new job responsibilities and the trip to Africa. The plumbing and electricity weren't connected yet, but the house was close to being finished. Saina would finally have an indoor kitchen sink. As we walked through, he excitedly described the details yet to be completed—bathroom tile, inside paint on the concrete block walls, landscaping, and a concrete sidewalk. Years before, he'd planted foxtail palms by the seaside house. When we lived there, we'd talked about how it was his favorite palm, and mine too, and he'd placed young ones in front of the new house.

After another luxurious night at Sinalei, I went to see Roma and Wilma, driving the way 'Afakasi used to go, along the southern coast to Mafa Pass and down the lush mountain slopes. Everything in Manunu seemed just the same. In three days, it would be exactly three years since I'd first arrived in the country, apprehensive and nervous. As Roma, Wilma, and I sat at their kitchen table, talking in Samoan while their house girl brought us tea and tuna sandwiches, I marveled inwardly at how easy it was now.

Donna La'itiiti as an adorable three-year-old.

We caught up on family news and talked of the biggest change in Manunu, a church hall which Roma was anxious to show me. When we walked in, it still smelled of new wood and fresh paint. The cream-colored concrete block building had a stage so the youth could perform, or practice for the next fiafia or White Sunday. During his years as pastor, Roma's love and devotion to Manunu's youth had guided many young lives. While we were trainees in the village, we'd danced to the beat of *Sau Malu*, the church youth band. Roma drove the band (and its successors) in the church van to play for hire in neighboring villages and took the boys and girls to soccer, rugby, or track and field games. But mostly he taught them respectful fa'aSāmoa and how to be grounded in the Congregational faith—attributes which served them well.

After tea, I walked to the intersection with the main road and on to the huge banyans and back. It was one of those days when the air was gauzy and gray but not threatening rain, cool with a slight breeze. Even though I kept up a brisk pace, I didn't sweat in the cool air of Manunu. We whiled away the rest of the day, talking, eating, greeting villagers who stopped by to see me and playing with Donna La'itiiti.

For the remainder of my stay, I explored 'Upolu with a freedom that I'd never had. Near the end, Hemara and I set off on a day trip around the eastern tip of the island. At almost fourteen she felt very grown up to be out of sight of her family with her indulgent aunty.

*I'm going to buy stamps and envelopes to leave with Hemara. She said she wanted to write me a private letter but didn't, because she had to give it to her dad to mail.*

She and I stopped whenever we felt like it along the way. We walked the meticulously groomed grounds of the Baha'i temple, got huge ice cream cones at Scoop's, and watched rainbows form out of storm clouds as we drove along the coast. We detoured off the government road to Manunu so I could say goodbye to the family, promising that I'd keep in touch and come back soon. We lunched at a tiny seaside restaurant where we ate our crispy fish and chips with ice-cold bottles of orange Fanta. But as we traveled the southern side of the island, our fun was dampened by the frequent sight of destroyed villages and left-over tsunami rubble. We stopped and talked to two hardy women from Habitat from Humanity in New Zealand who were helping to rebuild homes. Eight months later, it was far from over.

One-on-one "car time" is conducive to meaningful conversation and we made the most of it. No, she didn't have a boyfriend, school was good, and we did much musing and dissecting about the tsunami and the forever changes to Poutasi.

Hemara at fourteen posing in Poutasi.

Despite the lingering impacts, homes and lives were being rebuilt. And although I hadn't realized it when I'd decided to make the trip, I needed some reintegration too.

*My visit isn't over yet but winding down. I've found closure in more ways than I expected. I've realized some measure of finality in seeing Poutasi, changed as it is, mourning Tui and the others. But unexpectedly, I've also found closure to my Peace Corps experience. Letting go of what once was, accepting what happened in the past, and honoring the transition to something new. I left before my time was officially up, and although Mom needed me, I really left because I wanted to go home. And, although I'd been thinking about it for weeks, because I didn't tell Peace Corps or the village until just before I left, it seemed incongruously that I left in a rush.*

### Renewal Begins

While I was there I had conversations with Niu and Tuatagaloa Joe about the Marine Project, which carried on at least in part. The buoys and the concrete anchors that marked the Marine Protected Area had been washed away but the village planned to replace them. Sadly, the power of the waves damaged the coral. Mangroves can survive a tsunami, and indeed there's evidence that these odd, stilted trees reduce tsunami impacts.

The Homework Center at the church hall had continued successfully after I left, staffed by Niu and the village teachers. Indeed, they'd expanded it to create a quiet study area and library. Niu told me that on weekends it was a busy place where the children did homework and spent time on the computers. And the younger kids had been there too, coloring and making puzzles, like they did before.

When I heard the news that the village planned to build a bigger, better, and air-conditioned library/homework center, I was filled with joy and satisfaction to know that this little project would go on. Coordinating with Niu, Associate PC Director Kellye, and a Group

80 volunteer who was still in Samoa[13], we applied for a Peace Corps Partnership grant to purchase equipment for the new center. A few months later, Peace Corps presented the village with a new computer, a color printer and a monochrome printer, boxes of ink cartridges and paper, books, and miscellaneous learning materials.

Kellye and I had also done some personal fundraising for the kids of Poutasi and received nearly $2,000 USD from generous friends. On my visit I introduced Saina to Kellye, and they began planning a fun day for the children with crafts, games, prizes, and ice cream. It happened in September, three months later.[14] I wish I could have seen their smiling little faces! The remainder went to the new homework center.

*Only one more day and night in Samoa. I don't know when I'll come back. Probably in a couple of years. Even facing the destruction and loss, it's been so relaxing to be here without my Peace Corps hat on. I could be me and not the pisikoa from Poutasi.*

When you're a PCV it feels as if you're wearing a sign on your back constantly advertising your status no matter where you are in the country. Whether the observer knows you're just a pālagi or a volunteer, *you* know, so you do nothing that would reflect poorly on Peace Corps or America. It's your job. But now I was just a tourist, a white lady in a lāvalava. I still went to church in Poutasi and Manunu in my white puletasi, and I wore a lāvalava over my shorts when walking in the village. Because if I'd learned only one thing when I was in Samoa, it was respect.

---

13 Erica lived down the road from Poutasi. She literally outran the tsunami when it swept into her village and the house where she lived was destroyed. Her Samoan family moved to New Zealand and Erica left the village.

14 For an article about the kids' fun day and accompanying material about Tuatagaloa Joe's post-tsunami experience, see http://pacific.scoop.co.nz/2010/10/paramount-chief-welcomes-new-life-and-fresh-hope/

## Life in Samoa Moves Forward

For every Samoan and Poutasi villager—and for me—there will always be "before, and after the tsunami." It will never again be the same village that I lived in, and I grieve for it still.

The next chapters continue to be written. I've visited Samoa three more times, the latest in 2017 for the celebration of the 50th Anniversary of Peace Corps in Samoa, and coincidentally the 10th Anniversary for Group 78. For most of the more than one hundred returning volunteers celebrating the anniversary, it was their first time back in years or decades and I loved hearing their stories. I organized a meal for fifteen PC friends at Sinalei. It was fiafia night at the resort, highlighting Samoan food and entertainment for the guests. These few, and only a handful more, were the only people in the world who knew what it had been like to be a pisikoa in Samoa. We toasted past and future, sang along with familiar Samoan songs, watched the blazing fire knife dancers, and the moon rising over the ocean.

It was wonderful to see Meghan (a technology engineer at Disney Studios), meet her French husband, and see baby photos. Erin didn't make it to the reunion, being pregnant at the time. I'd met her husband the year before when I visited them in Baltimore where she was a research scientist at the University of Maryland.

Hannah was there. She and Leleiga lived in New Jersey where Hannah was a Program Associate at Rutger's University and Leleiga was taking classes at the local community college. Back at the beginning of my training in Manunu, Leleiga had lived with the family at Roma and Wilma's. He was a college student at the National University of Samoa (NUS), smart, funny, and a talented musician and dancer. Hannah had a crush on him—but relationships between young people in Samoa are tricky things. So, believing that there was mutual chemistry between them, I told Roma at breakfast one morning that one of the pisikoa girls liked Leleiga. He asked who, and I said I couldn't tell him.

That evening, Roma told Leleiga and Roma Jr. to go out to the grassy malae in the center of the village and talk to the pisikoa. Several American young people would gather there in the evenings and some Samoan young people would join them. But Leleiga and Roma Jr. were the pastor's kids, who wouldn't otherwise do that without his permission. Hannah and Leleiga spent the whole evening talking, and the rest is history. Maybe they'd have ended up together anyway, but I like to think that I helped a little.

In 2012, I flew to Āpia for their Samoan wedding celebration. They'd wed in the States the previous autumn but repeated their vows with Roma officiating. At the marriage feast in Manunu, Hannah and Leleiga beamed as the village presented a huge roast pig, coconut frond baskets with more food, and cases of pisupo accompanied by long speeches. Seated at the head table with Roma, Wilma, and the happy couple, I marveled at the fortunate confluence of events that five years earlier had brought us together.

With Leleiga and Hannah in Manunu in 2012.

In June 2016, Tuatagaloa Joe sent me an email to tell me that Niu had died in his sleep, a terrible shock for everyone. He suffered a brain aneurism at only fifty-one years old. Niu was a good friend and wonderful support for my Peace Corps endeavors. I know our village projects wouldn't have succeeded without him.

During my return visits, we'd become closer with the ability to spend time as just friends. On my last night in 2012, he and Saina and I had been the last guests, past closing time, at the restaurant on the pier at Sinalei. Saina and I laughed and danced a siva to the strains of the guitar-ukulele-bass string band, while Niu toasted Saina's skill and my many missteps.

A memorable evening shared with Niu and Saina on one of my return visits.

I'd received an email from him one week before he died:

---

RE: Visit to Samoa
Niualuga Evaimalo
Wed 6/8, 11:36 AM

Tālofa Donna,

Firstly thank you for this email. Secondly thanks God for keeping us all well now we have many chances of sharing and of course, will have more times of meeting each other. Thirdly my apology for being so long no words from here but I'm sure this does not break our consolidated family relationships.

Finally, we are very happy to hear that you are soon coming back to Samoa. That is great news and very happy indeed. Well, anytime is always good to us.

Looking forward to seeing you here soon

Alofa atu,
Si'a Niualuga

---

I did visit three months after he passed away. On a previous trip I'd brought the family six solar lights and batteries as a gift. Saina had put them by his two-tiered grave covered with smooth, fist-size, black lava stones, in front of their new house, next to the foxtail palms. I replace them occasionally and send extra batteries.

In 2017, Saina stopped working nights at the store to spend more time at home in Poutasi. As always, she's busy with family, village, and church affairs. She's my dear friend and Samoan sister. I love hanging out with her, gossiping, laughing, and shopping.

Daughter Aileen received a scholarship from New Mexico State

University. After graduation, she went back to Samoa, married a handsome professional rugby player, and works for the family business in Āpia. They live with Saina in Poutasi and have a daughter, Paugata, and a son, Niu, who are well cared for by Grandma Saina and ʻOfisa. Hemara got her Bachelor's degree in 2019 from NUS and works for the Ministry of Natural Resources and Environment in the Land Management Division. Fetū works at the family compound, in the gardens, and in Niu's orchard. Niu planted dozens of cacao and fruit trees on land adjacent to the house to provide food for the family with excess produce to sell. Tia is studying business at NUS.

When I visited with Tuatagaloa Joe the year after the tsunami, he'd told me that despite his heartbreak, he'd begun a friendship with someone "because an *aliʻi* needs a *faletua*." (*Faletua* literally translates as "back of the house," and means the wife of a high chief (*aliʻi* ), who traditionally has village responsibilities as well.) He'd invited me to meet her at Paddles Restaurant overlooking Āpia harbor at sunset. Tammy Mauala was in her forties, full of energy, and had pretty dark eyes. She'd recently returned to Āpia to work at her family's business, having lived in New Zealand for many years. As the evening progressed, a group of visiting Samoan New Zealanders joined us. When Tuatagaloa Joe and I exchanged a few words in Samoan, one young Kiwi asked him, "You speak Samoan?" and I thought, "You have no idea that you're speaking to one of the highest-ranking chiefs in Samoa!"

I was disinclined to like Tammy at first with my grief for Tui still fresh, but I could see that they'd become easy friends—the best place to start—and they married a few years later. I've been able to get to know and come to admire her over the years, occasionally staying with them at their house in Poutasi or at Sinalei. They're both actively involved in the Poutasi Development Trust (the "PDT"), established by Tuatagaloa Joe after Poutasi began recovering from the tsunami. It's run by a team of leaders from the village as an umbrella for several projects. These include continuation of the overseas worker programs, now augmented by small business opportunities in which to invest when they return to Samoa; greenhouses which employ villagers and sell produce to hotels and restaurants while providing healthy meals for local school children; and an arts and crafts center which sells handiwork to the public through its small workshop and store.

The PDT was a nominee for the *Samoa Observer's* Person of the Year in 2018. Quoted in the newspaper regarding the nomination, Tuatagaloa Joe said: "I believe if you can't sustain something, don't even go there. You're wasting the time, effort and money of the donor and what good is that going to do to the community?"

There are many new houses in Poutasi, but still very few by the sea. One year after the tsunami, the Marine Protected Area was back in place—a lei of red and white buoys floating in the bay. The village built a memorial hall to honor the tsunami victims, and in front is a small commemorative flower garden for Tui created by the women of the Pan Pacific and South East Asia Women's Association. The hall was built by young men from the village as trainee carpenters who went on to work in construction, some as foremen. Inside is a commercial kitchen used to cater for the school canteen and village functions, and as a training kitchen for Poutasi residents. In the same *Samoa Observer* article, Tammy was quoted as manager of the PDT saying that the kitchen is a way to get families away from eating chicken and noodles and choosing healthy local options instead.

Next door to the hall there's a preschool. And adjacent to that, a sleek, modern homework center with a well-stocked library where kids can come and use laptops at real desks—online! Using public and private funding, the government built a desperately needed new district secondary school to replace the buildings destroyed in the tsunami—with a nice, shiny computer lab. Another member of the leadership team (and former house girl) Leiloa is quoted saying she's seen the changes in her village, and she likes them. "I am looking and seeing that Poutasi is good, with a school, library and garden. It feels good to deliver vegetables from our garden to the hotels."

On my most recent visit, the fale 'i tai was still an overgrown grassy mound but Tuatagaloa Joe said he planned to build another fale in its place one day. I want to be there when it's dedicated!

My namesake, Donna La'itiiti is a beautiful young lady with a shy smile and dark, enchanting eyes. When I went to her primary school play on one of my visits, parents were recording the event with mobiles and tablets. What a change from our training days in Manunu when the only sporadic cell phone coverage was in the middle of the malae!

Donna La'itiiti dressed for her school play.

Even today when I visit Roma and Wilma, I slip back into the comfort of the Samoa that I first knew, when the adventure was new, I was filled with anticipation and excitement, and learning fa'aSāmoa in Manunu. Congregational pastors must retire at age seventy, so Roma and Wilma will move close to Āpia near his extended family when that time comes. That'll be a new journey for them, and Manunu will change for me. Life moves on.

# Chapter 14

## In the Wake of my Adventure

*Toe timata le 'upega*
*"Make the net over again"*
*Start a new life.*

I'm not a self-help guru and this book is much different from *Eat, Pray, Love*. There wasn't enough eating, there was *a lot* of praying, and too little romance! I expected to discover new things, travel, and have an adventure. But I didn't expect it to change me in the ways that it did, and to become part of two Samoan families.

I'm a different person than that homesick pisikoa. I don't fret as much about the small stuff in my life, because I know that I'm among the privileged in this world. Every time I go to Samoa, coming back makes me appreciate how much I have. I remember once reading that if you have money in your wallet and spare change in your house, you're among the richest people in the world. I certainly haven't lost my desire for nice (and sometimes frivolous) things, but I'm less materialistic now. I have enough and that's all I need. I don't keep anything that doesn't make me happy or that I don't use. I understand that culturally we Americans are stuff-oriented, but I still frequently find it distasteful. And yet . . . surrounded by a consumer society, it's easy to get sucked back into America's overabundance and overindulgence.

Despite my criticisms, living in Samoa made me appreciate America even more. I love our freedom and opportunity, and yes, our individualism. And it's important to acknowledge that when I complained about not having a stocked pantry, or the lack of a refrigerator, or waiting for a bus, that this was only an inconvenience for me. For many people on this earth, including some in the United States, these "inconveniences" are a way of life.

I came to Samoa as a normal American . . . go, go, go, get the job done. Do it right, and on time. I was a recently retired profession-al businesswoman who had all this managerial talent to use. I found those capabilities didn't help until I slowed down, understood the cul-ture, and put my faith in the village to carry our projects forward. Not that I wasn't often exasperated by fa'aSāmoa and the pace of life, but I learned patience—*onosa'i* in Samoan. Now when tempted to be impa-tient—waiting in a long line, bored in a board meeting, or stopped by road construction—I tell myself, "Onosa'i." I've learned to slow down and be more intentional in my choices, and I smile fondly at that ear-nest woman who wanted so much to "do a worthwhile project."

When I'm feeling frustrated, I ask myself, "Remember back in Peace Corps in Samoa?" You can deal with a broken hot water heat-er—you showered in unheated water for nearly two years. Don't feel like driving the half hour to town to run errands? Remember when you couldn't drive and had to wait in the sweltering heat for a bus that might not come. Feeling bored? Get over it!

One of the challenges that surprised me was the homesickness. When I read my journal after not looking at it for years, I felt a tiny pain in my heart. I was pretty low. I'm a fixer, a figure-this-out kind of person. I have been for as long as I can remember. But this was not something that I could figure out or fix. I wanted so badly to go back to my comfort zone, to forget about how hard it was, and to celebrate the experience like I do now.

Of course, I thought I'd miss home, but I never thought I'd be devastatingly, "I want to go home now!" homesick. I thought that was just for kids at summer camp, or something that happened in the first weeks when you move to a new place until you meet new friends. I thought I was old enough and wise enough at fifty-seven that

I wouldn't be homesick. When you can't have what's important to you, you may learn what's truly important to you.

What was I thinking?! That I wouldn't miss my life as it had been for the past forty years? While in Samoa I wrote that "we're all in transition." For me it was the beginning of figuring out what's next. It'd be wrong to say that I figured it all out in Samoa, or all at once. Or that I've figured it out once and for all. I'm still open to possibilities! I believe the possibilities change as we do. And, when we're out of our comfort zone, stripped down, we can find out who we are and what we really need.

When I left for PC, I knew it would impact my life, but mostly I thought it would be over and done when I returned. Maybe I'd stay in touch with some new Samoan friends, but they wouldn't be an integral part of my life. Naively, I assumed that I was a fully formed individual—the loving mother, the lifelong avid student, the passionate community advocate, the meticulous professional, the devotee of all things Hawaiian. But identity is sometimes as invisible to us as the air we breathe. Although we may not realize it at the time, when we go through drastic change—marriage, parenthood, divorce, retirement, Peace Corps—we respond to our world based on that current image. However, we may find that our old persona doesn't work anymore. We need to refresh, reboot, debug our system from time to time.

For me, the "elephant in the room" was my loss of control. I was the oldest of my siblings, the bossy big sister. At work, I was in charge of my department. I'm an American—we decide, and then get it done.

Then I went to a place where barely anything was under my control. Peace Corps volunteers are entirely vulnerable to the whims of whatever country, village, school, project, or people they encounter, including a new language, isolation, unfamiliar foods and customs, mosquitoes, diarrhea, lice, no refrigeration, minimal plumbing, stifling heat, and the pressure of expectations. I had no control over any of these except my ability to respond, which I didn't always do without difficulty.

Nevertheless, in Samoa, and way out of my comfort zone, I found a sense of compromise with myself on "the control thing." I'll always be the kind of person who writes lists and organizes, but I've learned not to push myself so hard and go with the flow instead—or at least I try to call myself on it when I don't. It's okay to just sit and listen to the rain.

The roller coaster of my life in Samoa—the joy, wonder, sadness, fear, excitement, anxiety, contentment, loneliness—made me keenly aware of my emotions. I learned to maximize the positive and manage the threat of letting the negative overtake me, even if that meant going home early. Loneliness was a symptom telling me something was wrong, and it was time to go back to my tribe. But working the emotional muscles used to cope with change strengthens them. I now ask myself: What is this emotion I'm feeling? Shall I revel in it and be appreciative of it? Or if I don't like it, can I figure out a way to adjust it?

One of the major ways that Peace Corps changed me is my clearer focus on how others' points of view differ from my own. We all know the saying, "Walk a mile in someone else's shoes." More than ever, with a heightened awareness, I try to think how the store clerk may have a sick family member, or a broken car, or . . . and that's why she's cranky with me today. Look at that man on the corner—maybe he's a millionaire, or maybe he's one paycheck from being homeless. We never know entirely what point of view someone else brings to a situation. That's possibly one of life's most important lessons to learn and remember to apply, often when we most need to do so. The life lived by every one of us is unique, colored by our culture, our family, our country, our food, how we worship, who we love, what makes us sad, and what makes us happy.

## *Back on the Big Island*

Mom came through the surgery well with some back-pain relief. Since my home was rented to my youngest son and his roommate, her house in Colorado became home base. I spent the first year after Peace Corps traveling in America. I flew to the east coast for my oldest son's wedding, to the west coast to see my little grandson, to Hawai'i to see Uncle Bob, and drove to Nebraska to see my aunts, uncles, and cousins. It was a time of wonderful celebration of family and friendships. We get busy. We get lazy. We forget. We procrastinate. And we risk losing these elemental links to our people. Never again will I take those connections for granted.

I returned to the Big Island to stay in January 2010. When I stepped off the plane in Hilo, the soft, fragrant air welcomed me home. Uncle Bob also welcomed me to stay at his guest cottage for as long as I wanted. I'd missed our long conversations seated at his perch facing the ocean. On my first night back, as we drank rosé wine in the cool evening breeze, I began to tell him the stories of my Samoan adventure.

Although I'd brought back with me a new realization that I could be happy and fulfilled each day without a job, the Great Recession had coincided with my Peace Corps service. I'd only heard murmurs of it in Samoa and was a bit shaken when I came home to a shattered economy and a burst real estate bubble. I'd planned to sell my Colorado house when I returned and begin to build my own house in Hawai'i, but there was no equity left. I'm not whining, because so many were devastated and I was okay in the long run. But it wasn't a good time to sell and I had bills to pay, so I continued to rent the house to my son and looked for work in Hawai'i.

I found my perfect final-transition job at the Legal Aid Society of Hawai'i. For three years I was an elder-law paralegal assisting seniors with wills, end-of-life documents, landlord/tenant issues, and other legal matters. With my law firm background and teaching skills, it was ideal for me, and I presented workshops on Advance Health Care

Directives and spoke on the subject at conferences in Hawai'i. Besides, I was an elder myself—though *only* sixty.

One of the best things about the job was the freedom I had. If Big Island clients were unable to come to the office, I went to them, and along the way explored old plantation towns, seaside villages, and rainforest tracts overgrown with vines as thick as your wrist. I found my clients in a wooden sugar shack with holes in the floor; in a long-ago church, its stained-glass-adorned sanctuary now a living room; and in a concrete block house by the ocean bursting with children, aunties, and uncles.

It was satisfying to know I was helping seniors with vital services, but as always, it was the people themselves who made it worthwhile. The ninety-year-old whose family had fled the pogroms in Russia to live in Mongolia, then Australia, and finally in Hawai'i; the veterans, including women, who were always delighted to hear that I'd been in the Air Force; the one-hundred-year-old Japanese lady who I expected to be frail, but bustled like a busy ant about her tiny home full of Asian antiques; or the Hawaiian cattle rancher whose front door opened to a sweeping vista of lush grasslands at the base of Mauna Kea.

A few years later, I realized that I wanted to actually "retire," and I was able to sell my Colorado house for a profit. I settled into the me who sat on that Nebraska porch swing so long ago dreaming of living on a Pacific island. Uncle Bob died in 2012 at the age of eighty-two and I was immeasurably grateful to inherit the house he built forty years earlier. I'm restoring and updating it, having fun growing orchids and other tropical flowers, reading with my book club, studying Hawaiian language, traveling, volunteering, writing, and enjoying long conversations with friends sitting by the ocean.

*Hawai'i! I knew it was meant to be since the day I first set foot on the island. It's the only place I've ever lived where I feel connected to my surroundings, innately and substantially. I have fond memories of other places—the home where I grew up and the house*

*where I raised my kids. But there's nothing like the contentment
I feel when I listen to the birds sing from all directions and the
wind rustling the banana tree leaves, as I sit and contemplate the
vibrant, dynamic rainforest and my slice of ocean view. Even from
ten miles inland I feel connected to the sea.*

I live alone, and I like it. I look forward to the times when family and friends stay at the guest cottage, but I relish the quiet time when they're gone. Actor/writer/playwright Donald Glover once said, "You're only really you when you're alone." Much food for thought in that statement!

I have a better understanding of the collectivist lifestyle lived by seventy percent of the people on the planet, and what individualism really means. How confusing we are to the rest of the world, even as they're confusing and challenging to us. And yet, "individualism" is one of America's most successful exports. What a complicated world we live in.

I'm also more appreciative of the depth and uniqueness of Polynesia of which Hawai'i is a part. There's a bond between peoples throughout the Pacific, as there should be, for they share common ancestry, language, and history. I understand Hawaiian culture better after living in Samoa—not only the language and the legends, but the communal lifestyle that the Hawaiians lived until only a couple of generations past, and what that means even today for family life, respect for elders, and the fundamental connection to the land and the sea. Before I went to Peace Corps, I considered myself a North American despite living in Hawai'i. Now I'm a resident of Oceania.

On a recent trip, one of Saina's cousins offered to take me to the airport. I told her I'd give her some gas money, and she said, "Don't think like a pālagi." In other words, because I'm family this is simply what you do. I suppose I'll always think like a pālagi; I'm so American. Yet I can be fa'aSāmoa when I need to be. On that same visit, Saina introduced me to a high chief who was visiting at church. I greeted him in perfect Samoan with the appropriate honorifics for his title, and she told me later that he was impressed and that she was pleased. And I also always love the surprised looks when a pālagi speaks proper Samoan!

Samoa is a part of me now. I feel its influence daily. Samoan siapo adorns my bedroom wall. Radio Australia is still one of my favorite stations. Sometimes when I don't know a Hawaiian word, I can translate it into Samoan, and then into English. My dogs are bilingual in English and Samoan! And thanks to modern technology, I can keep in close touch with my Samoan families.

So, this was MY view from the fale 'i tai—that very special house by the sea. All the people in my life saw it differently. From the viewpoint of the Peace Corps staff in Samoa, I was smoothly sailing along until my ship veered off course. My friends and family back home were always concerned for my welfare, but confident that I could handle it. And the kids at the Homework Center? Hopefully they'll remember me as that pālagi lady who taught them how to use a computer and cared immeasurably about them.

Life is a continuing story, and its arcs are set by its noteworthy moments—the peaks of joy, the valleys of melancholy, the unexpected forks in the road. In this story the finale isn't written yet. But the expansion of the circle of my loved ones to include two Samoan families has added another unexpected, happy twist. For in Samoa, as in all of Polynesia, if you are related by blood (even the remotest cousin), by marriage, by adoption (formal or otherwise), or by simply being welcomed into the clan, you are family, now and forever.

> We leave something of ourselves behind when we leave a place, we stay there, even though we go away. And there are things in us that we can find again only by going back there."

—Pascal Mercier, *Night Train to Lisbon*

# Epilogue

## We Come Full Circle

*'Ua sanisani fa'amanuao*
*"The joy of welcome is like birds greeting the dawn"*
*Seeing one's friends or loved ones brings great delight.*

"Aunty, these are soooo good!" exclaimed Hemara as she ate her first corn dog, slathered in mustard and ketchup. In 2019, I kept my long-ago promise and flew her to Hawai'i for a three-week visit. I'd asked if there was anything she especially wanted to eat here in America, and thus we were in Hilo's mall eating corn dogs, about to go for her first mani/pedi. She was twelve when I first left Poutasi, and she arrived in Hawai'i as a beautiful, mature, twenty-two-year-old university graduate having just completed her Bachelor of Science in computing, with a dual minor in physics and archaeology.

As an adult she has the tall stature and bearing of a Samoan chiefess with her dark, wavy hair flowing down her back. When we first met, she was a bright, plump, smiley ten-year-old who wriggled her way into my heart. From the beginning, there was something incontrovertible about our friendship. Maybe we got along so well because she was an inquisitive book worm like me—she reading books about American life and I about life in the South Seas.

I'd considered letting her stay in the cottage as I do with other visitors, to give them (and me) some privacy. Then I thought, "For a Samoan that'd be so odd and uncustomary that it would seem rude." So she slept on the living room's pull-out sofa and we talked late into the night about anything and everything.

I asked about her impressions and memories of me from the days when I first became part of her family. She said that I was the first pālagi that had ever stayed in the house, and she was extraordinarily curious. She said that I blended right in with the Samoans. I know that wasn't true, but it was nice to think that I did from her point of view, and it showed that I'd made an effort. She said because of me she had started writing, was motivated to get a good education, and adopted an "I can do this!" perspective. She recalled the Homework Center fondly and remembered me with my camera constantly strapped over my shoulder.

There was so much I wanted to share with her about my life, my island, Hawaiian culture, and America. I explained how car insurance works when she first noticed a dented car, rarer here than in Samoa. She asked, "Why did Americans elect Donald Trump president?" which led to an American history lesson, which led to a full-throated duet of the Samoan national anthem as we drove down the highway. "Why is that building sign 'YMCA?'"—a perfectly logical question when you've only heard it on the radio in the popular Village People song. "Why are the trees in that yard laden with unpicked fruit?"

Each day as Hemara discovered my country, I didn't know whether to laugh out loud trying to teach her to use chopsticks (she didn't know Hawai'i has a large Asian population and was surprised by that), be touched with her excitement seeing her first zoo animals, taken aback at her amazement that I have heirlooms from my great-grandparents, or shocked that she thinks dolls are scary (she didn't have dollies when she was young, and had mostly seen them headless and bloodied in horror films). She visited during our winter, when temperatures at my 1,100-foot elevation average $70^0$-$75^0$ during the day and cooler at night. She said it was like living in air conditioning. I never saw a Samoan house with a bathtub, so she had her first bath ever—and of course I made sure it was a bubble bath! After I went to bed, she was thrilled to have unlimited internet late into the night. My VR headset blew her away to other worlds and she marveled at my four-burner kitchen range with oven. She said my cooking was like eating in a restaurant every night, tasted her first zucchini and liked it, but didn't care for mashed potatoes.

She was here during a lunar eclipse which evolved over the ocean on a cloudless night as we drove down the mountain toward town. At the Foodland parking lot we sat in the car, ate pepperoni pizza, and marveled at the reddish glow of the full eclipse. Her visit surpassed the one that both of us had excitedly looked forward to. It became a time of discovery and rediscovery, sharing memories, enjoying the present, and looking forward to the future.

Just before Hemara left, we went to a hula performance on the Hilo bayfront and met Noe, a young Hawaiian dancer. She invited us to be her special guests at that evening's performance at Hulahula's, the restaurant and bar at the Naniloa Hotel. From a table up front by the band, we admired Noe's graceful hula numbers, then at her request, the musicians played a lively Samoan song and Hemara danced with cheeky abandon. Patrons eating in the restaurant came over from their tables to watch as locals yelled, *"Cheeeehooo!"* the shout of Samoans when they're happy, as a challenge to fight, or during rituals and dances.

On my last two visits to Samoa, I'd met Hemara's boyfriend Justin, a fellow student at the National University of Samoa. They married in 2020 at the Congregational church in Poutasi, officiated by Letone. I was sorely disappointed that I wasn't able to attend because of the worldwide coronavirus pandemic. Samoa enacted a swift and strict national quarantine, and as of this writing was one of only a handful of countries in the world with no cases—in stark contrast to the devastation wrought by the 1918 influenza, remembered each year on White Sunday.

On the eve of finishing this memoir I've learned that there's a little one on the way. Cheeeehooo!

Donna and Hemara in Hawaii.

## *It's Never Too Late to Find Love*

In addition to all the insights and gifts from my Samoan adventure, I'd hoped for romance. But circumstances and my own ambivalence had kept that out of reach. Then a few months after Hemara's visit, even that tide turned, when I met John.

Mutual friends intuitively invited both of us to a party. They didn't mention that they intended us to meet each other, although when I arrived, our hostess pointed out the tall, slender man about my age, and told me that he was writing a book about Hawai'i. For most of the afternoon, we both talked with others and then I asked him about his book. When we looked up, we realized that we were among the last at the party, seated at the picnic table, leaning close to one another engrossed in our discussion. He said, "We should get together and continue the conversation," and I agreed.

When I read Whoopi Goldberg's book *If Someone Says "You Complete Me," Run!* I thoroughly concurred with her witty opinions on why marriage isn't for everyone, how being alone can be satisfying, and how what's most important is understanding who you are and what makes you happy. I'd decided I was just fine without a "relationship." And I was, and I would be again, but then John came into my life.

A retired university professor, he too moved to Hawai'i in the 1970s and traveled in the South Pacific, including Samoa. We go for long walks in Hawai'i Volcanoes National Park, watch old movies, and talk for hours about everything and nothing. We discuss what we're writing, and I love listening to him read his latest chapter as I curl up beside him on the sofa. He brings me strawberries from his garden, and we eat them with vanilla ice cream on the balcony where Uncle Bob and I once sat, looking toward the ocean.

On her great adventure, Elizabeth Gilbert ate her way through Italy, prayed for enlightenment in India, and in Indonesia she found Felipe, her Brazilian lover. Near the end of the book as she holds Felipe while he sleeps, she has a memorable dream in which she sees her Indian guru across a crowded New York restaurant. Their eyes meet, he smiles, raises his wineglass in a toast, and mouths the word, "Enjoy." I plan to do just that.

*Fai le lā! Lelei le matagi!*
Make sail! The winds are fair!

# PLACE NAMES

Āpia:          Capital city of Samoa on ʻUpolu Island
ʻIli ʻili:        Rocky point of land between Poutasi and Sāleilua
Mari's:        Cafe in Āpia owned by Saina's family
Manono:        Small Samoan island
Manunu:        Group 78 training village
Nuʻusafeʻe:    Tiny island offshore of Poutasi village
Pago Pago:     Capital of American Samoa
Poutasi:       Village where I lived on southern side of ʻUpolu
Sāleilua:      Village to the west of Poutasi
Savaiʻi:       The largest of the Samoan islands
Sinalei:       Resort owned by Tuatagaloa Joe and Tui
Siʻumu:        Village at the end of the cross-island road
ʻUpolu:        Most populated Samoan island
Vaovai:        Village to the east of Poutasi

# KEY PEOPLE

| | |
|---|---|
| 'Afakasi: | Neighbor and bus driver |
| Aileen: | Daughter of Saina and Niu |
| Donna La'itiiti: | (Urima) Daughter of Roma and Wilma |
| Fetū: | Son of Saina and Niu |
| Hemara: | Daughter of Saina and Niu |
| Leleiga: | Cousin of Wilma's from Manunu |
| Leiloa: | Tuatagaloa Joe and Tui's house girl |
| Letone: | Pastor in Poutasi |
| Logo: | Letone's wife |
| Mataomanu: | Friend and neighbor |
| Meleisea Seti: | Mataomanu's husband, village chief |
| Niu: | Father of host family in Poutasi |
| 'Ofisa: | Friend and family house girl |
| Roma: | Father of host family/pastor in Manunu |
| Saina: | Mother of host family in Poutasi |
| Soloao: | Friend in Poutasi |
| Tamamasui: | "Grandfather" of Poutasi family |
| Tia: | Daughter of Saina and Niu |
| Tuatagaloa Joe: | Poutasi high chief, Saina's cousin |
| Tui: | Friend, wife of Tuatagaloa Joe |
| Tumema | Friend in Poutasi |
| Wilma: | Mother of host family in Manunu |

# SAMOAN TO ENGLISH GLOSSARY

There are fourteen letters in the Samoan alphabet: a, e, i, o, u, f, g, l, m, n, p, s, t, and v. The vowels have the same sounds as Spanish: a as in water; e as in they; i as in eek, o as in hole; and u as in cruise. The consonants are the same except for g which has the sound of ng in English, as in the word sing. A macron over a letter (ā) gives it a longer stress. A glottal stop (') is marked by an inverted comma where the voice pauses, as in the English oh-oh (o'o). Syllables always end on a vowel and the second to the last syllable is emphasized.

'Ava:      AKA kava, a drink made with the root of that shrub
Fa'aSāmoa:      The Samoan way of life
Fa'afetai:      Thank you
Fale:      Any building, but especially a house
Fale 'i tai:      House by the sea
Fiafia:      Enjoy, be happy, and a party
Laufala:      Leaves of the pandanus tree
Laumoso'oi:      Flowers used to scent coconut oil or for a lei
Lāvalava:      A wraparound skirt or sarong
Malae:      Open space in the middle of a village; village green
Mālōlō:      Rest or relax
Masi popo:      Coconut biscuit (large shortbread cookie)
Matai:      Village chief
Niu:      Coconut right off the tree

| | |
|---|---|
| Pālagi: | A foreigner, especially a Caucasian |
| Palusami: | Taro leaves stuffed with seasoned coconut cream sauce |
| Pisikoa: | Peace Corps volunteer |
| Pisupo: | Corned beef in a can |
| Puletasi: | Woman's dress worn for business or formal wear |
| Tālofa: | Hello, greetings |
| Umu: | An above-ground oven of heated lava rocks |
| Umukuka: | Cook house behind the main house |

# ACKNOWLEDGEMENTS

First and foremost, this book is for my families in Manunu and Poutasi. I can't imagine the story of my life without them. Thanks! Fa'afetai! You welcomed me when I needed family the most. When I was forlorn, you were there. When I was delighted with the discovery of Samoa, you were there. When I was so very *not* fa'aSāmoa, you were there. Helping me, teaching me, entertaining me, frustrating me, leading me, respecting me, teasing me, praying for me, loving me.

Thank you to my awesome family back home who supported me always while I was in Peace Corps and listened to endless stories about Samoa when I returned. Your faith and confidence that I could write this book buoyed me many times. Thanks to my three best friends, Sue Miller, Dana Weddle, and Julie Goettsch. In all the stages of my life you've always been there for me and believed in me.

In Samoa there were so many people who assisted me while I was in Peace Corps—more than I can thank here. I hope that my gratitude is adequately expressed in this memoir.

Fa'afetai to the members of the Poutasi Peace Corps Committee: the mayor Luafutu Leipa, Meleisea Seti, Vaeila Suesue, Saina Niualuga, Lesaisaea Niualuga Evaimalo, and Valasi Afi'a Tauloa. I'm also indebted to Rev. Letone and Logo Uili for all of their assistance with the Homework Center and more.

I'm grateful to Laura Moses, Christy Peace, Janet Hagerman, and Wally Grant, who struggled through early drafts and gave me important feedback. Julie Carpenter, Jennifer Muller, Ben Neivert, and Catherine

Robbins were invaluable readers whose insight and acumen made this a better book.

Tom Peek, my amazing editor and writing mentor, helped me develop psychological layers that I didn't know were there. He encouraged me to keep going and I couldn't have written this memoir without his guidance and wisdom. Mahalo nui loa to Nancy Kahalewai, my book coach, who helped me polish the manuscript and understand the big picture of self-publication.

And my most loving thanks go to John Culliney who listened, and gave me never-ending encouragement, insight, and support.

# ABOUT THE AUTHOR

Donna Marie Barr could only dream of living on a South Pacific island as a Nebraska farm girl. At fifty-seven, after raising three sons and a successful career, she joined the Peace Corps and was assigned to the South Pacific islands of Samoa. This memoir of that life-changing adventure is her first book.

Donna lives on the Big Island of Hawai'i where she grows prize-winning orchids and hosts travelers from all over the world in her guest cottage.

Made in the USA
Columbia, SC
22 May 2023

16475715R00204